FACE TO FACE

FACE TO FACE

FRANK MICHAEL CORTINA

COLUMBIA UNIVERSITY PRESS
NEW YORK AND LONDON · 1972

COPYRIGHT © 1972 COLUMBIA UNIVERSITY PRESS
LIBRARY OF CONGRESS CATALOG CARD NUMBER: 76-184745
ISBN: 0-231-03635-3
PRINTED IN THE UNITED STATES OF AMERICA

TO GARY SMITH

"Ah, my closet is full, each shelf
spread with my mummer's array."

PREFACE

"There are those who don't fit into any program. They simply can't be contained. And that would be the case even if they didn't abuse drugs, Frank Michael. You've worked with them yourself. They range from the unpredictably hostile to the totally alienated. They can't be reached. Most programs of necessity have got to limit themselves to the approachable."

Dr. Rolland was a slight man who spoke slowly, quietly. We sat together on his terrace, the blue-green ocean shimmering in front of us, the white sand, the palm trees, the crescent of beach all fixed in the glistening West Indian light. "I've encountered them over the years," I agreed.

"In prisons and in exclusive sanitariums, if they have the money to afford them. Isn't that so?"

He was right. Then I said, "I can't accept that they're unreachable. Difficult, requiring more time than most institutions can give. . . ."

He interrupted: "And oftentimes so obstreperous that they can disrupt a whole program. No, we haven't gotten to the place

where we can handle all types successfully, Frank Michael. Perhaps
we will never reach that place. Perhaps there is a degree of damage that cannot be repaired?" His slender fingers caressed a shell.
"I have seen many failures."

"But I'm sure after a good try."

"Try?" He looked toward the ocean. "For all the time you've
spent with drug abusers you have a remarkable butt-headedness
about you. I won't say that you're naïve."

I have known him so long that I could detect his note of pique.
"All I'm saying is that one has to take every step."

"Drug dependence is at best a perverse subject. It creates repugnance. Your last book was written to mitigate that very thing.* I
doubt if it succeeded. Who wants to read or learn about these self-
doomed people who have brutalized themselves? Drug addicts
have renounced their central uniqueness, that which separates
them from the lower orders."

I was astonished to hear the quiet fervor in his voice.

"A drug addict consciously suspends his reason, his spirituality,
his involvement with life. Drugs permit dissociation, suspension.
Nothing is more basically opposed to man's life force! Drug addiction is a renunciation of life." He carefully put the shell down on
the sand. "It's a denial of our instincts. There is that which is very
perverse about drug abuse, Frank Michael, and your books will not
prove it otherwise."

He glanced at me. I said: "I've always felt that they were just
the way we are, only more so—our drives but exaggerated."

"Or perverted," he insisted. "Have you ever had a bird collide
with you? It goes into shock, becomes rigid, appears dead. Is it the
impact or in the nature of the creature? Have you ever seen a rabbit expire from the slightest accident? A mere feather's touch is
sometimes enough to make it roll over and die. Now man is not
like that! He can be pummeled, shattered, literally crushed, and
yet he will struggle with his last breath. It's his instinct, his un-
quenchable vitality, his will to live. It's this instinct, this vitality,
this will to live that the drug addict casts aside. This is perverse.

* Frank   Michael   Cortina,   *Stroke   a   Slain   Warrior*   (New   York:
Columbia University Press, 1970).

That's why the addict is loathed—because he has rejected his uniqueness, his heritage as a man."

Jean was very excited and this was unlike him. He obviously had to carry his point about perversity. "Isn't it possible that some of us have an exaggerated humanity, for whatever reason, and this throws everything out of balance?"

He stared at me tiredly. "Who can devote all his time to perpetual intervention in a person's life? And that's just what it requires for this type of individual."

"But what makes you say that it has to be perpetual?"

"I know," he said flatly. "When you intervene, they demonstrate change, for a day, a week, a year, as long as you're around; but when they're alone again, what happens then? You know as well as I."

"Well, I have a new assignment. I'll be following a random group of addicted individuals over a year's time. Perhaps I'll learn something, Jean."

"You'll learn what you know already, Frank Michael. Drug addiction results only in overwhelming, incalculable loss."

I looked at his ravaged face. His loss was calculable: wife, children, career. But what he said about intervention and perversity stayed with me—it became *Face to Face*.

Frederiksted, St. Croix,
American Virgin Islands

CONTENTS

ON
SLENDER
ACCIDENT

1

The room was a perfect setting for the assignment: oak paneling with embossed swirls, closets concealed in the wall, arched window embrasures, high ceiling with plastered ornamentation, and all of it tied together by the huge mural on the back wall. It was the painting, that fantasy of the medieval period, that set the tone. How appropriate it was! Affected, imprecise, luxuriant, false with ringing energy, how like the drug addict, that rococo figure.

"Fascinating *mise en scène,* I think, Mr. Cortina."

"It sure is," I said, taking in the man opposite me. He had fine cheekbones, straight, strong nose, noticeably small ears, white kinky hair, mahogany colored skin, and a savage scar incompletely hidden by the beard he wore.

By any standard, Russell was an impressive-looking man, actually an extremely handsome man even now. And he had a voice in keeping with his appearance—what I have come to call a deacon's voice, suited to give the listener balm. He held up a hand, as if to soften a dazzling light. "That painting holds me . . . that road, turning, twisting, carrying one higher and higher into that

blue sky and those white clouds to that castle at the summit. . . .
Hardly attainable one thinks, hardly attainable," and Russell let
his voice ebb away.

"Unreal, though, isn't it, Russell? . . . The perspective is curious, don't you think? Look at that road, look at those figures . . .
sort of terribly inaccurate, the whole thing, or not inaccurate
enough."

"Yes, that's a very perceptive criticism, Mr. Cortina. I've been
troubled by something about that picture since I've been here . . .
vaguely troubled, don't you know. . . ."

"How long have you been here, Russell?"

"Almost three weeks. Seventeen days. . . . Yes, seventeen days."

How poised he was. He "sat" a chair, as a good horseman his
mount. His flannel slacks, the blue sport blazer. We could have
been sitting on a sound stage, or rather he could have been because
I was jacketless and anything but poised—I had too many ad-
justments to make on my equipment. "There, perhaps we'll at least
get decent voice separation. It's not a good room for recording.
How old are you, Russell?"

"Fifty-two. . . . Yes, I'm fifty-two, just. . . ."

"You look about thirty-two."

"Thank you," he said smiling. "I'm a physical fitness expo-
nent. . . ."

"How do you reconcile that with your abuse of drugs?"

"Well, to be utterly candid, Mr. Cortina, I feel that my drug dependence began as a result of disillusionment I suffered . . . heartbreak I had with a girl who I was infatuated with. . . . Let me ex-
pand that. Any problems any of us children experienced we
brought to our mother, as our father had died when we were very
young, eight years old in my case. Therefore all of my problems I
brought to my mother, you see."

"How old were you when this 'heartbreak' experience occurred,
Russell?"

"Seventeen years old. So I brought my hurt to my mother. I told
her that this girl had rejected me and she said to me: 'Don't
grieve, son. These things do happen. It's the everyday roles of life.

You're not the only one. It's not important. What is important is being able to ball up your fists, being able to carry on, you know, and being able to eke out a new life, or a new love, or what have you. But don't wreak out your vengeance on every woman you meet, because all women are not alike.' I accepted this because I adored my mother and I knew that she wouldn't tell me anything wrong, and I accepted it because I knew that she wanted me to. . . . But let me say in all candor, Mr. Cortina, that I was determined to get my revenge. . . ."

"So you really weren't candid with your mother in this instance . . . ?"

He nodded gravely. "Let's say that I had mental reservations. . . . I had respect for my mother and her pronouncements. I respected her role and understood mine in relation to her, but I had to make my own moves . . . my own moves. . . . So the first move I made was to drop out of school. . . ."

"You dropped out of school? This was part of your revenge or are you indicating that you were disenchanted with school . . . ?"

"No, to the disenchantment, yes, to the revenge."

"You were doing well in school, you were a good student . . . ?"

"I was an excellent student. . . ." Russell carefully selected a cigarette from his package, studied it, made sure there were no loose grains, and then with the same kind of deliberateness lighted it. "Let me digress for a moment, Mr. Cortina. I had been in an institution for wayward youth."

"You'd been put away for juvenile delinquency?"

"Yes, I had been guilty of an asocial act. . . ."

"A social act?"

"I was rebelling against my principal. . . . But let me deepen this perspective and go further back than that. I remember when I was attending an all-white school, grade school it was. I think I was in the third or fourth grade at the time. Then I came to realize that I was in an all-white school. I always have felt that I was a fairly level-headed fellow even at that early age. And I think I was a reserved child, or perhaps withdrawn more or less. I refer to the latter mainly because it was a process that continued . . . this being withdrawn. So rather than eat in the cafeteria and listen to the catcalls and derision. . . ."

"Because of your color?"

"Because of my race. . . . Well, I didn't want to fight or what not because so many of the tormentors were girls anyway. . . . So I started eating at a drugstore with a food counter. I was accepted there, and nobody who ever came into that drugstore bothered me in any way. So I'm going back to school one day, and two girls came up abreast of me and one says, 'Oh, Mary, there's your boyfriend.' And Mary, looking at me, says, 'I don't go with niggers.' And at that age that we were, who can control these types of currents, you know. Now, it was in the wintertime, and I lived in the East in those days, and it had snowed the day before and then rained on top of the snow. . . . So I packed a snowball, it was wet and hard . . . and then I rolled it in the water to make it even firmer. . . . And then I walked all the way around the block to meet that girl at the entrance of the school. And I leveled off about eight feet away and I flung that snowball at that girl and hit her in the eye. So naturally or consequently when I got back to my classroom there was a notification for me to go to the principal's office. And there this incident was discussed. Miss Fairweather, I remember her so vividly. . . . She always reminded me of a wax bean . . . pale and skinny and her face kind of waxy . . . Miss Fairweather, she demands to know why I attacked that girl so brutally. I told her that it was because she had called me a nigger. 'Well, aren't you a nigger?' says Miss Fairweather. I reached across that desk and slapped her across the face as hard as I could and ran out of the school." Russell brushed away cigarette ash. "I continued running for several days, never going home, because I know that my moms with her very proper orientation is going to insist upon my returning to school. However, a truant officer finally caught up with me, and all of the extenuations ensued. . . ."

"This was the asocial act."

"Precisely. I was removed from the school. I was placed under the jurisdiction of the children's aid society. I was removed from my home and placed in a foster home because they felt that my family was not a proper environment. I gather that they felt, well, that my reaction to this particular crisis might indicate that I needed a more supportive home milieu . . . that is, if I could be helped in an early enough stage, then I might be helped to develop without trouble. So they removed me from my home and from that school and placed me in another predominantly white school . . . there were six or seven other colored youngsters. . . ."

"They took you away from home because home was not suitable?" I asked quietly. "Must have been hard on your mother."

"It was a very simple matter. My mother was not a very robust person. She was suffering from a respiratory ailment and, being on welfare as well, the authorities thought that it might be better for her if she could relax some of her burdens for a while. They put her in a hospital. . . . And there would have been a home without a parent, don't you see."

"I understand. . . ."

"This business of the past, retrospect, the conjuring up of the old images, it appears so disjointed. . . . I should have mentioned that my mother was enduring this sickness at the time, simultaneous with my having these difficulties in school. This will account for the moves that were made. . . . Now I had a sister who was just a little younger than I and we were inseparable. . . . She and I were so close that when I wasn't around she would go into tantrums so that they had to take her and put her with me in the same foster home."

"How old were you at this time?"

"At that time I was in the neighborhood of eleven or twelve. . . ."

"And this foster home placement . . . was it acceptable?"

"It was like an average home—a home without children, however. . . . The woman was childless, but otherwise it was quite ordinary. But I learned that she was very possessive . . . perversely so," he said, with gravity. "That was my interpretation in those days, and years have only confirmed this opinion."

"She had a husband?"

"Oh, yes. . . . He didn't figure in anything that concerned me."

"That's curious, isn't it? You had been deprived of your real father and now you were deprived of a foster father. . . ."

"That is true, that observation. . . . But in the case of this latter man, he was a thing possessed as I was possessed, and the two possessions couldn't be shared. . . . Frankly, I don't think that the poor man much relished the idea of fostering strange children but he was, as I say, possessed. I was always a student of the female from my earliest years. Mrs. Danglois was a very interesting specimen for my microscope. . . ."

"I take it that you weren't happy there?"

"That is true, but I went along with it. . . . I didn't get into trouble, I tolerated the perversity of this possessive, dominating woman. . . . That is, I did until on one occasion when I returned home a little late. . . . Now, I am not talking about an absence, I am talking about a tardiness . . . ten or fifteen minutes after nine o'clock in the evening."

It was like listening to a baroque organ . . . full, orotund, played masterfully, swelling into the room, mesmerizing an audience. "What happened?"

"Many children return home late. They have a distorted time sense. . . . Children are not careless, they are carefree. . . . However, when I returned home after this insignificant tardiness, she was outrageously harsh with me. I can't to this day recall what kind of instrument she raised to strike me with, but I can recall my sheer panic: 'Oh, my God, if this woman hits me with that weapon, she may fracture my skull, dislocate a shoulder, or injure an eye. . . . If I throw up an arm she might break that.' So I abruptly turned and escaped through the front door. Someone caught me, someone from the neighborhood, a gentleman, and he brought me back. This time she took a strap and she beat me, I mean, she put herself into it and beat me. And my body remembered that beating for days. However, when she had exhausted herself and her fury, she locked me in my room. . . . But I knew how to get out. . . . Raise the window, down to the porch roof, and so out into the yard and escape. . . . I disappeared for a month . . . I went to live with some other people."

"You said that your sister was living there, too?"

"Yes, but Blanche didn't seem to arouse the strength of feeling, this fury in Mrs. Danglois. . . . Quite candidly, Mr. Cortina, now from the vantage point of time, I think it was quite sexual in motivation. I think Mrs. Danglois was sexually repressed and, though she was not aware of it, I, innocent child that I was then, seemed to sum up for her, rejection. . . . In my innocence, every time I failed to follow her dictates religiously her sexual repression emerged and she had to beat me. That is, of course, my mature analysis of the situation." He put out his cigarette with care.

"Let me ask you, Russell. How many years have you been using drugs?"

He smiled. "Yes, that's a question that I've had thrust at me a thousand times. . . . I started on drugs in the early part of 1937. . . . Ironically enough, on Good Friday . . . Passion Friday, 1937."

"That would be. . . ."

He interrupted graciously, "Too long ago to reckon, Mr. Cortina . . . too long ago. . . . And yet I recall so vividly my very first drug experience. . . ."

"Was it heroin? Or one of the soft drugs?"

"Morphine. . . . It was given to me. I went to school with some Latins; one of them in particular and I were quite companionable. One day as I sauntered along the street we chanced upon one another and we talked for a couple of hours together, you know, trying to make up for lost time. He had a beautiful new car, was well-dressed, and before he left me out he asked me if I wanted to make some easy money, and I told him that it all depended upon what was involved. So he pulled out an envelope and opened it and showed me these half-grain morphine pills, and he told me that I could get between seventy-five cents and one dollar for each one. And he indicated that it would be to my best interests to get the higher figure. We would split fifty-fifty. He offered me a hundred pills to start off with, and in that way my first commission would be fifty dollars . . . a most munificent sum for me in those days, Mr. Cortina. . . . I had little hesitation in accepting this offer."

"Did you know what morphine was?"

"I had no way of knowing. I suspected that it was a narcotic . . . I suspected that. . . ."

"You suspected . . . ?"

"Yes. . . . You see, I had been using marijuana for at least two years prior to this encounter."

"Did he say anything about what it was you were going to sell for him? I mean, did he point out that it could become addictive?"

"Why should he? He assumed that I would never use it. It was for me to sell. . . ."

"And actually I suppose that you would have been of value to him either way. . . ."

"Exactly, because I was to be his salesman in the black community. . . . In those days my Italian friend was not very popular in that colored neighborhood because, you see, you hardly had any young drug addicts. . . . Hardly any young people on hard stuff, really."

"To whom were you selling?"

"To older people . . . actually elderly people. . . . Most of my first customers were in their forties and older. . . . It's difficult to grasp that historic fact in these days of characterizing drug abuse as a problem of the young—or more correctly, *the* problem of the young. . . . No, these were mature people. . . ."

"And you had· no difficulty in disposing of your hundred pills. . . . ?"

"Difficulty! I sold three hundred pills that first day. . . . I had, for the first time in my life, one hundred and fifty dollars in the space of seven hours. . . . That was my first real understanding of what enterprise meant. The prospects of a future were dazzling. I became an establishment. I developed basic policies and practices. I suited my techniques to my neighborhood. . . . Every fifteen minutes starting at eight o'clock in the morning I would be in a given location, then pass along to my next point of rendezvouz. . . . Then in the late afternoon I would appear at the distributor's place to replenish my supplies. . . . Then, of course, I had very special customers, people of prominence for whom I made custom deliveries. . . ."

"You'd developed a way of life. . . ."

"Indeed, you might say that I established an ethos, one that supplied me with a cosmos. I was something."

"How long before you were using . . . ?"

"Not very long. I know now that I was curious right from the very beginning. . . . I was drawn toward drugs from the very beginning. . . . Actually, what happened was this. It was summer, a particularly sultry day, and I was making a delivery to this musician. . . . His door was open in hopes of capturing a stray breeze. I walked in quietly, he wasn't there. I noticed that the bathroom door was ajar. I went over and peered in. . . . He couldn't see me. . . . He was booting. . . . You know what that is, Mr. Cortina . . . ?"

"Letting the blood kick back. . . ."

"Precisely. I watched him go through these changes, that expression of rapt concentration . . . that expression of orgiastic suspension that I had seen on women's faces at the climax of passion. Need I say more, Mr. Cortina . . . ? It was not more than a few hours before I was initiated, I was made one of that brotherhood. . . ." He stopped quickly and seemed to be searching back for something he had overlooked. He snorted. "Long ago, but so vivid in my imagination. . . ."

2

Russell had been fascinated by the sound of his own voice being played back. He sat so quietly, so raptly, that he appeared to be part of that rococo room, a carved figure. At the conclusion, he looked at me intently and said: "Remarkable instrument, the human voice. What it can encompass just through shadings. . . . I could detect the pain about some of those old memories in my voice of last month. . . . Remarkable. . . ."

"Russell, you indicated that you've been a drug-dependent person for almost thirty-five years, and in the previous session you intimated that marijuana was a kind of introduction. . . ."

"Yes, pot, and it wasn't called pot in those days—I knew it as reefer. . . . It must have been about 1935. . . . I knew this fellow, a very musical chap . . . in fact I think he was a musical genius. . . . Well, Clayton and I were the same age, but he had been induced to try reefer at an even earlier age than I. We were in his basement one evening . . . and I was watching him dance. . . . Now, he was grace personified, musical to his finger nails . . . a joy to watch him melt into music, like a bird melts into the air. . . . In any case, at the end of this number he lit up a stick of pot and asked me if I wanted some. I asked him what it was because I knew it wasn't a cigarette, not with that odor—and in those days it was a strange odor. . . . So he told me that it was reefer. . . . As I said, the name 'pot' was not current. . . . So, ever responsive to the peer compulsion, I told him immediately that I wanted some. . . . He demurred, saying that I really didn't want to tangle with this kind of thing. . . . And so on and on in that kind of ritual dance of enticement that young people engage in. The upshot was he gave me some. I didn't know what to expect, and quite frankly I felt that I had been hoodwinked: 'Hey, Clayton, man, I don't feel nothin' . . . I don't fer a fact. . . .' But I laughed about that . . . and he laughed about it. And soon we were convulsed with laughter. . . . I was holding my sides, I was laughing so hard. Clayton, he says to me: 'Man, you still don't feel nothin'?' All I could answer between guffaws was that I felt absolutely nothing. . . . And he then brought to my attention this uproarious laughter. What was its basis? And of course that provoked even greater hilarity. . . . And then I realized that I did feel this alien light-heartedness. I searched myself very closely about that sensation. . . . It struck me as being too altering, all that laughter; it struck me as perhaps something I should not use if I hoped to gain an understanding of myself."

"You didn't feel that it liberated you?"

"On the contrary, I sensed that it would only retard my true struggle, which was to realize myself. . . . And so complete was that conviction that I never used reefer again until I got a home visit from the youth institution that I mentioned on our last tape. . . ."

"And you had been placed there because of your being in need of supervision . . . ?"

"That is right," said Russell grandly.

"In those days, in that institutional setup, did the youngsters talk much about drugs?"

"No. . . . No. . . . These children, myself one of them, they knew nothing about drugs. . . . We're talking of over a generation ago, Mr. Cortina. Drugs were unknown except to a very small minority—I need hardly add, a very special minority. . . . Children weren't part of that scene at all. . . . That's all very recent."

"This reformatory experience . . . was that your first time?"

"Yes, that was my first asocial act . . . but I grieve to say, not my last. . . . I wasn't out very long when I was picked up on some misdemeanor or other—most likely petty larceny—and placed in the county penitentiary. . . ."

"Petty larceny?"

"You know the drill—things like stealing curtains out of the curtain salesman's car, or cigarette cartons from the cigarette salesman's car, things of that nature. . . ."

"Were there other institutions after that?"

"Many. . . . Many. . . . In a sense, I am that statistical entity, the institutionalized person. . . ."

"Had you jobs between these stints?"

"I worked in a locomotive plant, a steel foundry, a dry-cleaning establishment, in a restaurant, as an iron worker . . . I had one job in a shipyard, where I stayed for three years. . . ."

"What made you leave that?"

He smiled at the recollection. "It was a concatenation of events, that is for sure. It was payday; it was also the day I collected my two-weeks vacation check and in addition some retroactive pay. So I had in my hand something like fourteen hundred dollars. It was a rich mixture . . . I hadn't the stability to manage it. . . . So I left the job. . . . A week later, however, I got a job with the Pullman company, and I went to work immediately. I held that job for almost three years . . . and would have held it longer if it hadn't been for the scrutiny of the U.S. marshals."

"Scrutiny of the . . . ?"

"They're called in when interstate lines are crossed, and we were crossing between St. Louis and Denver regularly. . . . And we were beating the company out of so much money on every trip. When I realized that the bust had come and that I couldn't make as much money any more and that I would have to rely more or less on our regular paychecks and tips . . . I decided that I couldn't afford to stay . . . I couldn't. I was used to fast money. . . . You want to understand, Mr. Cortina . . . drugs were missing from my life at this particular time, and I filled this void with clothes and jewelry, women, cars, and other surface glitter."

"You started to use morphine when you were about seventeen?"

"Just about then. . . ."

"And you used it fairly steadily . . . ?"

"Yes . . . I did. . . . But there were interruptions. . . . For example, I used very little dope when I worked in the shipyard."

"Were you addicted?"

"Indeed I was . . . heavily addicted, but nevertheless I resolved that it was time to discontinue. I employed my mother to lock me in my room, to turn up her radio, and to ignore me for two days. . . . I told her that I had to go through a spiritual crisis with myself. . . ."

"Did she know that you were on drugs . . . ?"

Russell seemed offended by this question. He said tolerantly: "My mother was a lady. Why would I tell her about something so offensive?"

"What made you kick, Russell?"

"Well, I've kicked many times over the years. . . . At that particular time I just wasn't satisfied with what was happening . . . perhaps it was that that became a challenge. . . ."

"Is it possible that the stuff was no longer giving you the high it had . . . that you had become dulled to it . . . ?"

"Yes, that is possible because one is always seeking that first, virginal high. . . . You may be correct in your surmise in that regard, Mr. Cortina. . . . But for whatever reason, I cleaned myself up in three days. . . . I was peddling pills and other things. I had no money problems in those days. My extravagances were few. . . . I am a most abstemious man. I like women, but that never costs money—quite the reverse. I had to prevent them from showering money on me. . . . They really are so generous, so foolish. They are, if they crave you. . . . They can be filled with such folly. It's very touching, a woman's generosity; it moves me. . . . Excuse this tangent. . . . I had money . . . but I wasn't satisfied, as I related. . . ."

"Russell, had you ever been busted on a narcotics charge?"

"No, up to the time we are talking about I had never been picked up or even accosted by the narcotic squad."

"Was this a fear, the sense that sooner or later you would be arrested . . . a kind of inevitable part of the drug bag . . . ?"

With that elaborate ritual he went through, Russell lighted a cigarette, rearranged himself in his chair, and smiled. "That is a fiction, that fatalistic quote. . . . I never considered that as a possibility. The narcotics squads in those days were few and far between. The whole scene was different. . . . You mustn't conjure up a vast roundup kind of notion. It wasn't that way at all. . . . There were arrests, but drugs were very low key in those days. . . . None of the braying about them that we have today. . . . No, I had for some reason or another become disenchanted with drugs, and I stopped using them. . . . And drugs interfered with other important things in my life. . . . Women. . . . It was nothing for me in those days of my youth to suffer for a girl . . . I would catch a glimpse of a particular girl, and she would course through my system like fire. I'd make my moves, and I would chase her until I caught up with her and brought her down. It was nothing for me to lay up with her for two or three days, quite oblivious to the fact that I had forgotten to fix. . . . You know, the first time that this happened to me . . . she was an exceptionally sweet girl . . . lovely, tender, generous to a fault. Her father owned an undertaking establishment, and she had serious intentions to make me into a solid citizen, . . . but no matter. . . . I was addicted, but like I say, the chase had inflamed me and I was laid up with this inimitable girl. We were doing our thing, as the phrase is, and I gradually became conscious of a change coming over my body. . . . My energy is low, my nose is running, my back hurts me . . . and I perspire heavily . . . and my stomach is very disquieted, and the girl she's conscious that my ardor has been displaced. That was the first time I ever learned what it was to be addicted. I saw this friend, and I told him how I was suffering from this most peculiar cold. . . . He scoffed: 'Cold. You ain't got no cold, man. You're hooked.' Crudely put, but it was the case. . . . I didn't believe it. . . . He said: 'Why, you fool, that's a Jones . . . and I'll prove it to you.' He took me to his home, fixed up a load, and hit me. . . . I felt like a mountain . . . some grand peak . . . all the symptoms disappeared immediately. It was a wonderful and terrible experience at the same time. . . . The power of the substance over me was not comforting. . . ."

"You were a pusher, and you had never seen anybody strung out, anybody sick . . . ?"

Nonchalantly, he said: "That is true, not up to this particular time. . . ."

"That's astonishing. . . ."

"But it isn't astonishing . . . not at all, when you understand the context. . . . In those days, drugs were very cheap. . . . Heroin was even cheaper than morphine. Drugs were of good quality and of reasonable price, and so even the most indigent could afford them. . . . Cold turkey and street kicking were really not common in those days. . . . If a man didn't want the blandishments of the drug euphoria, he took himself off somewhere and kicked on his own or perhaps went into a hospital for a week, a practice that I followed more than once. . . ."

"Then, with all of this availability, why on earth did you even consider taking a job . . . becoming a member of the square world?"

"Because . . . simply because Russell didn't want to be involved with something that could so devastate him . . . with pain and discomfort. . . . And add to that, someone telling you that you're addicted, dependent upon something. . . . No, Mr. Cortina, Russell had to lay off . . . if for nothing else than to experience the impact, the full impact. You see, I took care of myself."

For a man of fifty-two, I had never seen a better looking, fitter specimen. In his knit turtleneck, no stomach bulge showing, the short sleeve revealing his muscular arm, Russell could have passed for the model of middle-aged beauty.

"Your mother must have been suspicious about this spiritual crisis that you claimed you were going through?"

"Not at all. . . . She knew that I was a very sensitive boy . . . deeply meditative. . . . At that time I sincerely believe that my moms had no inkling that I was using drugs. . . ."

"The sister who was so close to you. . . . Did she know?"

"No one in my family had any intimation of my drug use . . . no one. . . . And no one else in the entire family ever used drugs."

"That must be of interest to you. . . . You were the only one. . . . This includes reefers, too?"

"They used nothing . . . ever . . . any of them. I was the only drug abuser. . . ."

"But you concealed the fact that you were using drugs. . . . That indicates something. . . ."

"I can't deny that. . . . I did conceal it. . . . Later, at the age of twenty-one or twenty-two, when the community first began to wise up to the fact that narcotics were around, then and only then did my mother begin to suspect. . . . And I think she then began to understand some of my actions, some of the alien things that I had done. . . ."

"Did she ever put it to you directly?"

Russell chuckled: "My mother was just a little slip of a woman, worn as smooth as a bone by life, but she was valiant. She stood there. . . . 'Sullie, is you usin' that stuff?' Now, I can't lie to my mother . . . I mean, I can't lie and hope to carry it off. . . . So, when I shrugged off her question . . . well, right away she knew. . . . She knew. But she also knew her boy, and she knew that I would finally come out on top, which as you can see I have. . . ."

"You mean by being part of this rehabilitation program . . . ?"

"Precisely my meaning. . . . At last, in an organized way, at the proper time, I am doing what is necessary."

I suddenly wondered if it was because Russell had talked to himself a great deal, as some lonely people will, narcotic addicts as well, that his tone nearly always sounded didactic. . . . There would be a better time later on to ask him. "A number of very significant events occurred in those years between the time you started on drugs and now . . . the Second World War, Korean conflict. . . ."

"Yes, history like a curtain hung around me. . . ."

"Did you see military service?"

"No, I didn't," he said shortly.

"That was because you were in prison or because you were a drug user?"

"Neither. . . . Actually, when the impending hostilities became apparent to me, I cleaned myself up. . . . Got off drugs and went to an induction center to sign up for the Air Force. I was trying to volunteer. It wasn't an intelligent action on my part. . . . The sergeant at the desk said: 'I'm sorry. We can't take you. . . . We don't need you. . . . Furthermore, we have no place in the American Air Force for niggers.' That's exactly the way he put it. . . ."

"It's a word that's sprinkled throughout your life."

"Who would know better than a Black American? So now, after Pearl Harbor and the induction process began to gobble up men —black, white, green or orange—I got my notice. . . . Mine was a very simple decision. Since my color hadn't changed, obviously they had lowered their standards . . . but I hadn't, you see. . . . Once a nigger, always a nigger. . . . I wasn't going into their army. So I got me nine goof balls, about seven caps of cocaine, an equal amount of heroin, two morphine ampules, three tubes of benzedrine, and I drank all night . . . all this on the night before my induction examination. . . . And the last thing I did just before I appeared at the induction center was to smoke two heavy joints. . . ." He chuckled. "They rejected me as being unfit for military service."

"I'm surprised that they didn't discover that you were really dead after all that stuff."

"You're right, but in those days I had a remarkable constitution. . . . I could sit at home and shoot up four or five grains of morphine at one time, and my regular dosage was only half a grain. . . . That'll give you some idea of my robustness. . . ."

"Chances are, don't you think, that they would have rejected you anyway once they detected your tracks?"

"That's a fallacy, Mr. Cortina. . . . True, the doctor saw marks, pinhead marks, but no tracks, because we didn't make tracks in those days the way they do today. . . . And we used alcohol at the point of insertion. . . . No, this track business is fairly recent. . . . We couldn't afford to have tracks in those days. We were ashamed to reveal that we were drug addicts. We wanted to conceal that knowledge from our families, from everyone. I have a hunch that today some of these infantile heroin addicts like to show off their tracks as a kind of badge . . . a badge of kinship, battle citations . . . because they haven't got anything else of value to show for themselves. . . . No, Mr. Cortina, in those days we made no boast of our drug dependence. . . . All that is part of the recent scene. . . . Very different. . . . But, in any case, the army never troubled me again."

3

It was the third scheduled appointment, but I was detained at the reception lobby. They knew me there. I had been in and out of the facility for several years. Usually my reception was minimally polite. They suffered my presence because they had received instructions to that effect—although it was easy enough to perceive that they were very suspicious of any man who worked closely with "dope fiends," particularly one who spent most of his time listening to their tales or "webs," the premise being that only the real professionals, the custodians, understood how devious, selfish, vicious and contemptible the drug user really was. But this day the atmosphere was ever so subtly different. There was a current of tension. . . . No attempt was made at politeness. They ordered me to put down my equipment and wait. I would have to see the director, but he was engaged. A quarter of an hour passed, and then another. Mine was a fairly tight schedule, so I questioned the guard at the desk. He leaned forward. "There's a rumpus going on . . . some kind of strike. . . . You may not even get in today. . . . You'll just have to wait. . . ."

An hour later I was still cooling my heels in the lobby. I could wait no longer if I was still to get my interview and appear at another place in the city a few hours later. I asked the guard if he could get my liaison man on the intramural phone. . . . He tried to locate the man. . . . It was a grudging effort because the young man was plainly upset; he seemed almost afraid of something. He paged my contact over the public address system. "He'll call back if he can. . . . I'm sorry, just take a seat. . . ."

Shortly afterward, his telephone rang and he passed it over to me. "It's your guy. . . ."

"It's Cortina. . . . I'm here to see Russell for our monthly session. . . ."

"I'm afraid that's not possible right now, Mr. Cortina. We're having some unrest in the facility. . . . Roxy won't be available. . . . Roxy and some others are confined to their section. . . . You might have to reschedule your meeting."

Roxy. . . . Roxy. . . . That was an interesting variation of Russell. "Can I reschedule for tonight . . . ? I'm in Salt Lake City tomorrow. . . ."

"I can't say, Mr. Cortina. . . . Why not call me later in the day . . . ?"

I gathered my equipment and thanked the guard. He nodded at me grimly, as much as to say: "See, wise guy, the way it is? No time for amateurs."

The "Roxy" part fascinated me; it was provocative.

Later, after finishing my other interview, I came back. It was now in the late afternoon, a new shift had come on, and I spoke to the replacement receptionist. He admitted me but got me an escort. I was taken to an office where I waited, my equipment on the floor next to me. In a short time a harried young man, dressed up to the moment—long hair, sideburns, wide tie, semi-Edwardian coat and buckle shoes—came in and shook my hand. "I regret that you've had this experience, Mr. Cortina. . . . One of our days," he said soberly. "I think, unless you want to come back tonight, that you'll have to skip your interview this month. . . ."

"I'll come back tonight. . . . I'd just as soon not have a break in the sequence. . . . Eight o'clock too early?"

He looked at me—he was having a hard time understanding my persistence; obviously my kind had little or no appreciation of the problems involved in operating a facility for drug addicts. "Just a minute. . . . I'll have to call the director." After he made his call, he said, "It'll be all right, Mr. Cortina. I'll make arrangements. . . . The front desk at ten minutes to eight. We'll have a man sit in with you during the interview."

"That's no good," I said evenly. "No one sits in during the interview. . . ."

"That's the way it will have to be," he said, and he dismissed me.

"May I use the telephone, please? I'll call the director. . . ."

"You can't use the phone. . . ." He bit his lip. "All right, you can have your interview alone with Roxy. . . . But don't you realize how dangerous these sociopaths are?" And now I really was dismissed!

My equipment was ready, and I sat there in the old refectory, studying that mural. What a curious painting it was, that white winding road, snaking higher and higher up to the clouds toward that towered castle . . . and above that, in a swirl of golden cloud, a cross . . . a cross whose corpus was large out of all proportion.

Russell came in gravely. We shook hands and his was a firm, strong handclasp. It had impressed me before by its strength. "Well, Russell, I'm glad to see you. I had my doubts there for a while. Is it convenient for you to see me now?"

"If you can bear with my preoccupation, Mr. Cortina, we can talk together."

"Good. Have a seat. . . . I'll start the playback. . . ."

"I do enjoy these sessions with you. . . . They're very stimulating. . . . We've had some conflict here today. Fortunately, through my peace-making efforts things have been resolved. There was a knife missing and I found it. . . . Some of these young people today are very rash, not at all amenable to reasonable process. . . . But I've soothed tempers all the way around and perhaps made the director understand that, though we are in a sense inmates, we should be granted a little more say in the direction and operation of this facility . . . a little bit of autonomy or an idea that we have some." He smiled.

What a marvelous mixture of social-worker, psychologist, and chaplain jargon came from Russell. One knew immediately that he had been exposed over the years to a variety of institutional settings. . . . But I asked no questions, and shortly we heard the recording of Russell's voice on the previous month's tape. When it finished, he said: "The past is soothing, it's revealing. . . . You recapture memory for me, Mr. Cortina, and make it permanent. . . ."

"Yes, the tape will do that at least. I would suspect that it also offers you a chance to see if your perceptions are accurate. . . . Only you would know that. . . ."

He nodded: "Yes, it is something to be outside of yourself, questioning, reflecting on yourself."

"Do you have any family left, Russell?"

"None. . . . Lost. . . . Gone. . . . No wife, no mother, no sisters. . . . All gone. . . . But I do have children . . . children born out of wedlock. You see, I've never been married, but I have been living common-law with many women over the years. And there has been one more enduring relationship of some ten years standing with a very gracious person that I refer to as a lady. I have to refer to her as that, a person quite above my life. . . . She occupies this special place, a sanctuary because she has nothing to do with, nor does she know about, the sordidness of the street, the prostitution, the thievery, the narcotics. . . . She has never been part of this, though she is very curious about this part of my life, naturally. . . . I have told her that she is my only link with reality. That I need her to cling to because she is reality, someone who has the power to recall me to myself . . . to remind me: 'Don't go too far, because you know that this is merely a game you are playing, you just want to keep up with people and things through inflating your own ego and what not.' And she has thoroughly understood this role that I have given her in my life."

"Is she the mother of any of these children?"

"No," he said wistfully. . . . "No, she had an inverted womb; she couldn't bear children . . . though they would have been beautiful. . . ."

"How many children have you fathered, Russell?"

He went through the ceremony of taking a cigarette and lighting it. There were seventeen of them, fifteen of whom are still alive. Two died of diphtheria. . . . Most of them are grown now. I have twin sons, thirty years of age. . . ."

"Do you keep track of these children. . . ?"

"Yes, I do. . . . I admit it's rather haphazard, but I think I know where each one is. . . ."

"Have any of them gone to drugs?"

He said slowly, dispassionately: "None of them. . . . Wait, let me take that back. . . . Up until several of my sons were sent to Vietnam, none of my children took drugs. . . . But I grieve to say that those sons will be exposed to the greatest bargain-basement offering of heroin the world has ever seen, exceeding even the most flamboyant fantasy nursed by any junkie. The White imperative —and I am not a bitter man, Mr. Cortina—to destroy my people will have spoken again. . . ." Russell chuckled grimly. "But what a backlash this will have. . . . What a backlash. . . . There's moaning and crying about the drug problem now . . . just wait until these young men, exposed to heroin in that sink of war, return to their communities with that hunger. . . . We will see the greatest heroin explosion of all time. . . . No one will be spared. . . . And you will be able to thank the United States White Army for 'Onward Doped-up Soldier.' "

"The army is aware that it has a problem. . . . They admit it, Russell. . . ."

"Of course, since they can't conceal it. But they lump together the soft drugs and the hard drugs as if they were exactly the same. . . . They bust men for use, never realizing that drugs are spread like chicken pox or anything else contagious. . . . Ah, yes, the white communities all over this glorious nation will have a debt to pay to the U.S. Army that will be well nigh incalculable. . . . Another brilliant achievement by that sterling corps. . . . So I suspect that my boys will come back with a habit . . . for a better reason than the other White boys who'll have habits. . . . My boys will be niggers in uniform, just like their father was a nigger going up for service. . . . But these niggers were accepted. . . . Black flesh bleeds darker . . . not as much contrast as when white flesh bleeds. . . . Besides, what difference does it make . . . ? the nigger breeds like a rabbit anyway. . . ."

It set my teeth on edge to hear the emotionless, quiet pronouncement. It was as near as I had ever heard Russell come to involvement with something other than himself. And I had to agree with his feeling about the Army badly mishandling what was potentially the most dangerous menace to the country to emerge from the Vietnam conflict. "This concern that you feel, Russell . . . did that extend to your support of these children . . . ? You had to provide for them?"

"I was instructed to by the court on several occasions. But most times I was able to persuade the grandmothers, that is, the mothers of the girls whom I had made pregnant, I was able to demonstrate to them that, while I was smitten by their daughters, I was constitutionally unsuited to be a husband. . . . I revealed my shortcomings—dope fiend, criminal, social outcast. . . . I illustrated to them that I would not be able to cope with the responsibilities of husband and father . . . that it would be a wanton ruining of a lovely girl's life to saddle her with me. . . . So you see how I made my moves, Mr. Cortina."

"Bigamy would have been. . . ."

He stopped me with his upraised hand: "You can't be imprisoned when you're already imprisoned. . . . This was exactly my point in explaining my ineligibility to my putative mother-in-laws. . . . You see, I have spent twenty-five of my fifty-two years in institutions. . . . Even if I'd wanted to, I couldn't have provided for these girls and my children. . . . It was impossible. . . ."

"Actually, you were away while they were growing up." Russell nodded solemnly. I filled my pipe. "Just about half of your life spent in confinement, Russell. All drug-related commitments?"

"Right. . . . All drug-related. . . . But about the years out of my life, surely you realize in your kind of work, meeting so many people, that some of us have a capacity for living what life we enjoy very intensely. . . . Some of us can live more in six months than others can live in six years. . . . This is my life style; there's nothing that I turn my hand to that I don't live to the fullest. This is why at my age I have a well-kept body, a broad outlook, a philosophy, a tolerance. . . . Life fascinates. . . . Though a lot of the youth here say 'The Old Man,' they have respect . . . for they'll never experience what I have and reach my age as I am. . . . I'm not putting myself on a pedestal. The truth must be faced without false modesty. . . ."

"Well, certainly I don't often follow fifty-two-year-old heroin abusers."

There was a small grunt. "For good and adequate reasons. They're dead or immensely skillful in handling their addiction. . . . They're around and I have met them. . . . Usually they're White, with money, and they can control their habit. . . . But they really haven't lived. They can't understand that they have been gaming all these years, gaming themselves, not coming to grips with the essential self-deception. They've been playing off of other people to get what they needed and feeling it a necessity to live that way. . . ."

"Usually they're very well defended . . . very well, indeed?" I glanced at him, wondering whether I had pierced his defenses. Either he seemed to find my question irrelevant or I had been too subtle. I said more directly: "One can build a lot of walls in fifty-two years. You wonder after a while what those walls conceal. . . . Perhaps the fear is always that if the walls come down the person hiding behind them will be destroyed. . . ."

"Maybe they don't feel that they will be destroyed. . . . Maybe it is that this roaring lion will be revealed as a purring kitten . . . an image destroyed. . . . You see, Mr. Cortina, group therapy is something that I have embraced during every one of my incarcerations. I have taken every opportunity to participate in group therapy."

"To gain insight into yourself. . . ?"

"Precisely. My quest is unending. . . . I keep looking and probing because I'm not going to give up until I have wrested a cause.
. . . I will not give up. I will continue to try . . . because one day,
if I can live, I will know. . . . You remember your Bible? 'I had
not thought to see thy face.' I will finally see my face."

"Are you saying that you feel there are specific problems that
you have which keep you on drugs?"

"A slight correction—that *kept* me on drugs. . . . Otherwise
you're right. . . . There are a number of dark corners in myself
that I can't come to grips with. . . . How can I associate with the
people I do, for instance . . . ? Now, I have used my years of in-
carceration very productively. . . . I studied voice production, Eng-
lish composition and literature, history, and music, and psychology.
. . . I think I'm not boasting when I claim for myself a certain
poise and ability to handle situations, such as this confrontation
today. . . . Inevitably I was looked to for leadership. . . . It was I
who was sent as representative to the director of the facility, and it
will be I who will administrate the new limited autonomy. . . .
But how can I associate myself with drug fiends, people who have
no pride, no image of themselves as anything but cripples, failures,
pariahs? The drug addict is a person forever off balance, his life
poised on slender accident. I'm not like that. Why do I allow myself to be entirely seduced by heroin? Am I afraid of my own
power? Let me tell you of an occurrence in my life." He chose his
cigarette with care, lighted it. "I was approached by a fellow who
had access to quite a bit of narcotics. And he commented to me:
'You seem to be a pretty cool dude, and since you're up in age, you
should know the game inside out. How are you making it?' This
was an interesting opening, so I asked him what he meant. . . .
Well, we talked, you know, one word leading to another, and the
first thing I knew he was giving me fifty bags, you know. And you
understand how the game operates, Mr. Cortina: When you sell
out the fifty bags, you turn in the money and you get yourself another bundle. I was doing this with such success that I was disposing of four bundles a day. So you can see that I'm making a good
dollar. I'm taking care of my own habit; as a matter of fact, being

somewhat of an extremist, I was using more narcotics than what was really necessary. . . ."

"Getting greedy is the usual phrase used by addicts."

"Yes, precisely. . . . I was getting greedy. . . . And also I had a lot of compassion for people out there who needed straightening out, who were getting sick and had no money to pay for their fix. . . . Now you know there are all of the moralists who would attack me on this point—let him kick and take it, et cetera. . . . But when an addict is sick and suffering, that's all I see, a sick man. . . . In any case I provided for these kinds of contingencies far too many times—this, plus my being greedy. . . ." He dusted off the ash from his cigarette.

"So you found yourself short in your money turn-in to the dealer. . . . And I imagine that this was brought to your attention."

"It's a pleasure to talk to an intelligent man, a man who savvys the drug subculture. . . . That's it, exactly . . . The man he told me not to act the good Samaritan . . . it could be a position of no return. . . . I agreed, for the man was right, and I explained to him that I would square it all up before the week was out. . . . Now, this situation went on for more than I anticipated. . . . And business was good; I was up to moving seven bundles a day. That's a lot of stuff. . . . And a lot of money when you consider that he's getting eleven dollars a bag, because the going price is fifteen dollars in my city. . . . You see, my cut was the four dollars; so you see, for every fifty bags I'm making two hundred dollars clear profit, plus he was very generous, the man, he was giving me ten bags for my own habit. . . . These I could turn into another one hundred and fifty dollars a day. . . . So you can see I am in high grass up to my chest. . . ."

"But you continued to use heavily yourself . . . ?"

"Exactly. . . . But I was taking care of a lot of habits . . . something that certain people looked forward to each day. . . . However, the narcotic squad ran down on me one night."

"Had you been ratted out . . . ?"

"I don't think so. . . . It was pure accident. . . . I just happened to see them in the nick of time. I turned around and started running. They took off right after me. Now, I had the stuff, how was I going to get rid of it . . . ? I knew that if they saw my arms in a throwing gesture it would be all over . . . they'd find the stuff and that would be the name of the game. . . . As I'm running, I'm making my move. . . . I take the bags in my thumbs and flick them like coins into the doorways. . . . All the time I'm leading these fellas down different blocks, and then I suddenly stop and let them catch up with me. . . . I'm put up against a wall and frisked. . . . I'm clean, and they're tearing their hair out. . . . They're fat and out of shape, they've been running for blocks, and for what . . . ? They're blowing off like whales, and they search me again and again. . . . They can't come up with a thing, and I'm a Black son of a bitch and a no-good nigger, but they have a job to do and I know that they are laboring under frustration in this particular instance, so I don't take no offense. . . . And by and by they let me go. . . . What else can they do?"

"They didn't knock you around?"

"No, they were gentlemen. Besides, we were in a colored neighborhood, and they knew chances were that they would have to come back again. . . . No, there are accommodations in all walks of life, Mr. Cortina. . . ."

"So you escaped unscathed. . . ."

"Far from it. . . . No, my troubles now really began. . . . Where had the heroin landed? How much had I thrown away . . . ? I searched for what must have been hours, and I couldn't come up with it . . . what in the excitement of the chase and me running like a youth and not a grandfather. I hadn't an idea of where that stuff had got to. Besides, I had been hawking it so intensely, using so much personally, and drinking as well, that I really hadn't been taking care of myself. . . . I was burning at too high a flame . . . and it was me that was the candle that was being consumed. . . . I needed sleep. . . . So, I had to make a move. Right away I made it. A woman is always available somewhere, it's been my experience, and Royola was my choice. I went to her place, and I was just barely high, but fatigue was closing in on me mighty fast. I took the five bags that I had found after my searching and the money from the collection and put them in my left hand, and I put that hand in my pocket in a fist. . . . I knew I was going to pass out, but I felt somewhat protected here with Royola because she and I had had our thing together for a long time. But how careful I was, though I was far from being alert. I knew that she was an outgoing type, a lot of people came to her house to use her works or some just to lay up because they had no place else to go. . . . So I calculated that they would see me asleep with my fisted-up hand in my pocket and they would automatically hook up the score. . . . But I prided myself on being such a feather-light sleeper that I was convinced that, before they could get that hand out of my pocket, I would be wide awake. . . ." Russell disposed of his cigarette. "I wasn't taking into consideration that I had been on my feet for more than forty-eight hours, I had shot up far too much narcotics, and I was utterly played out. . . . I woke up seven or eight hours later. . . . I was lying face down on the couch, and my left arm was hanging over the side, my wrist watch just dangling from my wrist. I understood at once what had happened. They'd taken my watch off, examined it, and put it back on my wrist . . . it was too cheap for them to keep. I knew that there was no point in checking my person because I would find neither money or narcotics. . . ."

"So you were beaten out. . . ."

"Yes, I was beaten out of stuff and money, and this is the complication: I'd thrown away almost a bundle because of the narcotic squad, I'd lost collection money, and I want to emphasize that I felt responsible for this double loss. . . ."

"Responsible to your supplier, you mean?"

"Exactly, I felt completely responsible for what had happened. . . . My dealer said to me when he gave me the last bundle that I looked kind of tired and high and since it was raining out I should go home and rest up for a while. . . . 'Because I know that you're taking care of business for me. I'm more than satisfied,' he says. . . . But I wouldn't take that good advice he passed out . . . that's why I felt responsible. And being in the game so long . . . I know just how he's going to reason. I'm behind in my money anyway, I've just blown another collection, and I've tossed away almost a bundle. . . . He would figure in only one way: I had become slick. Roxy has become slick, he's made too much money, and he thinks he's got me cornered now. . . . So consequently, I figure I better put something like distance between us until I can square up accounts. . . . I figured something would break for me, because in the past I had found that when I tried real hard to scare up some money I got things set in motion so that money was generated. I found another dealer who gave me some dope—now, what with one thing and the other, some six days had passed since I had welshed out on my regular connection—some dope, mind you, not enough to build a new route with, not enough to supply my own habit. Consequently, I was almost always sick or on the verge. . . . I was laying up at this female's place. . . . She was a very generous person . . . she had given me what little she had of dope but I was still sick. . . . And I'm troubled, you know. Dope addicts have the highest instinct for suspiciousness of any group . . . it's a sixth sense with them. So I'm troubled. I know in this tight world of addict and pusher that my old connection has got to be looking for me to avenge himself, and I also know that other addicts has seen me circulating and they are not above sharing my whereabouts with this pusher, so I am most apprehensive. And then being semisick from not getting enough stuff. . . . It was a wretched man who lay in that apartment. . . . So I slipped off into this sick drowse, and I felt myself being lifted up, I felt myself walking down the stairs, I felt myself being seated. . . . I couldn't break through this drowse that I was in, but I sensed that these things were happening to me. Well, when I came back to actuality, and God knows how long I had been out, I was in a car and it had just pulled into an open field. . . . To this day I don't know where that field was. The windows had been lowered in the car and the air was striking me in the face, and this is what had brought me to consciousness. And right away, with that quickness of defense, I knew what was about to happen. . . . Right away I hooked it all up because I looked at the dude behind the wheel, I looked at the dude sitting next to him, and I looked at the dude sitting next to me, my old supplier—an open field, the greyness of night, and these three—you don't need ESP to understand that Roxy is ticketed for a long, one-way trip. So right away I hit the door on the left side and out I go, but they had calculated this move. . . . I was no sooner out than one came at me from around the car, another from the front, and the third one right on me. . . . But I'm so sick and I had deteriorated so much from the narcotics that I was down to about a hundred and twenty pounds. I know that these dudes are going to smash me into unrecognition just as soon as I raise my hands in defense. The best thing I can do is to use a psychological overlay and defuse them: 'Hold it, man. I don't know why you're doing this without having a conversation and confronting me to find out the reasons for what I have done and the motivations for it . . . I think it is very necessary.' They weren't listening. I was hit from behind, I was hit from the front, I got kicked to the ground, stomped on. . . . And I kept pushing myself up, only to get beaten to the ground. . . . And one of them is saying through his heavy breathing: 'Let's get out his eyes, let's kick them out so the son of a bitch will walk around with a tin cup.' Three of them struck at once. . . . I was just raked with blows, and then suddenly it all stopped. Maybe they were scared off. God knows. All I know, I lay on the ground, a lump of flesh, and I was alone, and I could smell soil and dampness. See, I wasn't sure whether this was a game on their part, they were laying for me to try and get up so that they could come at me again, so I was very cautious. . . . I lay there still, and then I made my move. . . . I got to my knees. . . . Nobody there, just me in that big field, and over the way I saw an occasional scrape of headlights . . . that would have been the road. Somehow, I managed to drag me over to that road and to get some kindly soul to take me home. . . ."

"Where were you living?"

"I had these various female associates who I shared facilities with. . . . So I got to one of them. . . ."

"Why didn't you go to a hospital with your wounds?"

"The man who picked me up wanted to take me, but I didn't want anything officialwise to be put in motion. . . . So, as I related, I got to Sidna's place, and she's high but nonetheless filled with concern. . . . And she does what she can to ease my sufferings, and I lay there, and I thought about what had happened to me and what I had done to catch such a beating and have my eyesight threatened. . . . I had made that supplier an awful lot of money in a short time, a great bundle of money. . . . Now, I was wrong in what I did. . . . And I should have gotten a re-buke like his cutting off my commission for a week, or drying me up for a week, or rap to me, 'Roxy, you're forever playing games, and that's why you wind up in the penitentiary, but you don't play games with Milo.' This kind of reprimand would have been in keeping and I would have profited by it. . . . We were only talking of two Gs at most in money. That's all the money involved, two Gs. Now, I understand that some people put more value on money than others. . . . I could never have attacked a man for something like this. . . . But, being in the game so long, I knew that worse things had been done to people for less—acid in the face, body disfigurement . . . and worse. . . ."

"You're fortunate that you weren't killed or permanently disabled. . . . Were these men addicts who assaulted you?"

"Only one of them. . . . The driver and my supplier were nonusers. . . . That's the difference, because I've played the game with other suppliers who were users, and the most they would ever do in the way of wreaking revenge was a reprimand . . . never violence. They would rap: 'Now, listen Roxy. . . . You're messing up. We're not going to lose friendship, we're not going to fight, we're not going to go through all these changes. You looking for me and me looking for you, that's folly. You're blowing a good thing, . . . but you're the loser, Roxy. . . . Sure, you hurt me a little, but I'm the man with the stuff and I never lose money. . . . You got to be the loser, Roxy.' That's the way it was handled by the addict supplier. . . . It's the nonuser supplier who's the beast in the jungle. . . . Very few addicts get behind that violent image, Mr. Cortina. . . ."

Muscular and fit as he looked now, I thought that Russell might be a formidable opponent. I wondered how calm and nonviolent he might be in a confrontation. "How did you get that scar? From a street fight?" I watched him trace the scar with a finger; it extended across his throat. . . . Russell said: "No man did that. . . .

It was a woman. . . . A woman in her fiery, jealous rage uncovered me with another broad, and she slashed me with her shears. . . . But I could see that it was an act born out of love. . . . She's a very dear friend of mine to this day—though now she's a grandmother. . . ."

"Yours has been a life punctuated by violence and confinement, Russell. I'm surprised that you are in a program like this. . . . You had to volunteer. It's been my experience that most old-timers look upon prisons as the place to clean up. . . ."

"That is true, but I'm not like them. I've always tried to interject thought into my life, thought and planning. . . . And I would like to add another dimension to my life, Mr. Cortina. . . . You said it has been punctuated by violence and confinement—an apt couplet—but also sprinkled in there has been love. . . . I have been loved by many women . . . and I say that with gratitude to them, for their influence has kept me reasonable. . . . Into my life at a moment of crisis has always stepped a woman . . . even in the case I related to you a moment ago. It was Sidna who made me let slip the revenge I was carrying in my heart for this supplier. I had made up my mind to kill him . . . to kill him. But Sidna, who was a young thing—and I think I became a father image for her—Sidna, even though she was a user, prevailed upon me to drop them images of revenge. . . ."

"Maybe you had also come to the end of the line, Russell, and you knew it. . . ."

"That is a sound conjecture."

"Let's face it—you had allowed yourself to run down, you had become a very heavy user, and you had lost your supplier. . . . That all adds up to the end of the line. . . . But even so, for you to come in here . . . a self-committal, that's quite a reversal. With all your prison experience, loss of freedom would be a genuine hangup."

"But you remember what I said earlier today about always seeking insights into myself, always being on the alert as to understanding myself and my problems. . . . All these factors go into understanding my moves at this particular time. . . ."

"When did this fearful beating occur?"

"Relatively recently . . . just about a month before I signed my-self in here. . . . Sidna, this young thing, was a great help to me. . . . She restored my perspective, made me ease off my revenge thing, and helped me to see that I had to give over this drug thing; I had to, I was too superior to it, the company was beneath me. . . . I began to cut down on my amount, and I hooked up with a doctor on the north side and he was giving me some metha-done. And as the days went on, my system was feeling it and not the heroin, and because of this I am getting to be more and more rational in my self-evaluation. . . . My mind is clear now and I re-alize many things. I got this terrible beating because I had permit-ted myself to deteriorate mentally and physically. I found myself jammed into a plight because of narcotics. . . . I ran the whole scheme to myself. . . . I had laid myself out to all of what had happened because I had thrown in everything with narcotics, and it was time for me to reassert my hold over myself and over my destiny. . . . And I took Sidna one night, and we lay there in the bed and I told her: 'Sidna, I've got to give myself a chance. I must. Now I have been for cures before . . . I have cleaned up be-fore. I took four separate and distinct hospital courses. . . . It's time, baby, for me to come to grips with this intervener in my life, because heroin is holding me down now and I have always wres-tled my way to being the in-charge man.' "

"How had you learned about methadone, Russell?"

"On the street. . . . It has a specific kind of use there, you un-derstand. I've bought pills from people who had gotten them from their doctors as part of a prescribed medical treatment. Let me make methadone's place clear for the addict. Now you know that heroin's appetite is wolfish, and you got to feed that wolf Satur-days, Sundays and all days. . . . Now how do you handle that on those rainy Sundays when your opportunities are limited, when you can't raise up the bread . . . ? And maybe you're tired and maybe you're not getting that old euphoria, that love-hate sensation, so you want to lay up . . . you want to perk up the old rapture. . . . That's where the methadone comes in. . . . Take your ten dollars and buy twenty pills, and that'll hold you for a weekend and save money and restore you as well. . . ."

"Had you ever considered methadone maintainence as an alternative to your heroin addiction?"

"Oh, yes, not only considered it but entertained it very soberly. . . . You see, after the beating, after seeing my grey hair, after laying up with this young beauty, I could see the jaws of that life that I had led for more than a generation slowly closing, closing with me in the grip. . . . But conditioning is a powerful force. . . . I was, in a sense, heroin . . . after thirty-some years, I was heroin. . . . And on the other side, I can take care of it, I can control it. When the worst comes, I'll go to prison and be cleaned up there. But my own native intelligence brought home to me that all of those maneuvers were just maneuvers and nothing more, designed to bring those jaws closer. . . . It was then I decided fatefully to find a program. It was time that Roxy met up with Russell, time for that fateful confrontation of these two. . . . It was time." The ribbon eased from the supply reel, the tape was finished. I removed his microphone. "It's fascinating, Russell. Your voice has a wizardry all of its own. . . ."

His face broke into a smile of complete delight, as if he had suddenly been lighted up inside. "Thank you. . . . That phrase spins a web . . . 'a wizardry all of its own.' Yes, that's quite a phrase, Mr. Cortina. . . ."

We shook hands. "I'll see you in a month. I hope that the unrest here will have eased up. . . ."

Still holding my hand, Russell said: "It's all over. You see, my finding that knife, my going to the director as spokesman, my becoming a representative of the residents here, my sitting on that board of staff and inmates . . . well, these moves on my part defused an ugly situation. . . ."

I watched his straight back, his erect shoulders, his relaxed, poised stride, his air of being equal to all contingencies, and I had the sudden feeling, that kind of swift intuitive realization, that it had been Russell who had stolen that knife and hidden it, it had been Russell who had indeed made his move, it had been Russell who had engineered that whole institutional rumpus. . . . It had been he, it was in his style as a mover of events. Whatever for? Whatever for?

4

Everything was ready for the playback. I sat there in that unbelievable refectory, studying that unbelievable mural. The thought of a
group of nuns having uttered grace before they ate, having peered
reverently toward that fresco, the climate of piety, and my waiting
for Russell with his history. . . . It was incredible.

On this ocasion I had had no difficulty getting into the institution. The old minimal kind of courtesy prevailed; apparently life
had settled back into its pattern of conformity. The door opened. It
was the young fashion plate who had spoken to me last time. . . .
He thrust out his hand. "Mr. Cortina, I want to apologize for my
rudeness last month." I assured him that there was no need. His
tone less chastened now, he went on: "They're such devious people.
Forever trying to alter reality—whether they're on narcotics or
not. They simply cannot accept things for what they are." I was
puzzled. Why was this young man bothering to share his theories
with me? His apology I could understand—it cleaned up a ran-
kling incident for him—but why the lesson? "Somehow," he
continued, "the narcotics addict only functions when he is managing reality, moving it around like a piece of jigsaw puzzle, to make
some kind of screwed-up picture. . . . It's an interesting phenome-
non. . . . Have they sent for Roxy for you?"

"Yes, they said he was on his way."

"Fascinating character, isn't he? Real, classical sociopath, don't
you find?"

"You indicated that the last time we met, Mr . . . er . . . er."

"Elkins, Pete Elkins. I'm the junior psychologist on staff. . . .
Roxy has got to be the most consummate sociopath I've ever met

. . . a genuinely dangerous individual . . . totally defended, basically disturbed, but with a kind of indefatigable cunning. . . . Is this your experience as well, Mr. Cortina?"

I had an idea now why he was taking the time to conciliate me. "My brief contact with Russell wouldn't permit my having an opinion. I'm just an interviewer, Mr. Elkins."

He gestured toward the tape. "These will be available to us?"

"I really can't answer that question. Perhaps the director can."

"Doesn't it amaze you that Russell has survived after all of those years in the drug world . . . ? He's the oldest resident in the facility."

"And he's your client?"

"Oh, yes, didn't I make that clear? I meant to. . . ."

"You find him difficult to work with?"

"Not difficult, just characteristically sociopathic, unreceptive. He's just a slippery son of a bitch. And he'll get out of here and be back on drugs within a quarter of an hour. This is for him just another opportunity to show his cunning."

"It could be."

"What have you discovered through these exchanges with him, Mr. Cortina?"

"He's eloquent and, like most of us, pretty complex." Footsteps approached in the corridor. Mr. Elkins shook my hand again. "I think we should have a long chat together, Dr. Cortina. . . . Roxy has got to be made to cope with reality."

Russell entered the room.

"Good morning, Mr. Elkins . . . Mr. Cortina. . . . By the way, Mr. Elkins, have you a free quarter of an hour? There are details that we should discuss about the new governing board. How's your schedule? Mine indicates that this afternoon would permit me to see you. . . ."

The young man struggled with his own feelings and brought it off very well. "I'll have to see, Roxy. . . . I'll let you know. . . . I'll call your ward," he said as he went out the door.

"Thank you, Mr. Elkins. . . ." Russell seated himself, produced his cigarettes, and with a grave inclination of his head indicated that he was ready for our session to begin.

"When were you first called Roxy, Russell? How did it come about?"

"You mean, when was I first conscious of this other entity?" he asked, trimming his cigarette.

"That's exactly it. When were you first conscious of this other entity?"

"Well, I think it was about 1940 or thereabouts. I had been, or let me rephrase that, one of my pursuits had been that of sneak thief. I would go into a jewelry store and come out with some trinkets, rings, watches, pins, etc. . . . I was so phenomenally successful at this that after awhile I became known as the jewelry salesman, that is, I had this name in the projects . . . the housing projects in this colored slum—what's called today the Black ghetto. . . . When I'd show up in the projects, the children would chorus out: 'Mommy, here comes the man with the rings. . . .' This went on for quite a while, and as with everything that I turn my hand to, I studied gems. I had become fascinated by them. You know—planes and facets, weights, colors, mountings. I loved to sit and gaze at the stones . . . they mesmerized me. And there was something else about jewelry—it was a marvelous type of security . . . a few rings or stones or watches carefully hoarded up could ease the rainiest of days. You know, for the rent or for one of my women who had come on hard days, pregnant or some other human crisis. . . . It was my salvage money. . . . Now you can see that I probed this jewelry preoccupation pretty good. . . . Now the name came about in this manner. There was a woman I was paying some attention to, a tall, queenly creature, I'm sure that she was descended from some noble line in Africa. She was without doubt the most magnificently endowed woman physically that I had ever encountered. . . . She infatuated me. . . . I used to carry a little velvet tray in my pocket, and I would delight her by showing her these rings, permitting her to try them on. . . . She was all woman, she would oooh and aaah. . . . It was like her rolling around in soft waters. She loved the stones; they fascinated her. . . . And I used to say that these were my favors to her, and I'd give her a ring on occasion. When our son was born, I gave her a beautiful jade pendant. She whispered: 'Oh, Roxy . . . Roxy. . . .'

When she said it, I was struck by its absolute appropriateness. Struck."

"So that's how Roxy came into being? What happened to her?"

"There are two parts to your question; let me address myself to the former. . . . Resteena, that was her name, looked like a queen but she was not in actions. She was too talkative and too indiscreet. I had to back out of that relationship, though I often think about her. She was a wonderfully beautiful woman . . . and that should be enough. . . . Beauty shouldn't have to be responsible, Mr. Cortina. Who can blame a rose because it has a few thorns . . . ? Now, the second part of your question, now there is something very profound and significant. I was so delighted with the name Roxy that I mounted a small campaign to get people to call me that. I was successful, and I came to be called Roxy by nearly everybody I knew; even when I got to the penitentiaries I was known as Roxy. . . . But the deeper significance was there all the time, and I probed it. . . . Roxy was really that part of myself that was the narcotics addict, the sneak thief, the convict, the con artist, the panderer, the irresponsible asocial entity."

I sensed that he wanted me to question him. I knew that he would frame the question for me if I remained silent, as if I were at a loss to express it. I wanted him to say it. I moved a hand, as if searching. . . . Roxy leaned forward; he said helpfully: "I realized that I was two men, Roxy and Russell. That was the significance of that last declaration I made on that tape of last month. . . . I was two men."

"Yes, I understand. . . . May I ask if you were conscious of Russell?"

He inclined his head toward me. "Yes, I was. Very much conscious of him."

"When did you first become aware of him?"

"I've always been aware of him."

"You have been? How come Roxy became paramount, became dominant?"

"That's because, at the time, Russell was struggling to find something in life for himself. Something in life through which he could be creative. . . . And through this search, Russell became frustrated and confused and what not because a lot of the answers he sought weren't there. . . . They weren't there, Mr. Cortina."

"What were some of the questions Russell sought answers for? What were some of his goals?"

"In answering this question, a compound question, let me say this: Russell's father had disappeared out of his life at a very early age, and Russell did not have the father that he needed to identify with. I had often felt as a child that I was frustrated right there. I was confused as to what I was, with all those women around me. I didn't know what I wanted to be, what I wanted to get out of life. I wanted to be something. . . . I wanted to be . . . something. . . . But what . . . what? And I'd go round to the other kids' houses, and I would marvel at the closeness between the kid and his father and how when it would come up, maybe some grown person would ask, 'What do you want to be when you grow up, son?' 'I want to be like my daddy.' Or if this wasn't the case, the kid would say: 'I want to be a mechanic or a milkman,' because his father is a mechanic or a milkman. And here is this same longing in my heart to say the same thing, and it's not there because there is no father, there never has been. All that's there is the heart with its longing. . . . So, Mr. Cortina, when I came out of that reformatory, I realized that I had to find a new way. I was determined to find one, and in this confusion of trying so desperately to find something when I had no specific thing I was aiming at, I got lost, I got confused, I got to the point where I didn't care any more whether I found it or not. . . ."

"And this is where Roxy became assertive?"

"In a manner of speaking, yes, Roxy took over. . . . But I grasped the significance of this take-over. . . . It must have been about thirty years ago, I slowed down and I interrogated me: 'What's happenin', man? What are you doing? Where are you going?' And I replied to myself: 'Well, I really don't know which way I'm going or where this life of mine is going to lead, but I do know that if I am spared, as far as life goes, I am going to stop somewhere and go back and find out where I went astray. . . . I will go back and find Russell, sitting there confused and lonely and silent by the side of the road.' I knew that it would be necessary for Roxy to go through trial and adversity in order to come to this point of going back to Russell in order to make his moves. And then I would get fearful: 'Will it be too late, will too much of life have passed me by?' And then I would try to establish where I was, right at that moment. . . . You see, there never was anyone to say: 'Well, young man, don't do this,' or 'Listen, I don't think you should do that,' and give me direction and explanations and what not, and whereby I could gain respect for someone and myself. . . . This is what I didn't have and what I continuously wanted. . . ."

He looked at me, trying to fathom whether I fully appreciated his exposition.

"These two entities of Russell and Roxy . . . they're quite a study in contrasts. Russell, you indicate, was confused, unmotivated, lonely, immature, alienated, uncomfortable." I paused, unwilling to push too hard, too far.

He said, a touch pedantically: "I thought that this was understandable. Roxy would have to get all the experiences that Russell would need in order to succeed in the wide world."

"So Roxy took the hard knocks for Russell, is that it?"

"Precisely."

"You make it sound like a conscious process."

"It had to be, of necessity. . . . It had to be in order to make it work. Roxy had to subject himself to all of the underbelly of life, the seaminess, if you will, in order to enrich Russell, in order to give him the experience to make his moves. . . . I can't say less. . . . Like I told you a few minutes ago, when I stopped momentarily to appraise myself and my life, its directions and goals, . . . I knew that in order to become motivated, to be secure, to establish goals, I had to undergo all of these rigors on the part of Roxy in order to come to this specific point in my development."

"So your entrance into this rehabilitation program signals the death of Roxy—or at least his loss of supremacy?"

"That is so. You are reading me correctly."

"Would you say, then, that the use of heroin was part of this tug of war between Roxy and Russell?"

"Yes, definitely. . . . Heroin helped me—let me rephrase

that—heroin served the purpose of helping me to escape from the constant preoccupation with why did I have to be this kind of individual. Heroin helped me to stop, to find that peace I needed to interrupt that maddening pace out there. . . . I was caught up in the game, spinning my webs, making my moves. . . . I was powerless to break out of that force. . . . I took heroin to hear me say quietly: 'No man is an island but me. . . .' I'm an island. You bet you. I'm an island . . . I am an island of loneliness. . . ."

"Heroin was a palliative, is that it . . . it eased pain?"

"It gave me pause to reflect on what my conflict was. . . ."

"You took these other cures, you said. . . . How much did Russell emerge at those times?"

He almost appeared to be speaking to himself as he said: "Russell at those times only returned for the purpose of analyzing what had gone by, to tally up the progress, to find out how much further, how much longer the search had to go on. . . . How much more did I have to subject Roxy to in order for Russell to begin to move . . . ? I'd say: 'Do you think this is the time?' and Roxy would say: 'Not yet . . . there's more that I've got to undergo. . . .'"

"This quest of yours . . . search for realization . . . it seems that you developed few enduring relationships?"

"Which one of me?"

"Let's take Roxy first."

"Roxy had many, many relationships. You couldn't be in the game unless you did. . . ."

"But the many women you loved . . . this was as Roxy?"

"Of course as Roxy. . . . All of them but the one that I mentioned previously . . . the lady . . . that was as Russell. . . . That was as Russell. . . ."

"And that was the only relationship for Russell, that single one?"

He repeated mesmerically: "That single one."

"There were no other relationships . . . not with sister or aunt or relative of any sort?"

"Those were all Russell of course."

"I'm sorry but I don't understand. . . ."

He smiled. "It's very simple. My people, when I had people in those days, never had met Roxy. . . . I was always Russell to them . . . always. . . . You see, at the outset they never knew that Roxy existed. . . ."

"But with all the other women except the lady you were Roxy?"

"Exactly. . . . No, that's not to say that I would not have become Russell with them if the relationship developed in such a substantial way that I could have trusted them to meet Russell. . . . But they never did . . . they never did. . . . So I always remained Roxy, the sport, the expert, the talker, the wizard. That's what they wanted. . . ."

"Why, since Roxy seemed to be a man for all occasions, why should you become Russell with this lady . . . ?"

It seemed so obvious to him that I was simple-minded that he had to smile at me. "Because Sola could penetrate to me, she could divine the Russell part. . . . And I could rest my burden on her for a while, feel peace and security, forget that I was an island. . . . When I left Sola, the door closed behind her and the Russell I left there. . . . I'd be back outside again as Roxy, the island."

"Will Russell ever come to dominate Roxy?"

"Dominate? That's not the word, Mr. Cortina. . . ."

"Let me put it in another way. Is it possible that because of all the years of Roxy's being uppermost that Russell has been erased?" I asked, watching him keenly. He didn't take offense. He merely paused and said, again almost pedantically, "I should think that you would not need to ask the obvious."

"The obvious . . . ?"

"Russell is impervious to Roxy. . . ."

"How can you be so emphatic?"

"Because I am Russell. . . . You are talking to Russell. You have been talking to Russell for four months now. . . . I am Russell."

Our eyes met for a moment. "Are you?"

"I am Russell."

5

As I set up my equipment, I found myself stealing glances at that mural. I think I was trying to discover whether there was more to it than I was getting and whether a glance at it from a different position might reveal something. Probably some devoted, pious nun had spent weeks in painting it, an act of adoration and love. . . . Why did she paint the corpus so large? It appeared so gross: so large a Jesus could not have been crucified on so small a cross —but undoubtedly I was overlooking something.

"Well, Dr. Cortina, back with us again," he said cordially, extending his hand.

"Just mister. . . . Good morning, Mr. Elkins."

"Why not call me Pete, everybody else does. . . ." He sat down with an air of permanence. I thought surely something had happened to my interview. "I'm fascinated by your method. Roxy has been telling me about it. Pretty random, isn't it?"

"I suppose so. . . ."

"That kind of milieu, broad and unstructured, would appeal to Roxy, give him plenty of room to operate. . . . Sociopath is like that. . . . You must get awfully tired being lied to, Dr. Cortina."

"I can't say. . . . I'm not always conscious when it's happening."

"Well, with Roxy you could pretty well plot it as being nine-tenths lie and one-tenth manipulation. . . ."

Roxy certainly had set this young man up for a kind of chronic smouldering. I was tempted to ask him some questions but I didn't; I wasn't paid to interview staff.

"I read your last book, Dr. Cortina, on communication. It's very impressive . . . Don't you feel, though, that with drug addicts you leave yourself wide open? They're always conning and operating.

One has to be constantly alert to that. . . . An addict by nature is a schemer—cut everything away, tie up every kink in his nature, and you are left with a schemer. For example. . . ." At this point Russell entered, and Mr. Elkins greeted him and said: "Well, there's never enough time, is there? I look forward to that get-together, Doctor."

I closed the door behind him and looked at Russell. He seemed disconsolate. He said: "I thought I'd find him here."

"Why is that, Russell?"

"I told him that I was able to reveal more to you in one session than I could reveal to him in ten years. . . . I figured that would send him trotting here. . . ."

"I see," I said noncommittally. One didn't choose sides in an institution when one was a visitor; there were too many variables.

"Well, let's hear the tape. . . ." This morning Russell listened with the same air of poise, but he seemed out of sorts, lacking energy. The playback was more than three-quarters through when Russell leaned forward. "Could we begin to talk now, Mr. Cortina?"

"Certainly, Russell. . . . You're not feeling well today?"

"I'm troubled . . . I'm troubled. . . ."

"Something on the tape that we were hearing?"

"Oh, no, that was very well organized and expressed. No, not the tape. . . . That was very revealing. . . . No, this has to do with here, at the moment. . . . I told you that I entered this facility on my own. . . . I volunteered, a self-commitment. I had reached that place in life that was a crossroads and I knew it. Roxy knew it. . . . Roxy had finally gotten to that place in life, squeezed out that sum of experience that Russell needed in order to begin to function. That's why I came here. . . . I, Russell. . . . Now, when I started out here I was given methadone, and I was elated to think that I would flush my central nervous system of heroin and be free of its demands. . . . I suspect that the doctor, seeing my age and understanding that I had been a user for so many decades, prescribed a larger dose of methadone than I really needed. And pretty soon I had a new habit, a methadone habit, and that methadone habit working into my joints was worse than any habit I ever had in thirty-four years on heroin. Mr. Cortina, when I kicked methadone I was sick as I've never been sick in my life, and the mental distress was intense. . . ."

"Could it have been the combination of events and the methadone . . . ? Knowing that you had come to a crossroads, you were thrust down into a community of young drug abusers . . . you were back in an institutional setting again. . . . All those factors, Russell."

"Quite right. . . . All contributing to my aggravated reaction. But my point is this: I did suffer intensely, for quite some time. . . . But I had the wish to get well. . . . I wanted to hurry up," and Russell's speech speeded up at this point, "because I was impatient to make my moves, to do the things that Russell is now equipped to do. . . . But the methadone held me for quite a while and I'm convinced would still have its grip upon me except for a minor operation that I had to have. . . . They administered a synthetic morphine, and I'm convinced that that drove the methadone out of my system. When I got back here after the surgery, I felt free of anything addictive. . . . So I started to build myself up physically . . . calisthenics, weight lifting, handball, working in the office. . . . And then, as you know, we had some strife over wanting to have some autonomy, and I assumed great responsibility there. Spent a great deal of time working with the director and assistant director of this facility, trying to keep things manageable and free of emotion and violence. . . . I assumed responsibility for many things, always inserting myself wherever there was a problem, wherever there seemed to be an opening for me. . . . Now this I did because, as I related, Roxy has helped Russell to make his move. . . . I'm opening up now. I've come of age. I'm seeing young dudes around me with problems that Roxy had, Roxy who had no father, no guidance, no one to look up to, so I'm seeing these young dudes suffering this. And Russell, he steps right into that role . . . right in: 'Can I help you . . . ? Can I help you, young dude? Can I assist you in seeing your problems, to understand where you have taken a wrong turning and misread the signs in your life's path?' Oh, I'm giving myself without reserve. I'm writing letters to the director or the assistant director . . .

notes to the chief therapist. I'm designing training procedures for the staff so that they can understand the psychology of the narcotics abuser. I'm doing everything, making moves in all directions. . . . Russell has burst into life. . . . And then when our autonomous setup was approved, I was voted into being chief representative of the residents. And also the staff asked me to undertake the additional role of lay counselor to talk to the young dudes. Now this is a heavy responsibility, a mighty obligation. And I'm asking myself: 'Do I have the ability to live up to this faith that they have placed in me . . . ? Do I have the confidence to perform all of these significant, important, essential services . . . ? Do I?' I asked my contemporaries these questions. I asked them: 'Do you feel that I am the man?' And they said to me: 'Roxy, you are the *only* man in the entire facility who is uniquely qualified to perform these services.' "

"Curious, isn't it, that they referred to you as Roxy and not as Russell."

This observation did not sit well with Russell. His voice hardened: "Everybody who gets busted, who's in a joint, gets a nickname. . . . And it sticks. It's the way of joints. . . ."

For the first time, some skin had flaked off and I saw revealed the Roxy of the prisons, of the streets . . . momentarily.

"So I responds with my thanks and a vow that I will faithfully honor their trust. . . . To myself, I knew that I could handle these problems . . . I knew it. I was up to it, I was prepared. This was beautiful. It would be the first time in my life that I would have a chance to do something constructive and go all the way with it. Solid, solid. . . . I'll really achieve something beautiful here by doing a beautiful job. . . . This is all the surroundings of my mission, Mr. Cortina. . . . All the surroundings." He shook his head, an expression of incredulity on his face. "It hasn't worked out that way, Mr. Cortina."

"You've encountered opposition?"

"Opposition I take as part of the mission. . . ."

"They question your motives?"

He sighed and nodded solemnly. "Yes."

"They resent your pushing yourself forward?"

Now Russell looked at me suspiciously. "Yes. . . . Did Elkins tell you about this?"

"No, I think it's perfectly logical to guess this from what you've related, Russell."

"You are one hundred percent correct in your deductions, Mr. Cortina. You are a very perceptive man. You have caught exactly what my predicament is. . . . I handling this mammoth job that was given to me, plus working in the office as well, in fulfilling these obligations, it seems those people who conferred this responsibility on me have forgotten that they appointed me to these tasks, it seems that they resent me and question my sincerity, my motives. . . . Now, I've been around long enough to know that any time a person is given large missions, he is exposed, and he's a standout, and he's on the spot and is thereby exposed to those little minds that ridicule and criticize and that are envious and jealous. . . . I understand that I am a target just because of the role that I have been given. . . . But this is Russell now and not Roxy. . . . I am no longer an island. I have dialogues with myself; I am self-conscious; I am saying to myself: 'What's the problem here? Can't they see that I am making all these moves in their behalf? Can't the administration read my activities and see that I am doing my best . . . ? It's obvious that I am so forthright and forceful in my attacking a situation, first, because I am a resident, second, because I am held in esteem by the administration, third, because I can provide leadership, and fourth, because I have been a drug addict for thirty-four years and as such have played all the games that have ever been played. . . . And nobody, resident or staff, can play their games and hope to take in Russell. . . . He's played them all; there ain't any new ones to him. . . .' You see, Mr. Cortina?"

"A matter of interpretation of your role, huh?"

"Basically . . . and something personal at bottom. . . . My leadership threatens them."

"Them?"

"The residents and staff as well. . . . You see, Russell understands staff very well . . . their hangups about working with drug addicts, always being suspicious of them, always expecting to be conned or schemed upon. . . . You see, underneath, staff feels superior to a bunch of men who would sleep their lives away on a narcotic, men who have to make up a kind of fantasy world to live in. . . . I understand staff; they don't like for a man like me to point out to them that addicts are just the way they are and that you can't work with them if you can't somehow overcome the fear of being tricked all the time. . . . What automobile mechanic can work his trade if he's afraid of getting grease on his hands . . . ? It's the same as with the drug addict. . . . Sure, he's a con artist. He's had to be. That's part of his survival. . . . But you see, Mr. Cortina, it cuts deeper than that. . . . *The staff has got to feel superior.* It's their hangup."

"You pointed all of this out to them?"

"Most assuredly. . . . I wrote a four-page letter to the director pointing all of this out . . . *and* I laid out the correctives to ameliorate this whole screw-up. . . ."

"And what's happened?"

"I imagine he's taken it under advisement."

"Tell me, how has the Russell part stood up under this kind of attack? Or should I more properly ask, how many times has Roxy been called upon to protect Russell?"

His voice dropped: "Roxy has waited there on the side for Russell to try and carry the ball all through this, Mr. Cortina. . . ."

"But the methods of approach, the wonderful grasp of organization, that seems to me to reflect more the Roxy than the Russell entity . . . don't you think?"

He hesitated and considered: "Yes, I can see how you might get that kind of interpretation of the situation but, you see, Russell has learned through Roxy, techniques, approaches, savvy. . . ."

"But Russell seemed so quiet, so unobstrusive, so thoughtful. . . . Energy didn't seem to be . . . pardon me, physical energy didn't seem to be his forte. Or perhaps I've misunderstood your thrust. . . ."

He lifted a hand to allay my fears. "No, no I can read you . . . I can read you. . . . But, you see, Russell has come of age. It is Russell's game now. . . ."

"Then you've cut Roxy, he's finished? No more Roxy, no more

drugs, no more . . . what shall we say . . . drug culture . . . ? You've turned your back on more than half your lifetime's experience?"

He was very serious. "I haven't turned my back on anything. I've used that experience to get to my present consciousness. Roxy has been outgrown . . . that's all. Roxy can't survive in this new world that I've entered. . . . He's all wrong as a style. Can't you see that, Mr. Cortina? That's why I'm so disturbed by what has been happening. Russell has stood up and tried to perform his job, discharge those responsibilities put on his shoulders. . . . No, see, I am accused of trying to work my wizardry, playing a game. . . . On all sides I am accused of playing the game. They yell at me in group therapy: 'You're gaming, you're gaming, you're gaming.' These eighteen- and nineteen- and twenty-year-old snot noses hurling these terms at me, accusing me of playing the game. . . . I invented the game before they were ever carried inside of their mothers. . . . They've used drugs one, two years, four years. . . . I've lived drugs for thirty-four years. I am a history of drugs. I'm gaming, I'm gaming they say. . . . On all sides, they accuse me. . . ."

"The staff, too?"

"Oh, yes, especially the staff, since I've dared to try and point out to them the error of their ways. . . ."

"So what do you do? Can you stand up under this kind of attack without calling upon Roxy?"

"I am at the fork in the road, Mr. Cortina. I'm fifty-two years old. I must hold on to Russell. . . ."

"Why do they think you're gaming, Russell? Don't they buttress that charge with reasons . . . ?"

"Oh, sure, they come out of that therapeutic bag. . . . You know, that grab bag of phrases that every junkie commits to memory after his first bust in a rehabilitation program. . . . They can out-social-worker the social workers; they know all the jargon. . . . But they say I'm gaming. . . . And I keep asking them: 'If I'm gaming, what's the prize . . . what's the prize I'm seeking? I'm an intelligent man—persuade me, convince me. . . . What's the prize I'm spinning my web to snaffle? What's the prize?' "

"What do they answer?"

"They can't answer . . . they can't answer. They can't tell me where they're coming from. . . . They can't do it. When I put it right to them, all they can fall back on is that they feel it, that they sense that I'm gaming. . . . Now what kind of a reasonable, logical response is that, I ask you, Mr. Cortina?"

"I've never seen you so agitated before, Russell."

"Because I've never been so misunderstood before. I put myself on the line and I've been scorned. . . ."

His poise had been shaken. I touched his knee. "I wonder how they could misunderstand so grossly? I wonder. . . ."

"If they can't see what I've tried to do . . . I'll just go back and do my thing. . . ."

"What's that, Russell?"

"Continue to improve myself, recognizing me and my new insights about me. . . . Yes, I'll just be totally self-supporting. . . ."

"Sort of like the old days when you were on heroin. You were alone then. . . ."

He didn't accept that. . . . "It's very, very radically different. . . . When I was on heroin, I wasn't alone. I was always making my moves, out with people, arranging. . . ."

"When you were on the nod?"

"My mind never stopped, always planning, planning. . . ."

"Russell, I've never asked before, but since you've mentioned going back into your own self-supporting world, do you ever have any visitors?"

"Visitors?"

"Or are visits not permitted?"

"They have visiting privileges here. . . . But I frown on them. . . . Why should people come in to see me here . . . ? I'm here to do a job. I'll visit those people I want to see when I finish my task here."

"There are people, then, who have wanted to come and see you. . . . Your children perhaps?"

"I'm sure my children would want to come and see me, but I've carefully kept away from them any knowledge as to where I am. . . ."

"And that goes for the woman you always refer to as the lady . . . ?"

"Most assuredly. . . . Because she is the lady. . . . I wouldn't permit her to walk into this contagion. . . ."

"So you see no one . . . no one from the outside . . . ?"

"I see you once a month, Mr. Cortina."

I was touched by the way he said it. Apparently it meant something to him. "And you don't feel lonely and left out?"

"Lonely? Yes, but then that's nothing new. . . . Left out? Left out of what . . . ? See, that's like my gaming. . . . What's the prize . . . ? What's the prize . . . ?"

He left. The old air of assured confidence was absent from his walk. His handshake was less firm. Russell was under attack, uncertain and confused. I got my equipment together and put on my raincoat as the director came into the room. We had known each other for many years. He was a man who had been in the field for a long time.

"You have our number one prize there, Frank Michael," he said, pointing toward the tape box under my arm. He smiled. "Roxy has got to be the clinical study of all times. Have you ever worked with a more totally defended man? He has turned this place topsy-turvy . . . absolutely upside down. . . . He's got some of these staff members, the younger ones especially, talking to themselves. He's arranged private consultations for staff and residents; he's arranged training sessions. He's invited in the mayor to see addicts putting themselves together. . . . He's an incredible example of the sociopathic personality . . . Roxy the magnificent! I had to pull the rug on him, I had to. . . . I abolished, by direct fiat, this whole autonomy scheme that he had foisted on us. . . . I had to, Frank Michael. . . . He had this place going around in circles. . . ."

I lighted my pipe. "What better way to hide, Sam? What better way to hide than in a rushing crowd . . . ?"

"Exactly, exactly. . . ."

"But I think you've pierced his armor, Sam . . . I think you have. . . ."

"Maybe that frightens me. . . . Break down that constant need for superiority . . . break him out of his entrenchment. . . ."

"What will be left . . . is that it?"

"Can he survive? Can he survive that way?"

"He survived for thirty-four years in the most savage jungle conceivable, the jungle of the drug abuser. . . . I think he'll surprise you, Sam. . . . He may even surprise himself. . . . I've got to get to the airport."

6

One of those ravaging West Coast fires was raging. Already most of the lower slopes were charred and, like some doomsday canopy, the sky was black. Inside the facility the odor of smoke, that burned-out acridity, hung heavily and made it disagreeable to breathe. The director had asked me to talk to the young psychologist, to share with him some of my experience with Russell.

Mr. Elkins was saying, "But you credit this Roxy-Russell charade?"

"Why not? You're dressed Hawaiian today—last time I saw you, a month ago, you were dressed Edwardian . . . your safe personal manner of changing yourself. . . . How different is that from Roxy-Russell . . . ?"

"But I know what I'm doing. I wear my clothes consciously. . . ."

I looked at him. The director hadn't asked me to argue or to persuade. "Mr. Elkins, this man has been a drug addict for thirty-four years. What kind of change do you want for him? It can only come from him . . . not from a set of imposed values. . . . It can only come from him. It's sheer reflex for him to try and engineer, to manipulate. . . . He can't help it. . . . So it seems to me that one engages this capacity to the full. One sets him to engineering himself. Only his own change, the change that he feels he has brought about, will be enduring. . . . But after thirty-four years. . . ."

"But he can go out at any time. He'll bounce back here so fast. . . ."

"Yes, that's his whole history. But maybe he's just slightly less defended from himself now. Maybe he's just a little more sensitive, self-conscious, if you will. Maybe, Mr. Elkins. . . ."

"What would you do with him?"

It was time for my interview. I was getting impatient. "I'd give him some kind of menial job for a few weeks. . . . I guarantee you that he will work it into something prestigious and important. . . ."

"I don't understand you, Dr. Cortina. . . ."

"I'm not a doctor," I said flatly. "It should prove to you that Russell is a fantastically adroit, energetic man, who will always prove superior when he is placed in a situation beneath him. He's always pitched himself that way. . . . The trouble is that no one has ever been able to make him see that. . . ."

"I see. . . . So after that. . . ."

"Sufficient unto the day is the evil thereof. . . . After you've seen it for yourself . . . then I'm sure you'll come up with the next step. . . ." And I had to smile as I said: "Or as Russell would say, 'You'll be ready to make your move.' "

The tape had just finished. I leaned forward and switched it over to the Record mode. "Remarkable man we've just heard . . . clever, adroit. . . . He has a fantastic capacity to weave a spell. . . . I wonder how much of that weaving ability comes from being deprived?"

He studied his hands. "I don't know, Mr. Cortina. . . . I've had many experiences that hurt when I've tried to offer love. . . . Maybe I was too young. But that was of no consequence when it came to the next time, because I would always offer love. Let me give you an illustration: Look at my face. . . . You can't help but see that savage cut across my throat. . . . I told you about the jealousy that provoked it. But that woman, when she came to see me in the hospital . . . when the police caught her . . . I said nothing. I wouldn't identify her. . . . She almost killed me, but out of love. . . . I'm the way I am out of love for other people. I'm battered because I've given love. I've protected people, that's why I've been scarred. . . ."

"Is that because Russell, as opposed to Roxy, had to seek love very directly?" That smell of scorched air pervaded the room. "Because Russell lacked confidence in himself?"

"You've said that before, Mr. Cortina, that Russell lacked confidence. . . . Russell had plenty of confidence, but you must remember, which I'm sure you do, that the only thing Russell was hung up on was, 'Where do I go from here?' Russell didn't see any great need to send himself through school because he couldn't see himself hooked up with a future. Russell had to be able to hook up his feelings and his convictions together in order for him to make his move. What was the point of going through it without seeing the need . . . ? I'm still like that to a degree. I still have got to be subjected to a certain part of life. . . . That's what brought me in here, a voluntary committing of myself to this program. I never thought that I would openly surrender myself. But somewhere along the road of life you get jolted, thrown to your knees . . . like St. Paul on the road to Damascus . . . thrown to your knees, and you are forced to look deeply into yourself and into life. . . . You have to scrutinize reality, not scorn it. . . ."

"Does this scrutiny ever lead you to suspect that Russell was left at the starting post . . . ?" I held up my hand to forestall his reply. "You just said that Russell couldn't motivate himself except in terms of an immediate reward. You said Russell didn't know what he wanted. You said Russell waited for Roxy to do things for him. . . . Do you recall that old prescription about heroin users being immature, unmotivated, dependent? Sounds terribly like Russell, doesn't it? Almost to a T."

"Just a minute. . . . What makes you think that Russell was not active, was not mature, was not independent? Who do you think the lady fell in love with? Not Roxy . . . not Roxy. . . . She first met Roxy, but she fell in love with Russell. . . . It was Russell she cherished. . . . And I wanted it that way. . . . When you say you fall in love, man, you have to fall in love with something. It's no vacuum. The lady fell in love with the revealed Russell, who was me. . . . Yes, Mr. Cortina . . . with the real me, Russell." He felt that he had scored heavily and was prepared for my rejoinder, but I said nothing. He resumed, an air just short of cockiness making itself apparent: "No, Mr. Cortina. . . . Once a situation got really started, and Roxy did get the situation started, then Russell always took over. . . . All this happened now because in effect the woman was saying: 'Let Roxy go, let him go. I've found Russell and he is beautiful. Maybe I looked into Roxy first because he was forbidden fruit. His brushing with notoriety, his dangerous life maybe thrilled me, I liked that brush with danger . . . because mine has been a quiet, steady life. . . . But now that you have revealed to me Russell . . . let Roxy go . . . let him go. . . .' That was her reasoning. I know, Mr. Cortina. Ain't no woman ever lived that I couldn't read like a simple book. . . ."

"Which one was the heroin addict, Roxy or Russell?"

"Roxy. Roxy was the heroin user. . . . I thought I made that clear."

"But why did Roxy need heroin? He could function very well. He was able to meet almost all contingencies. He was skillful, energetic, he enjoyed a reputation. . . . Why did he need heroin?"

"I explained all of that. He needed it to gather the experience in order for Russell to make his moves. . . ."

"Or did Roxy need it in order to make Russell feel superior to him?"

"Would you repeat that again?"

"Did Roxy need heroin in order to make Russell feel above him, superior to him?"

"That's a surprising thing you say. . . . I'll have to meditate on that because it hangs in with something the lady once said. She was talking of how she would explain me to our children if we ever had any—a kind of lover's make-believe—you know, Mr. Cortina? The lady said: 'Children, your father has been an escapist from reality all his life long. . . . Yes, your father has been an escapist from reality all his life long . . . !' " And Russell elongated the words as if he relished them. I looked up at the mural; it had grown dusky, it seemed to me, from the smoke seeping in through the windows.

Suddenly I pushed forward and turned off the Record mode, rewound the tape and set it for playback. "I want you to listen to this, Russell . . . I want you to listen to Russell for a moment. . . ."

And we listened together to this entity, a suggestion of pleasure wrinkled his face, he nodded his head.

"An esca-a-pist from rea-a-l-ity all-l his li-i-fe lo-o-ng," came from the loudspeaker in an attentuated emphasis. I quickly switched the machine back into the Record position.

"Did you hear it, Russell? Who said it . . . ? Who said it?"

"The lady . . . the lady said it. . . ."

"She was mistaken, was she?"

Russell was uncertain. But he had to answer, he was made that way. "No, she wasn't mistaken, she was caught up in that lover's vapor when you just croon out your thoughts."

"So she was in a vapor, and the group was in a mass lie when they told you you were gaming. . . . And everything that Roxy does Russell shifts off himself. . . ."

"Tell me where you're coming from, man. I don't catch your bag. . . . I hear you rappin', but I don't heed your bias. . . ."

"That tape captures Russell and Roxy. It has no axe to grind. . . . A microphone is totally indiscriminate, it just picks up sound, any sound. . . . It's your voice, it says something beyond the words used. . . . We've captured a shadow, Russell. Are you aware of that . . . ? We've done the impossible, we've captured a shadow."

His face was grave, thoughtful, and unexplainably youthful— perhaps it was fearful.

"Roxy, or Russell, that tape just played back for us a man incredibly fluent, incredibly facile, a man who can use words like a magician. Now you see him, now you don't. I suggest to you, Russell, that that man or men uses words like a smoke screen. . . . He latches on to ideas, to thoughts, with a coruscating brilliance, with a fantastic talent for blocking out truth from himself. I suggest to you that Roxy-Russell, as you wish, is a device that some third entity has created to keep you from grappling with yourself. . . . I suggest that heroin was the cement that bound together an image, that heroin made it possible to survive, because neither Russell or Roxy could sustain that superiority." I waited apprehensively for what would happen. I watched him struggle with what had been said. " 'An escapist from reality all his life long.' "

The room was silent, the scorched, burned-out odor between us. . . . I said softly: "Russell, is there any truth to that?"

Slowly, his voice smaller, his head cocked as if he were listening to something remote, "I must think about it more deeply. . . . It is deeper. . . . Think a little deeper. . . ."

I looked up at that fantastic painting on the wall.

7

Russell had been laid up for more than a month. As a consequence, some eight weeks had elapsed between our sessions. Mr. Elkins had left a note for me at the desk. It told me that Russell had been assigned to the kitchen as dishwasher, a job he'd been holding down for the last few weeks, ever since his recovery from the flu. The fire in the hills had been extinguished weeks before, and that sunny warmth of the Pacific billowed out the curtains in the former refectory while I waited for Russell. He was thinner, noticeably so. He was dressed in white, his kitchen uniform. He smiled as we shook hands.

"You had yourself quite a bout, huh, Russell?"

"Yes, I did. I just couldn't seem to shake it. . . ."

"Flu is all over. I seem to fly in and out of it each city I go to."

"They diagnosed it as flu, . . ." he said pregnantly.

"It wasn't flu?"

Ceremonially, he opened his fresh package of cigarettes and selected his smoke. He tapped it against the table top, cleaned away the loose shreds, and said, looking at the pack, "It was a crisis, a spiritual crisis I went through, Mr. Cortina, . . . aided and abetted, you might say, by a few flu germs. . . . But it was a spiritual crisis. Indeed. It was our meeting the last session that brought to a head a lot of what I had been probing on for a long time."

"Why don't we listen to the playback, and then we can refresh our memories with exactly what was said?"

He held up his hand. "Please, if you'll permit. . . . What was said is scorched into my mind. I would as soon omit the playing back this time, Mr. Cortina, if you'll permit. . . ."

"That's yours to say, Russell. Let's just start recording then, shall we?"

"Definitely. . . ." He drew on his cigarette.

"What was it that brought on this crisis, Russell? I mean what particular point that was raised?"

"The capturing of that shadow . . . the point about the superiority. . . ." He smiled ruefully and said: "Imagined superiority, that was the way it was phrased. . . . A superiority I couldn't sustain and that made me go to drugs. . . ."

"Is that why you went to heroin?"

He said, very deliberately, emphasizing each word: "It sounds reasonable. . . . It is the first reasonable clue I've had. . . . You can't use heroin for thirty-four years without everything in your life becoming damaged. . . . But I can use that reason to probe even deeper now, on account of the fact that it strikes me as being possible. Do you see where I'm coming from? That's why I had my crisis."

"How do you feel right now . . . ? I mean, apart from your being weak and thin?"

"I feel very beautiful . . . cleansed and strong. I am my own man now. . . . No Russell-Roxy, but just me. . . . I've been back in the group meetings now, and I've told them about what's happened in here between us. . . . How I've been helped to see a me outside of me. . . . I admitted that they were right, that I had been gaming unbeknownst to myself, that it was a way of life for me. . . . I told them that I realize now that I had been running with all of my insecurities and inabilities headlong into failure, self-defeating failure, which was heroin. . . . You see, almost all of my life I have always pitted myself against people I knew I could master. This is how I developed up for myself that sense of superiority that I had to have, but underneath I was paying for that because I knew in my bones that it was all a flimflam, and I was handling that with heroin. . . . Because, Mr. Cortina, every time I had a victory at some other dude's expense, somebody who was below me, I really had another defeat. Do you read me?"

"Yes, I do."

"In short, every time I had a doubt as to what would happen to me in a confrontation, I would skip it, I would round on it. I did not want to be weighed in the balance to be found wanting. . . . Just a week ago, with this new awareness of myself, a young dude, a new resident just come in off the streets, thinking he was giving me a junkie compliment, said: 'How old are you, Jack . . . ?' I told him I was fifty-two." Russell cleaned away the ash from his cigarette. " 'Man, but you're in great shape for your age. . . . That white hair of yours don't mean nothin'. You got wisdom and you've lived a life so passionately like no lame I've ever met.' Sweet words, Mr. Cortina. How I could have spun a web around that. It was just like a high to me . . . a wonderful high but I squashed it . . . *I squashed it.* I said to him: 'Yes, I've come a long way, Jack, to reach the point where I'm seventeen years old all over again, or perhaps for the first time. . . .' It's a hell of a thing to be seventeen years old, Mr. Cortina, with a fifty-two-year-old heart, liver, and system . . . knowing that twilight is just before me. . . . It's a hell of a thing to feel inside so weak and halting. . . ."

"What do you hear about leaving here, Russell?"

He put out the cigarette. "Very shortly."

"Are you ready to go?"

"Frankly, no, but then I don't have the time or the luxury of feeling a security that I've never felt . . . in my life. . . . I don't know what it is. . . . So I've got to go out there where it's at. . . . I have nothing to throw my rope on, nothing to clutch hold of, Mr. Cortina. . . . The core of my life was heroin and now that's gone. . . . When I was a boy I had an uncle, he was a dancer and a street poet. He wasn't on narcotics. He was a gifted man. I looked up to him, but he never could catch hold. He used to have the most beautiful words and phrases—beautiful. I looked up to him. . . . And then one day I was dawdling along the street, and I spied him down in a pit using a short-handled shovel. . . . He was working for the W.P.A. He was a slight man, doing hard labor. He wasn't built for it; he wasn't made for it. He was made to dance, to recite poetry. . . . But there he was, digging away. I could imagine his muscles crying out, his heart beating fast, his mind pressing down on him like a big rock. . . . Something tore inside of me. I heard the voices say: 'Good to see the Black son of a bitch do a decent day's work for a change.' Something tore inside of me that day, Mr. Cortina. I knew that I couldn't go that way. . . . That's where the Roxy part of me began to take shape. . . . Oh, I can see now how I trapped myself, but that's one of the critical passes in my life. . . . I didn't want that because I thought I did have something unique, Mr. Cortina. . . . I did, so help me God. . . . But nothing was going to make me put it on the line in that way."

"But that Black community is still out there, Russell. And in that community the pusher is still making his way. . . . I can't think of any contribution that he's making to Black activism by addicting young Black men and women. . . . ."

"Funny you should mention that. . . . Just the other day one of the staff members, I've been friendly with him for some time now, he asked me when I was getting out, and I told him, and he asked me if I would consider leading a youth group. . . . You know, to talk about the drug bag and crime and delinquency and all of the deviant bags. I accepted. I said to myself that it was just what I needed . . . something to build on. It would give me one of my first moves. You see, it so happens that I had tried this kind of thing once before and I had failed badly. . . ."

"Failed? Nobody could know more about it than you, Russell."

"Oh, I failed. It was one of those times when I had made a half-hearted attempt to put myself together. I had joined with a local minister to talk to kids . . . and to adults in the community about the menace of drugs. I found myself up on the stage, and I want to tell you I had that audience in the palm of my hand. I had them crying and shivering and feeling their flesh rip open from that spike, smell the urine and filth from the dirty clothes the junkie wears, pant with that skeleton as he ran his game of boosting and deceit . . . I had them, I had them right here," he said, balling up a fist. "They had never been so moved . . . *but I was high on heroin while I was filling them with this passion.* I could see the minister, those children, and their parents thinking that I was a man who had returned from the brink, I was a man reborn. . . . Oh, Mr. Cortina, I burned like acid inside. . . . Now, at this moment . . . I think I wanted somebody to shout me down, to humble me, to yell liar, liar . . . cheat. . . . You know, a lot of addicts take this road, they become evangelists . . . but so often they're high while they're exhorting others. . . . They use that avenue. . . ."

"But then you know so much, Russell, even though you say that you're only seventeen. . . . How will you handle that nagging need for superiority now? You say that thirty-four years of heroin abuse have damaged your life. . . . So what chance do you have?"

"The same chances everybody else has. . . . But I've got to turn around my thrust. . . . I have been, without boasting, the most successful negative leader I've ever known. I've got to turn that around. I've got to polish up those values. . . . I've always been a marvelous calculator. I have launched more schemes than Boeing has airplanes . . . and nearly all of them were successful. . . . All negative schemes. . . . I've got to turn all of this around. Do you see? It's really the same thing, but it's got to be reversed."

"You're really a very lonely man, aren't you, Russell? Do you have any relationships you can build on?"

He studied the recorder, the reels glinting in the sunlight. "There are my children, but frankly I'm not up to that, not yet anyway. . . . No, aside from the lady there's nobody."

"Well, you do have her, that's something."

"Well, I don't know. To be truthful, I don't know what is there between me as I am now and her. . . . See, she was a challenge, too. She was a schoolteacher, way above me. I took her to bed, I spun my web in that way to give me superiority. Do you see what I mean when I say I don't for real know what's between us . . . ?" He paused. "I don't know if I can meet her as I am. I don't know if I can stop myself from putting it over on her. I'm afraid of being successful with her because it might be another fail-ure for me. . . . Does that make sense?"

"Yes, it does. . . . But that Black community out there should have a need for a man like you. You have fifteen children, and they in turn have had children. . . . You don't know really whether or not some of your own kin haven't started on drugs."

"True. . . . I don't. . . ."

"Isn't that a relationship . . . a critical one? So, what you're say-ing now is that the big difference is in your awareness of yourself?"

"Definitely . . . my self-consciousness. . . . That and the sense that I have to make choices . . . that I have to bypass the easy ways. . . ."

"Jesus, Russell, you really have the horn in you. . . . Can you do it?"

"Man, I've got to do it. . . ."

"Aren't you biting off more than almost any man could chew . . . ? You used heroin for thirty-four years. . . . You don't know yet its enduring compulsion."

"True, and I don't underestimate it. . . . I'm going out and make a new life . . . new friends, new relationships. . . . I'm start-ing all over again. . . . I have to. . . . All life is fragile, for you as well as for me, Mr. Cortina. . . . That plane you spend so much of your time in, nothing says that it's pasted up in the sky. . . . Same as for me. I know heroin. Nobody better. But I've cut it away."

"Methadone would support you, Russell."

Angrily he said: "Another cop-out, a cop-out. . . . You're offer-ing me a whore instead of a woman. . . . If I got to go that way, I don't want to live."

I leaned toward him and put a hand on his shoulder. "Russell, you're going to be the loneliest man in the world—no heroin, no heroin world . . . and you seventeen years old in an alien world . . . a nondrug world. . . . A displaced person."

He snorted. "A Wandering Jew."

"What happens if you mess up?"

"What happens if your plane falls, Mr. Cortina?"

The interview had a disturbing effect upon me. I sought out the director. We sat over a cup of coffee. "Sam, what about Russell?"

"I don't know. . . . I think we're all surprised and suspicious. He looks almost too good. . . . Of course he's got the kitchen totally organized. He's got those women down there waiting on him hand and foot. They save special food for him. I wouldn't be a bit surprised if he hasn't knocked up a few of them, but I don't know. . . . But you didn't drop in for that, Frank Michael. What's on your mind?"

"Give him a job, Sam."

"A job. What kind of a job?"

"Some kind of paraprofessional job working with the youngster coming in off the street . . . some of the young abusers. . . . Give him a job with problems, a job that's too big for him, a job where he'll be under attack."

"Humph. . . . I suppose I could manage something."

"He's fifty-two years of age, Sam. What do we want . . . ? He might make a remarkable contribution."

"I'll think about it . . . talk it over with the staff. . . . You'll be back . . . what? In a month or so?"

Before I left I went back to look at the mural. It certainly was unreal.

8

What with delays, schedule changes, former addicts who could not be located, and others who could—but in jails or morgues or hospitals—my appointment with Russell was postponed. I called the director of his institution to arrange the meeting when I had booked my flight. He sounded rueful. He wasn't sure that Russell would appear. Was he working? Yes, he was working part time there at the facility with young addicts. What was wrong then? Russell was changed, suspiciously changed. . . . He was too subdued . . . subdued. He was probably using again. That would account for his being let down. It was easy enough to determine that—urinalysis. . . . Sam scoffed. Any bird who could use all the years that Russell had could figure a way around that and I knew it. But he would try to get Russell to come in. He was not hopeful, but he would try.

That conversation disturbed me deeply, perhaps because I was halfway persuaded that Russell could never make it and really never had the slightest hope of staying away from drugs . . . so what disturbed me was to hear Sam voice my own suspicions. I had listened to all the tapes that Russell had made over the months, in a kind of audio recapitulation. Frankly, I was uncertain whether he hadn't spun me into a web . . . hadn't effectively flim-flammed me into treating him as if he were somebody else. It is baffling and disconcerting to work with long-time hard-drug abusers because they have for so long used the mechanics of deceit, fantasy, and adroitness that it is part of their way of life even when they've renounced drugs. . . . And something else—was I not by now so conditioned by the drug-dependent psychology that I, too, was no longer objective . . . ? The whole thing was disquieting, and I left for the West Coast tired and dispirited. That was standard for last interviews, though. I bought a detective story. It would be a pleasure to discover who the culprit was for a change.

He arrived on time. He sat like that fine, dark-hued carving of the early sessions. He was dressed well, carefully groomed, but he was thin, and he had removed his rufflike beard so that the savage scar stood out like a poorly sewn seam. . . . And Sam was right, he was subdued. I looked into his eyes. . . . How many thousands of times had I heard from users: "I defy you to detect when a person is on the stuff. I defy you." God knows, that is true. . . . He met my glance and smiled tentatively. " 'I had not thought to see thy face,'" he said in that baroque voice, but it didn't have the old richness.

"Well, you know, Russell, my last interviews with people take all kinds of time. . . . Sometimes you chase them for months without success. How're you doing?"

He shook his head: "I don't know, and that's a fact, Mr. Cortina. . . . I don't know."

"What's it like out there?"

"Well, it's a hell of a revelation to be out there after being in here all these months, not that my stay here was long in comparison with my other institutional experience. . . . In fact, in terms of days, being here was one of my shortest stretches. . . ." For the first time I realized that Russell was no longer young. It was incredible that I should have had the notion that he was somehow a young man. He resumed: "Do you know that I feel so totally different, so different that I'm not sure of myself . . . ? I'm not sure of myself at all. . . . This place has done that to me. . . . You've done that to me with that machine," he said.

There was no trace of bitterness . . . no taunt, no innuendo. . . . It was that that gave me a pang. He had uncovered for me my real conviction, my real fear in his regard: that he was too old in the drug culture to be broken out. . . . He was what now? A zombie, a kind of vegetable left after the lobotomy. "How about your children, or the lady . . . have you seen them?"

"I haven't seen anyone, Mr. Cortina. I do my work. . . . I've conducted a few therapy sessions on the outside, and I go home. . . ."

"Home?"

"I have a room on the North side. . . ."

"And Sidna, Royola . . . ? Sidna was the young girl who meant so much to you."

"No, Mr. Cortina . . . no, that's the difference. What kept me alive before when I emerged from a penal institution. . . ."

He said "emerged." That sounded like the old Russell. Anyone else would have said "released" or "gotten out" or "discharged," but only Russell would "emerge." My spirits perked up and my suspicions were aroused. Russell continued: "I sought two things, a generous woman and my first bag of stuff. It was the prospect of these two pleasures that sustained me behind bars. . . . Not this time. I'm a lame for sure. It's the same world out there but I'm a stranger. . . . I'm a sort of Wandering Jew."

It was an old ruse, the building up of adversity; it was an addict's pet device for setting himself up for a ground swell of sympathy so that he could go back to heroin with a resounding justification—he had been victimized. "But didn't you know it would be this way, Russell . . . ?"

"Of course I knew, in here," and he tapped his head. "But what about the rest of me . . . ? I get drawn back to the old precincts." (That was vintage Russell.) "When I was in here, I used to think that I would never return to that environment . . . I couldn't. . . . Now I get drawn back just to stand there and search faces."

"Have you been tempted?"

"I have sat the night in the park watching them on the nod, with every muscle in my body crying out, with my mouth trembling, my whole soul on fire, my brain weaving for me the romance of rapture, rapture . . . just one bag, one bag. . . . I'm clean—one bag and then rapture. . . . You don't know the sudden joy that swells up inside when you think of that euphoria, that love tryst, the excitement, the sudden catch in your breathing. . . . Have I been tempted, you ask? For shame, Mr. Cortina . . . for shame. . . . You know I have been . . . you know it."

I could see the pitfall. It was in front of me. Here was the time for me to give him his way out. Say to him that he would probably have relapses that would send him rushing to the nearest cop-man, or say to him that he had to be strong and determined, and that would send him out to fix as well. . . . He was waiting for the cue, I thought. It was one of the classical exaddict ploys. And I was startled by his remark: "You're asking, really . . . have I used? Isn't that it?"

"Yes, that's it. . . . Have you used?"

He rose, removed his jacket, pulled off his shirt, and held out his arms . . . first the left one and then the right one. It was dramatic, melodramatic, especially with that slow, solemn, ritualistic flavor he imparted to everything. "Well, Mr. Cortina . . . you know the game. . . . You know it as well as I. Well, tell me. You're not the only one. Everyone else thinks of Roxy . . . of Roxy . . . but you know of Russell. . . . Them I don't care. But you . . . I want you to see. So look."

There were no signs. And he insisted that I examine his flesh closely. No signs. "Was that really for me, Russell?"

"I had to have you see. You must understand. For thirty-four years I used drugs . . . thirty-four years. . . . What life is left for me?"

"You said yourself the last time that life was fragile at best."

"Exactly . . . exactly. . . ."

"So what is it you want me to say to you, Russell?" I asked quietly. "You see, I'm caught in the same limbo. I know you from the tapes, I've been conditioned to think about you as you have revealed yourself to me. . . . So I'm jammed, too."

"Jammed, a junkie word. . . . Jammed. . . . I'm jammed. . . . Exactly, I'm jammed. I'm handcuffed to myself. I'm handcuffed, Cortina. I'm in custody of myself. . . . Before, there was Roxy. And there was Russell. . . . Now I have this silent antagonist with me, this silent, unsleeping antagonist. . . . Always there, always alert, always poised, always weighing me in the balance . . . and if I am found wanting, I shall be slain."

"You said that you were seventeen again, Russell. You knew that you would have to live with this heightened consciousness of yourself. You wouldn't take methadone. The bag is empty, Russell. All the games played. Here you are now, squarely in the middle. You had to come to this place, this position. . . . Tell the kids about your antagonist. Let them know. Tell your own children. Tell your Black community. Take off your shirt for them. Show your arms."

Russell gave me the most searching glance I have ever endured from another human being. Slowly he clothed himself and without a word left the room. A fly buzzed against the screen. The sunlight lay in pools on the floor. I looked toward the wall. . . . It was blank . . . blank. The mural was gone. Over in a corner, there were paint cans and brushes, a floor cloth, and a roll of canvas.

Mechanically I unrolled the canvas. . . . It was the painting. It was down.

Three months later I was at Seattle Airport. My flight had been diverted there from Vancouver. I hadn't heard anything about Russell in that time. I called the director long distance.

"What about Russell, Sam . . . ?"

"He's here. . . . He's here!"

"He messed up?"

"He claims not. . . ."

Angrily: "For Christ's sake, you can determine that, Sam."

"Nothing shows up . . . nothing shows up. . . . He's here, working full time."

"He's giving you trouble?"

"Not at all. That's what bothers me. I'm using him with the young addicts and to help train new staff. . . . But I simply don't understand, Frank Michael, I don't understand. . . . He's a sociopath. . . . I don't understand. . . ."

"You don't understand why he hangs on, is that it, Sam?"

"Sure. He used for thirty-four years. . . . If this is maturation. . . . I can't believe it. It's too mystical. Him and his 'antagonists.' I can't accept it."

"Is he effective in his work?"

"Oh, yes . . . yes, he is. But I can't understand why . . . I can't understand why. I keep waiting for him to fall back. I don't see what he has to live for. I don't see, Frank Michael. . . . What is it?"

"Why don't you ask him?"

THE
UNEXPECTED
BRIDE

1

"Bitter . . . bitter; I can taste the real essence on my lips, bitter.
. . . Like when I was a kid and they wanted me to stop biting my
nails, they coated them with bitter alum . . . bitter like that, some
aunt or relative. I don't know any more who was a real aunt and
who was this woman they had to give some name to so that I
could be there without getting anybody into trouble with the authorities. . . ."

She was short and squat, her hair cropped and bristly, her heels
run down, her stockings bellying out, her face puffy, her complexion blotched, her mouth curled, and her dress too small; her body
appeared bulged, and one pale breast dangled out of her dress. It
was pushed back in unceremoniously, as one would remove a shred
of lint from a garment. "Yeah, bitter, man, bitter . . . I taste it."
She threw it at me, a half-hearted bravado about it. "That was
until I was about eleven, when my gracious mother decided that
she would hold out her arms and take me back. . . . Up till then I
bounced in and out of families like a fat cat, my mouth
always full, my lips always greasy from the last food I could
stuff in my face. I used to eat and eat and eat, always figgering

how I could get that extra piece of anything. . . . In and out of families, in and out of cities and states, in and out of schools. . . . I went to school in Florida, in Texas, in Washington, D.C., in New York, and now back here in the land of sunshine," she said, and then yawned and picked at an ear. "I guess I was pretty stupid all right. I was always at least one grade behind for my age."

Her speech, despite the overlay of coarseness, couldn't conceal the registration of a fine voice. If I had closed my eyes, I wouldn't have summoned up that picture of belligerent dowdiness from hearing her voice. "So you went to a number of schools."

"I was a student in a camper . . . just overnight or over two months or over six months. In and out and very stout, that was my little song. . . . I think I went to about nine schools. . . . You got a cigarette?"

She grabbed my hand to bring the match closer and waited for me to react, as if she expected it to be quickly withdrawn. She sighed heavily: "I was a very gullible youth . . . gullible. . . . I'm still gullible, as a matter of fact." She sat back in her chair, her breast sticking out again. She tumbled it back inside.

"Gullible? That's your opinion, or have others remarked about that to you?"

"I'm gullible. . . . If I look at you and you show me a sense of sincerity, I will trust just about anything that you say to me. Anything you tell me, man. . . . If you tell me the sky is purple and I know it's blue, I'll say, 'Okay, it's purple.' "

"But why would you do that?"

"Because you said so, and I saw the sincerity in you."

"But why would you deny your own sense of reality and say that it was purple when you knew it was blue?"

"Because it would be the way you would see it."

It was so artless, so unexpectedly artless. She was young . . . I hadn't realized it before. I asked: "In other words, you'd humor me in any way just to please me, just because you would want me to like you so much . . . ? Is that it?"

"Yes and no. . . . You see, man, I would agree with you, but in my mind I'd still see that that sky is blue, but I'm saying in verbal terms the sky is purple."

Yes, I could see that she couldn't permit herself to appear confused. . . . She had to look as if she could at least maintain her position, however tenuous. "Is this the way you are as a person, Mae . . . agreeing on the surface and holding inner reservations, do you know what I mean?"

"Yes, I'll say that I have mistrust. . . . I have never been a deep-down, hard, hopeless drug addict. . . . But I have suspicion and I have distrust and I am gullible."

"Pretty uncomfortable combination."

"I'm suspicious, and yet I'm trusting if I see the sincerity in you. . . ."

"With this kind of ambivalence you must nearly always be uncertain, I suppose."

"Yeah. . . . That's it, man. . . . I see where you're coming from. . . . You get yourself hung up in a spot, and you're not even sure yourself. . . . But the only time I really get that way is when I use drugs."

"How old are you, Mae?"

"Eighteen . . . eighteen and seven months."

"And how old were you when you started using drugs . . . I mean, any kind of drug?"

"Um. . . . When I was twelve. . . . That was when I was in New York."

"When you were living with your mother?"

"Yeah," she said, trying to sound very bored and distracted.

"How did it come about?"

"How's anythin' come about . . . ? It happens. . . ." Again she brushed me off. She looked at her dirty fingernails. "I just wanted to try it . . . you know, man?"

"When you were with your mother, who else was there? Brothers, sisters?"

"Nope. . . . Just her and me and my stepfather. . . ."

"You were happy to be back with your mother after all those years of knocking around?"

She shrugged her shoulders and uttered a small I-couldn't-care-less grunt.

"Then home with your mother was not a place you enjoyed?"

"Why should I enjoy it? She and my stepfather, they didn't get along. . . . And I wasn't getting along with them either. . . . At that time I had very strong feelings against my mother. I felt she hadn't taken care of me up to the age of eleven, so what was so God-damned sacred about her that I should listen to everything she told me. . . . I was very rebellious. I wouldn't do whatever she wanted done or I would do it half-assed so that she would get choked up."

"And what would happen then . . . ?"

Mae shrugged and looked at her nails. "She'd hit me."

"And what would that do?"

"It made me hate her just a little bit more," she drawled, too bored by the question to look at me.

"Where does your stepfather fit in this, Mae? Did he stand up for you, take your side?"

"Oh, sure. . . . Sure. . . . And there was always somethin' behind his taking my side, too. . . ."

"What would he gain by protecting you . . . ?"

She opened her eyes wide and scowled at me. "This man was a pervert. . . . I was just something to be used by him. I knew it from the first time I met him. I didn't like him at all."

"Did he abuse you?"

She stared very hard at her nails and uttered that curious grunt —perhaps it was more like a squeak. "Yeah. Yeah. . . . Grabbed me in the kitchen, threw me on the floor, pulled it out and shoved it on me. Right there in the kitchen. . . . Oh, he was a pervert."

"And you were how old?"

"Twelve."

"How long did you stay there?"

"Until I had my daughter a couple of years later." She gazed about the room, yawned several times, scratched herself, and then leaned forward to stare into my face.

"You had a daughter?"

"Sure, why not . . . ? I'm normal."

"And it was your stepfather who . . . ?"

"Oh, no, no, man, you're in the maze. . . . He wasn't the father, it was some boy at school. . . ."

"This boy meant something to you?"

"Yeah . . . a helluva lot of trouble. . . . He meant to me what any fella means to a thirteen-year-old. . . . Just that. . . ."

"So you were pregnant at fourteen. . . . What happened when your mother found out?"

Mae gasped, falsified her voice: "Oh, I had did the ultimate wrong. . . ." She cocked her head on one side and yawned. She began to hum.

"She had never had any experience that way . . . ?"

"Oh, no, of course not. . . . She'd had me when she was fifteen. . . . Same darling, draggle ass as I was . . . just I had had my kid one year before her. . . . Generation gap, man."

"You were born out of wedlock?"

"Oh, come off it, man. . . . Wedlock, for Christ's sakes. She was knocked up. . . . I don't know who my father is. . . . Maybe he's really the king of a small country and I'm a princess royal."

"What did she say to you?"

"What didn't she say . . . ? She let me know that she was hurt, hurt, hurt, like hurt, man. . . ." Suddenly the voice sharpened, her jawbone quivered. "I had threatened her, I had warned her, I had told her if she didn't let me go out with boys, if she didn't let me do the normal things that most kids did, that I would end up that way. But I really was only putting that on. . . . I was only trying to retaliate with a normal statement at the time, but when it happened. . . . Whew! If I'da had normal relations with boys, I woulda ended up pretty straight today but that pervert of a stepfather, he hurt me . . . he hurt me. . . ." She squirmed in her chair. "I was deprived of going out, the knowledge of how to conversate with a boy, knowing what to say, how far to go and everything else without going to that deadpan thing, sex. . . . Oh, yes, my mother really protected me. . . . Stupid bitch. . . ."

"Had she any idea that your stepfather was molesting you?"

"Nope."

"Why didn't you tell her?"

"Why? Just so I could catch another beating . . . ? She loved this lame. . . . She wouldn't have believed me, and I could do without the clouting."

"You weren't trying to to spare her feelings?"

"Oh, my living pelvis. . . . You sound like a book, man. . . . Spare her feelings . . . not hardly . . . not hardly. . . ."

"With that kind of setup, I suppose you ran away quite a few times?"

"You best believe I did. . . . How about one of your cigarettes?"

I gave her the pack. "How many times did you run away, Mae?"

She said through clenched teeth: "Every time I got the chance."

"And you'd be picked up by the police each time?"

"Enough. She finally put a warrant out for me. . . . And they brought me before the court. . . . And that was a break, because they agreed with my mother and said that I was a damned bad kid, a obstreperous child. And they sent me to a home. That was a break. . . . So I stayed there until I was just sixteen, and I blew the state. . . ."

"You were discharged from the home?"

"I split. . . . I lived on my own. But I was hanging around in bars, and finally the parole people got wind of me after I got picked up in Connecticut, and they returned me to New York. . . . So they sent me back. . . ."

"For how long?"

"Just long enough to find out that my mother had left my little daughter with my stepfather. . . . Now, that I couldn't stand. . . . See, my mother's a drunk, and I went wild when I thought of that baby of mine being taken care of by that pervert. And I figgered, "Here we go again, all over again, history repeating itself. . . ." I couldn't let this happen, so I ran away, grabbed my kid, and I had her put away in a foster home." She laughed with embarrassment. "Then I had a nervous breakdown and they put me in the looney bin. . . . The looney bin. . . ."

"You were how old now, Mae?"

She yawned. "All of sixteen. . . . It was nice in the looney bin. . . . You could be anything you wanted. . . . You could stare out the window all day. . . . You could pretend you were in convulsions, and they'd rush all over for the doctor. . . . You could talk to him by the hour. . . ."

"You weren't disturbed by the fear that you might have something the matter with you?"

"Oh, how you talk, man, you are a living history book of a hundred years ago. . . . Something had to be wrong with me, huh . . . ? Had to be. . . . There I was in that happy land where everything was one big circus. . . . We were the sideshow."

I asked her very quietly: "How long were you there?"

"Two months, and my mother came for me. . . . And she brought me home," she was speaking in a singsong, "and she told me if I didn't do what she said that she would send me back to bugville so fast. . . . Yes, she told me exactly where I stood . . . because she was the one who set the rules and 'That's the way it's going to be, my darlin' daughter.' So I just up and said: 'Shit on you. Forget it.' And I blew, and I didn't stop until I got out of New York State. . . . I had made some friends in another city. . . ."

"So you lived on your own?"

"Yeap. . . . Uh-huh. . . ." She smiled. "I even got a job working as a clerk. . . . I even got a job. I had my own room. I had my own life. . . . At sixteen. . . ."

"You mentioned friends. . . ."

"The wrong kind . . . the ones I had met at the home . . . the kind that society frowns upon . . . prossies, boosters, hop-heads, pimps. . . . Yeah." She stretched and yawned again.

"Did you begin to pross, then?"

"Yeap, yeap, yeap. . . . I began to pross. . . ." And she had made it into a little song. "I prossed from sixteen until just the other day. . . . Hum . . . hummmm . . . ta-ta-ta-taaaa. . . ."

"Two years and some months. . . ."

"That's absolutely good addition, dad. . . ."

"You said that your first drug experience was at twelve. . . . What was it?"

"Bush."

"Did you smoke it much?"

"Just three or four times. . . . I didn't like it . . . got in my lungs." She slouched in her chair, trying to assume as gross a position as she could. "I . . . uh, didn't use again for years. . . . Nope. . . . no booze. See, my mother I can thank for that, since she was a bottomless bottle. . . . No, I was pretty straight all them years . . . until then when I was turning tricks. . . . Then I had a G. shot. I didn't like it too tough . . . made me sick. Whew! I threw up for days. . . . I just threw up. . . . Ah, damn, that was it. I didn't want any more horse after that. . . . Jesus . . . what a gut-roll that gave me."

"But you did go back to heroin?"

"Oh, sure . . . and it came about because of a very irrational affair. I met a friend of mine that I had known for a little while, he was a male," Mae said, leering at me. "Like I said, a male. And it was the funniest thing; I found out that he was using. . . . And I liked him; in fact we got pretty crazy about each other for a while. . . . He did something to me. . . . And I knew that I meant something to him and that, because of this, he didn't want me using drugs. . . . But one night, I found out that he was selling me out to this other stupid broad . . . just selling me out. Explaining to her that I wasn't anything but his stable broad. He rented me out; I was running for him. . . . That was all I was, his stable broad, his hired cunt. . . . You know how pimps talk. . . . So I figgered I'd fix him. I found his works and a bag he had stashed away, and I don't know how I did it but I fixed. . . . And I didn't get sick. I gave myself my wings, you know how it goes. . . . And when he got back and he saw me. . . . I was floating, but I had my pride. I got up, high as I was, and I flicked my ass at him and said: 'Goodbye, Charlie. Shit on you. . . .' "

"And that was your introduction to regular use?"

"Nah, I don't know. . . . I used it on and off. I liked it. . . . I was mainlining, all right, but I wasn't hooked . . . not yet, anyway . . . but I was using. . . ."

"And this man . . . ?"

"He was dead to me. . . . I had my pride, too."

"How much did you know about drugs, Mae . . . ? I mean, you had been around. . . ."

"Not much. . . . Oh, I heard a lot about . . . but I never had no course in school or nothing like that. . . . Do you know, really and truthfully, when I first found out anything about junk? When I was picked up and thrown in the house of D. Oh, to see all of them drug addicts laying in them cells almost drove me mad. . . . See, I watched them go through all these changes . . . groanin' and hollerin' and rollin' on the floor, and they had those big, running sores and swollen faces and bodies. . . . I was scared to death to be in with all them monsters."

"Ironic. . . . You became a drug addict yourself. . . ."

"Like hell I did. . . . Lot you know about it. . . ."

"They why are you here?"

"Possession. . . . Possession. . . . Possession of seven grains of marijuana. . . ."

"Were you selling?"

"Reefer? You're crazy. . . . Some of my customers liked to smoke pot when we turned tricks together. . . . You know the way you give away cigarettes—I gave away reefer to my customers."

"You weren't smoking yourself?"

"I didn't need it while I was using stuff. . . ."

"But I thought you said that you weren't a heroin addict."

"I wasn't. . . . I just used it."

"I beg your pardon. . . ."

She smiled archly. "You know, stuff makes you do some really crazy things, like irrational, that you wouldn't do if you weren't flyin'. . . . Like, say you're a very easy going, gullible person when you are yourself. . . . Now, you take stuff and stuff can make you very ee-vil. Like you might never steal, if you were facing reality, but when you were in this fantasy because of stuff, you'd think: 'Well, I'm just the smartest booster in the world. . . .' "

"So heroin made you a good booster?"

"I was a good booster without heroin."

"Then why did you need it?"

"I was tryin' to explain to you, daddy, what stuff does. . . . I'm sayin', like, it changes you."

"Why did you need to be changed?"

She tittered: "I liked getting high. . . . I liked the feeling I got. I liked getting high," and her voice fell to a hoarse murmur.

"How long have you been here, Mae?"

She was languid again. "Two days. . . ."

"How come you came into a rehabilitation program?"

"It was a terrible decision for me." She laughed. "The judge said that he was going to bust me or if I wanted to do something about cleaning myself up, he'd suspend sentence and assign me here. . . . Now, you can see it was a great decision I had to reach, either to go to the joint for maybe five years or to lay my ass up here in this country club for a few months. Listen, I ain't that stupid a broad. . . . I took this."

"Do you have any idea what's involved?"

"Just more bullshit, dad, just more bullshit. . . . You know, the usual trick bag where you learn group therapy, self-control, self-will, why you used stuff, why you should brush your teeth and say your prayers. And after you been here a certain allotted time, you'll go straight to heaven to sit at the right hand of the Lord . . . *bullshit*. And speaking of allotted time, I'm tired, dad, and you ain't soothin' my nerves any. . . . So long, Charlie!" And she hitched her breast back into her dress.

2

This time her dress contained her, so far. She had ambled into the room—an exaggerated prison shuffle, I call it—looked around with high and studied boredom, and at last glanced at me indifferently.

"Hello, Mae, I'm glad to see you."

She grunted. "Daddy, you gonna pluck my nerves again all morning?"

"Did I raise old ghosts, Mae? I'm sorry. . . . I got so interested in what you were saying that I just got caught up in asking questions. . . ."

She quickly became gracious, generous. She sluffed off her reluctance. "Gimme one of your smokes."

"Won't you have a seat? Here, take this one . . . it's more comfortable. . . ."

She straightened herself, her head held high for a moment. "Thank you. . . ."

When I turned on the machine for the playback of the first tape that we had made, I was prepared for another siege of yawns, scratches, grunts, cries, body contortions. . . . Mae belonged to that group of volatile responders who range between fury and submission, never able to let you forget that they are there— needing attention so desperately. The voice emerged from the machine, and again I was impressed by its registration. There was a richness, a fullness, about it that came through the bluster and drawling and swearing and exaggerations. It seemed a trained instrument. It was difficult to assign that voice to the squat, bristling figure opposite me, her figure even more dumpy after a month of institutional food. Throughout the playback, Mae was a study in lapsed self-consciousness. . . . Sometimes her voice was so persuasive that she was coaxed into forgetting that she was undefended, and other times she would twist about in the chair and mutter, "So, bullshit. . . . Do we have to listen?" But the latter was never said so convincingly that I would take her literally. A few times I even saw a very young child peering out from that square, puffy facade, the eyes glowing with pleasure, taken up with the magic of her own voice. "You have a lovely voice, Mae. Have you studied voice?"

"Oh, no," she said unguardedly, only to be followed by the denigrating, "Are you kiddin'? Study voice . . . fer what?"

"It's impressive. . . . Reminds me of a kind of thick, red velour, . . ." I leaned forward, "a red velvet, sort of a Venetian luxury. . . ."

She laughed with pleasure; perhaps I should say she purred. "Daddy, how you rap. . . ."

"You said you were both gullible and suspicious at the same time, Mae. . . . Is that still the case?"

"Have you got any candy? I think I got a cold. This place with all these split-tails is unhygienic. Colds get around awful fast. I think I got one coming. . . ." She cleared her throat noisily. I watched the recording needle bounce as she did it. Next time I would have something sweet with me.

"Now, what did you put to me, daddy?"

"Oh, I just wondered if what you had said last time about being both gullible and suspicious had changed at all?"

"It's changing slowly but surely . . . because my feelings are being hurt, and I'm tired of having my feelings hurt. I just don't take that layin' down . . . havin' my feelings hurt."

"Am I hurting your feelings, Mae?" I asked.

"Not you, Professor." She laughed. "You, hurt my feelings?" She shook her head, as if children really should be protected. "I'm talkin' about these cunts here. I'm being too gullible. I'm acceptin' people and they're not acceptin' me."

"You mean the other girls here with you. . . . I see."

"Certainly, that's who I'm talkin' about. . . . I despise this place. . . . I despise it. . . . And that feelin' will never change, daddy, it will never change. It'll only get worse."

"What is there about this place?"

"Well, I'm goin' to tell you, Professor. . . ." This was her second mention of me as a member of academe. She continued: "We have group therapy sessions here. You know, those phony rap sessions where all these stupid broads roll around like they got snakes inside of them. And this here one girl I liked, she came out of a very weird bag on me and I didn't approve, and I found out that outa forty-five women only five of them liked me." She shook her head grimly. "Five out of forty-five. . . . And I didn't particularly care for that at all . . . just to find five broads outa all of them, to find out that people didn't like me at all. . . . Phony bastards."

"Very distressing. . . ."

"You bet your ass it's distressing. . . . They say they don't like my attitude or my ways. . . . Dig that bag."

"I wonder why."

"Oh, you know what these stupid bitches are like in the joint. They've always got the flag wavin'. . . . They say I'm a phony. . . . They say I'm a phony!"

"Phony? You . . . ?"

"Yeah, me. . . . Ain't that enough to take the bread out of your nacker? So I started to think about it. Like, this mornin' when I was listenin' to myself there on that tape . . . I could kind of see that bag. . . . Like, I know there's sometimes, like there are some fronts that I'll put up, you know, like you'll dress it up a little. . . . But, hell, everybody dresses up just a little, but that ain't no reason to say that you don't like a person or to accuse her of being a phony. . . ."

"This group therapy . . . just what is it supposed to do for you?"

"Help me, daddy, help me. But I'll tell you for sure that they ain't helpin' me one damned little grain by tellin' me that I'm a phony and that they don't like me. . . . How's that grab you?"

"Perhaps they're trying to rile you . . . huh? Perhaps they want you to lose your cool . . . huh, Mae . . . ?"

She glanced at me. "Hey, maybe you got somethin', Professor. . . . I didn't think they were all that jive. . . . I'll have to watch that. . . . The sly bitches."

"Maybe they're trying to test you . . . you know, to see if you project images. . . . It could be, you know?"

"I really haven't been projectin' too many images though. . . . I been trying to be truthful with these people. . . . They're down on me . . . they're down on me. Just a bunch of jive people . . . that's what they are. . . . Just look at them nuns. Talk about projectin' images. . . . Who ever heard of nuns wearin' mini-skirts . . . wagglin' their tails like they do? Now ain't that projectin' a image . . . ? Huh, Professor . . . ? Why ain't they dressed up like a nun is supposed to be dressed . . . huh? Ain't that an image?" she demanded, her face grim with righteousness.

"Makes you wonder, doesn't it?"

"You bet your ass, daddy, you bet your ass. . . . Well, I didn't ask to come here to no holy shrine to be made over. That damned judge never told me that he was pennin' me up with all these

sweet sisters and their mini-skirts and their sweet ways of callin'
you a phony. . . . They don't fool me . . . not Mae. . . ."

"Here. Have a smoke. . . ." Through the haze I said: "They've
certainly succeeded in upsetting you, haven't they? Do you suppose
that they wanted to do that?"

"Huh. I don't know why though. It's made me feel very hurt.
It's made me go back into myself, and I started to write poetry
again just to stay away from people." She suddenly shook
herself. "If they think I'm so God-damned phony, then they
don't need to be bothered with me. . . . I don't need their piece of
fat. . . . I can get by. . . . Bitches. . . ."

"What do you suppose makes them do this, Mae?"

"They're just a bunch of cats, itchy cats. . . . See, they come offa
stuff and they get itchy . . . they gotta do somethin'. Ain't no stuff
here, they get uptight, so they has to pick. And they picked the
right one to pick on. . . . I'll tear 'em up, the dirty bitches. . . .
And them phony nuns with their short skirts. . . . Jees, how I'd
like to tell that judge about this place." She mimicked the judge:
'You'll have an op-po-tune-ity to find yourself.' Oh, yeah, find myself in a snake pit with a whole lot of itchy broads. . . . Jesus."

"He said that? To find yourself . . . ? Strange how people express themselves. . . . Maybe he's found with other female addicts
that they don't know very much about themselves. You know, a
lot of them don't. . . . Now, we know that . . . I'm sure you see
that every day here."

"Oh, sure, some of these broads are so phony that when they
look into the mirror in the morning they gotta wait a minute to be
introduced to themselves. Oh, sure, the dope fiend he don't know
from nothin' . . . phony from the word go. . . . But, see, Professor,
that's never been my way. . . ."

"You don't have to be introduced to Mae . . . ? You know all
about her?"

She studied my face. "It ain't that I know everything about her
. . . not everything . . . but I watch me. . . . I watch Mae very
close. I put things down on paper about Mae. That's why, like I
said, I'm back to writin' my poetry now. . . . On account of I'm
putting me down so I can't get like the rest of this jive bunch."

"What do you write down about yourself, Mae . . . ? Can you share it with me?"

"My moods, they're very changeable, Professor. I can be very happy at one time, thinking different thoughts, and in a very depressed mood in the next second. But lately I been very morbid . . . mor-bid. . . . This place, you know. . . ."

"I'd love to hear some of your poetry, Mae."

"I brought one with me. . . ." She pulled out a folded sheaf of yellow paper from her dress pocket. "You want to hear it?" she asked sharply.

"Well, these interviews are all about Mae. . . . And your poems were written by you and about you. . . . Is there any question?"

"You're right, Professor." Figuratively she patted me on the head and proceeded to open her bundle of papers.

>"I have been alone like the sun and all the lonely stars
>   in that lonely sky.
>I have been alone like the seagull and all the lonely creatures
>   in that lonely sky.
>In the white snow, in the golden sand, I have traced the
>   footprints.
>Were they lovers who walked here and are now gone?
>Were they lovers?
>Oh, yes, lovers. They go two by two, the snow bruised
>   by the twinning feet, the sand brushed by their unknowing feet.
>Lovers they were . . . oh, lovers.
>And like the seagull's cry that shrieks in the silence,
>   that makes the loneliness howl,
>I cry. . . . I cry. . . . I cry.
>Why have I no lover? Why am I alone? Two footprints in the
>   sand of my life. My own.
>Then I whisper: 'God . . . You there. Am I so dirty to You?
>Why should You make me to be so terrible a sight to all? So
>   terrible. You there . . . answer me!
>I need someone, not just time and things. I need someone who
>   will breathe on me.
>Why do You have me alone?'
>So the sun rises in that lonely sky, and the gulls wheel
>   in that lonely sky.
>I wait on that beach, I hear the cries, there is no answer . . .
>   no sign.

Just footprints . . . two of them . . . my feet.
No sign, no answer. Footprints leading to the water. . . .
The tide thunders in, roars, washes. . . . No prints now.
No answer. Silence. Silence."

She dropped the papers on the floor and swore. She was profoundly uncomfortable and ill at ease. She gathered them together with exaggerated care.

I asked softly: "So, since there was no answer, she destroyed herself . . . ? No Mae . . . is that it . . . ? She walked into the water and into oblivion?"

Suddenly she stood up. "Me, I've walked into the water. . . . Me. . . . There was no reply to my pleas."

"Pity . . . self-destruction, huh?"

She uttered that funny little squeak that she had used in our first interview.

I continued: "Or withdrawal . . . ?"

"Well, there was no answer to my plea, was there? There wasn't. . . . No answer. . . . Only silence."

"So we have self-destruction or withdrawal or both of them sort of summed up in heroin use. . . . I suppose you could look at heroin in that light, couldn't you?" I asked very tentatively, not wanting her to blow up.

"Yeah, in a way I guess you could. . . . Yeah, I guess so. . . ."

"Now, what is the question that the person in your poem is asking of God or of life?"

She leaned forward, a smirk on her face: "What's keeping love away from me? Why haven't I been able to have it? And why hasn't somebody been able to understand me the way I want to be understood? What's keepin' it away from me?" she demanded belligerently.

"You've never been loved, and you've never been understood the way you've wanted to be understood. Is that it?"

"You bet your booties, daddy."

I asked quietly: "Is it possible to love you the way you want to be loved or to understand you the way you want to be understood, Mae . . . ?"

"Oh, Christ sakes. . . . I ain't unique. . . . I ain't unique."

"Oh, I'm sorry, Mae. Forgive me. . . . I get caught up in what you say. I didn't mean to offend you."

She patted my hand. "It's okay, Professor. . . . My nerves are very plucked these days. In this crib with these dizzy broads. . . . It's like you got the curse every day in the week. . . . But see, I ain't askin' for the impossible . . . when I want to be loved and understood."

"Mae, have you ever had a rewarding relationship? With anyone?" I asked mildly. "It might be of great interest for you as a poet to explore that."

"Yeah. . . . I did once. . . . With another woman. . . ."

"An older woman . . . ?"

"Yeah, when I was in the joint. . . . It was beautiful, beautiful . . . no dead-pan sex. . . . We had such feelings for each other. We were very close. She stood up for me. . . . It was so much more than I ever had. . . ."

"Intimacy?"

"If it'd been possible, intimacy woulda come into it. She understood me; she understood that my youth was on my side. And there were things that she explained to me, things that, like, nobody else ever even tried to explain. . . . I learned a lot from her, and she learned things from me, too, because youth can give wisdom to gray heads, too, you know, Professor. . . . We were together for four months and eleven days. . . ."

"What happened?"

"I got out and she went up. Hers was murder. She went up. . . . She'll be up a long time . . . a long bust. . . ."

"Have you corresponded?"

She snorted. "How? All her mail is opened . . . and so's mine, here in this house with these damned, mini-skirted, creepin' Marys. . . . Nah. . . ."

"What did she give you that you never had before?"

"Love. . . . Love. Emotions. . . . She gave me affection . . . because it's affection that makes it possible for love, to make love grand. . . . She was gay . . . a lesbian, a masculine-aggressive type," she said. That last phrase—she'd undoubtedly picked it up during one of her institutional stays. How naturally, how quickly the addict assimilates the professional jargon.

"She was a drug user?"

"Oh, God, she never wanted me to use them. Nobody wants the person they love to use drugs, Professor, because drugs comes between you like a piece of paper . . . a wall. . . . When you lay in bed at night with your lover, you don't want a third person there with you, and heroin is the white lady, she lays in there with you. Oh, no, Sheila wanted me never to use stuff. No drugs with her. . . ."

"When was this?"

"A few years ago. . . . Lots of footprints been washed out since then." I passed her the cigarette package. "I was gay all the time I was prossing. . . . Then I tried to kill myself."

"Because the relationship had been ended?"

She snorted again. "Ended? Yeah, my relationship with life. But it wasn't because it was ended, it was because it never even started. . . . Oh, I piled it on. I musta took almost a bottle full of double-troubles, some libries, and then shot up two cookers full of hot and cold." She chuckled. "Damned near killed myself."

"Wasn't from want of trying."

"That's for sure."

"You wanted to kill yourself . . . really?"

"I thought so. . . . I woke up in the hospital. . . ."

"Love affair, huh?"

"Nah, a hate affair . . . that's it, Professor, a hate affair. That's all I'm ever left with, a hate affair, a hate of me. . . . You know, my mother, and prossin', and another woman rejecting me. . . ."

"And no men?"

"Sure, how do you pross if not for men, but that's business. . . . A trick is like a job."

I said, as if making an offering: "There is your child, so we know that there was a time. . . ."

She interrupted me: "That was a long time ago . . . a long time ago. I haven't had a dude that way in years."

"Does being gay make you uncomfortable?"

"Why should it?"

"It shouldn't if it doesn't; I was just asking. . . ."

"No, it don't, Professor. . . . See, when I was in the looney bin after the nervous breakdown . . . there was this real tough, masculine-aggressive girl, and I was really attracted to her. We got real uptight together. I dug this. . . . See, I never reached a climax with a man but I reached one with her. . . . Then I did . . . because she looked out for me. . . . She stirred my emotions. . . ."

"Do you think that your experience with your stepfather soured you on men?"

"Oh, sure. That cut it, squashed it. . . . I don't enjoy men; I really hate them because of that cockroach. I really hate them, you know, Professor. . . . I hate them. . . ." All of a sudden, a wicked smile broke across her face: "You know, I really egged him on. I really did. I got him pretty steamy. I was a flirt. . . . But damn, he didn't have to take me like he did, do all them things to me. . . ."

"Ah, you add another dimension to yourself, huh? Who were you trying to get at by seducing your stepfather?"

"Hey, you ain't so dumb, Professor. . . . You can see that, huh? I was really jealous. . . . How come he had the love of her when I shoulda had it all . . . ? I mean, my mother should have loved me and not him, so I figgered I'd take him away from her. Oh, brother, I could be real wicked when I wanted . . . ee-vil, you know?"

"What would you say now? That that was an attention-grabbing tactic . . . ?"

"Most definitely," she said with infinite maturity. "Yeah, I was always looking to grab attention . . . always."

"You've covered a lot of ground today, Mae. . . ."

"Yeah, I don't know what got me started, Professor. The poetry I guess, and being with these damned females. . . ."

"Mae . . . before, you mentioned a mirror. . . . What do you see these days?"

She crinkled the cigarette package. "I don't see her too tough."

"You mean that you don't think much of her?"

"That's it. I don't have too many tough feelin's about Mae. . . ."

"Anybody could really tell that from your attempts on your life —and from that poetry. . . . And yet isn't it puzzling that what people think about you does bother you very much?"

"It does, it eats me out . . . really eats me out that they should downrate me and tell me that I'm a phony and all that female clack."

"That's puzzling. Since you have this hate affair with yourself . . . why should it bother you? You know?"

She paused, playing with a cigarette. "Yeah, hey, that is puzzling. . . . It is, Professor. . . ."

"You know they're just confirming your own opinion of yourself . . . so why get so mad . . . ? Or maybe it's not that?"

"I get so crushed so much. . . . Ever see them strawberry boxes . . . ? When I was a kid, we used to step on them just to hear them snap as we crushed them with our feet. Me, I'm a strawberry box. I'm always gettin' crushed. . . ."

"Mae, why do you dislike yourself so much?"

Subdued, her head cocked, she murmured: "I did some hellified wrong things. . . . I tried to take my stepfather away from that bitch, my mother. I was a whore and I never had good feelin's about that. . . . I did that because of that lame who I thought loved me, and he just kicked me in the ass. . . . And I had that little baby and I gave her over, too, and I'm outrageous in my ways. . . . I am, Professor. . . . Outrageous, always swearin' and throwin' my weight around. I still do wrong things . . . you know, really wrong things. I know they're wrong but I do 'em. And there ain't no need for anybody to tell me that they're wrong because I can beat them to it. I know that they're wrong, on account of I have a very good sense of moral value. . . . But I do it all just for the hell of it. . . ."

The interview was over. "I'll bring some candy next time, Mae."

But the door had opened, and I watched Mae suddenly slouch; her belly was thrust forward, she yawned and said: "Anything you say, daddy . . . anything you say. Oh, Christ, how borin' it all is."

3

"How long have you been here now, Mae?"

"Ohhhh . . . er . . . er . . . three months and four days. . . . Yep. Three months and four stinking, stupid, out-of-the-world days. . . ."

"Still angry . . . ?"

"Angry? I'm wild, wild. . . . Bunch of two-faced bitches."

"I must say that you look very smart today in that outfit. What do you call that, please?"

"Oh, this. It's a jumper and a blouse. . . . My old lady must have had the grabs after one of her bouts and broke down and spent some guilt money on me. What the hell do I care? It's clothes . . . I need them. What difference does it make?"

"A considerable difference, at least from where I sit. . . . You look very attractive. . . ." And she did. She had lost weight; her hair had grown, and she had obviously brushed it; she wore stockings and pumps; her blouse was colorful and it came up around her throat, no danger of her falling out of it.

"Thanks anyway, Professor." And she tried to make it sound nonchalant. But then, as if she had to put affairs in their proper perspective, she lashed out: "The stupidity of this God-damned place. You know, these females . . . all of them. . . ."

"Residents?"

"Residents and the staff. Oh, they're creeps, all of them, loonies, zonks. . . . You know what a zonk is? Somebody who gets jammed in a window and says that they're tryin' to find new ways of gettin' in their house, that's a zonk. . . . There was an incident that just happened recently. They thought they'd play a joke on me. They wrote me a very obscene letter. A very obscene letter

. . . which it resulted in my being very hurt. Very hurt through it.
. . . And I went through some emotional disturbance on account
of this. Like, you know, I'm the scapegoat on the grounds. . . . I
think maybe I put myself in this position in a way. You know, me
tryin' to help them out. I'd take the blame for them or let them
have my radio . . . little things. . . . But you can't put your arm
inside of a bear cage. The stupid animals only know how to grab
and pull off your arm. . . . I tell you, Professor, I been goin'
through some outrageous changes. Really, outrageous changes, and
I'm tender about cattiness and this kind of stupidity . . . I'm
tender. . . ."

"Because of attention-grabbing?"

"What else? My mannerisms. . . . You know, I come on like,
'Here I am, look me over. I'm somebody, and don't you dirty
bitches ever forget it.' Like, due to the fact that I'm new to this
kind of a setup. . . . Really, Professor, I'm new to all this group
therapy stuff. Some of this stuff puts you through an awful lot of
changes and you get jammed. . . . I'm . . . I'm more or less, you
know, lookin' for people to accept me. Like, I do need people. . . .
You gotta need people, huh? Don't you?"

I brought out the bag of hard candy I had bought for her and
extended it. She grabbed and tossed three pieces in her mouth.
"How much of you . . . Mae, how much of you do you accept?"

Her mouth full, she stared at me. "How much of me?"

"Yeah, how much of you do you accept? Remember, you were
telling me about looking at yourself in the mirror?"

"In a sense, I guess, I don't accept too much of me. . . . I don't
accept the fact, for instance, about my back, the broadness of my
back and the largeness of my breasts, and the bigness of my can. I
don't accept that, though I'm gettin' around to it. . . . To those
bitches making wisecracks about it. . . . They're calling me the
'seven course dinner.' Bunch of cruel bitches. . . ."

"Why do they do that?"

She took a piece of candy out of her mouth and looked at it.
"Damned if I know, just cats . . . just cats. . . ."

"Do you have any friends, Mae?"

"One or two. . . . I don't invite friends. I just don't want to

spread myself for them . . . you know, I don't trust them. I'm very
suspicious of them . . . suspicious. . . ."

"And gullible?"

"Yeah. And gullible. I keep tryin'. There is one girl . . . we're
pretty tight together, pretty tight. . . . We're very much alike. It's
her intellect, her understanding of me."

"Masculine, aggressive?"

"Oh." She was surprised by my question, and embarrassed, I
think, since she had provided the content. "She is, now that you
mention it. . . . But this ain't sex. She likes the zodiac and I'm
quite frequent with it, myself. I'm an Aquarius and she's an Aries,
and we both look at things and try to understand each other by
what astrology tells us. And she does understand me. . . . Now I
know for a fact what kind of person I'm supposed to be and what I
am."

"You do?"

"Certainly. I'm supposed to be loyal. I'm supposed to be understanding. I'm a very sympathetic kind of person, and I'm more or
less changeable, too."

"So how do you square up with this astrological projection of
your characteristics?"

"Well, these astrological prospects are pretty true to a certain extent, all right. . . . I'm loyal to a certain extent. I'm true to
whoever I'm associated with until I'm crossed, and once I'm
crossed I get very vin-dic-tive."

"You seem subdued to me today, Mae. . . ."

"It's just here lately my nerves has been getting the best of me.
This place is really getting to me. Like, these walls was meant to
be climbed. I kid you not—these walls were meant to be
climbed. . . . These mini-skirted Marys . . . they're too much. I
figger that they've got a scheme. They'll either break you or you'll
come out of here pretty tough." She put some more candy in her
mouth. "Oh, hey, Professor . . . have a piece?"

"You don't seem so resentful today."

"I been thinking. I'm coming out of my scheming bag. . . . I'm
sittin' back and watching. . . . I'm not bein' drawn into these con-
frontations where I suddenly flare up and grab for hair."

"You're controlling your temper?"

"I'm makin' different moves. Like, I'm going to the mini-skirted Marys and lettin' them carry the shotgun. Like I'm just as mad, but I block that to some extent. . . . I'll go to the authorities . . . tell 'em . . . let them handle it. . . . What the hell do they get paid for? Why should I do their dirty work . . . huh, Professor?"

"Looked at in a certain way, somebody might accuse you of joining the other side."

"I told you I'm coming out of my scheming bag. The hell with what they think."

"Or somebody might even get the idea that you were putting on a responsibility image. . . ."

"Look, the only thing this place might do for me, if I can stay down from the walls, is to maybe use my mouth instead of my fists. . . . That's the only thing."

"Wow, that's tremendous, Mae. Look at what it does. It gives you another way of handling things."

"Certainly. . . . A resource . . . a resource."

She wanted me to pick it up. "You use absolutely the right word, Mae. The right word."

"Now, we know, Professor, when I get back out on the street, it's got to be a very different bag. But in here I got to do like the Romans. . . . Out on the street it will be quite a difference, as you and me will agree."

"You'll have to go back to fists of course."

"I wouldn't exactly say that, but I'm the kind of person who can talk for just so long, and then . . . you know?"

"So actually you're experimenting. . . . A kind of tentative exploration of other . . . how did you put it before . . . resources?"

"Exactly. I'm very changeable. See, like now I think that I'm gettin' provoked pretty near to the breaking point. Like that obscene letter. . . ."

"You're still in group therapy?"

"Oh, that . . . the creepin' Jesus society for weepy women. I'm in four groups, four different rap groups. . . . There at those I started to bring up my resentment bag, but I was brought to understand that I can holler about resentment all I like, but I would still be here. . . . It's like trying to break into the movies, with those therapy groups—you got to go to bed with the producers, otherwise you can't act, get what I mean? See, it's a little game they run. Everybody chips in and nobody rocks the boat but me. I'm sincere and I want to break through those God-damned lyin' bunnies, but they don't want that. They're all playin' their games, spinnin' their webs. . . . You know, what's the percentage . . . ? All those dumb broads has got resentment. So what?"

"I suppose that's so. . . ."

"Sure, Professor. . . . Look, there are people here who've been in and out three and four times. You know, they lay up. They've seen the light of the Holy Grail. They got it made. They got concern. They're through with drugs. You know, typical junkie shit, and then they get out, go round the corner, and they score and they fall right on their stupid, lyin', gamin' faces and they get thrown back in here for another year. So there's a lot of broken pictures, a lot of them smashed images. . . . And there's a lot of bitterness and a lot of lyin' that's gotta go on for them to cover up their hurts."

"So the group really hasn't done anything for you?" I asked. "But you really didn't expect anything from them anyway."

"It's true, Professor. I didn't. Only thing they've done for me is to make me accept the fact that I'm here. Big deal, ain't it, after three months and four days. A bunch of zonks. Sure, I'm improved to the fact that I can understand some of my feelings—who wouldn't be with all these stupid broads around yellin' their heads off . . . ? But I know when I get certain signals that I want to be destructive, that is my nature talkin'. This is in me, and there's nothin' no group is goin' help me with. I can't pinpoint how I feel the way I feel sometimes. I can't tell you why I feel like I do right now, Professor. . . ."

"But I bet your poetry can."

She looked at me, and I was amazed by her smile. "How did you know? I brought one with me. I wrote it last night on account of I knew you were comin'."

"Would you read it to me?"

"Professor, I think it shows a change in me.

On my beat, along those lonesome streets,
My hips sway to some music I cannot hear,
Some voice calls, some hungry eyes seek,
I pause, and then the hoarse invitation,
And I hear the footfall next to me,
That silence that precedes my moment of intimacy.
Oh, if he be young and not bruised, with trembling
He'll come to me, unlearned and clumsy.
And in his bought moment a great light
Will burst between us, banishing gloom,
Giving to each full measure of insight
Into the other, into ourselves, into life.
For me he'll be less damaged than I, less
Knowing, less untrusting, less demanding.
I'll see me reflected in his face as a mirror.
I'll see me clean and free and unashamed.
I'll see me quiet and in repose, no gnawing hunger.
That hunger whose sharp teeth drive the body,
That filthifies the image, that sullies the mind,
That breaks the dream, that curls the soul. . . .
He'll strike and the rock of the sepulcher that
Hides the dead girl will roll away, will roll away,
And she will arise like some unexpected bride,
Blushing to face him who called her forth.
On my beat, along those lonesome streets,
My hips sway to some music I cannot hear,
To some music I cannot hear, music I cannot hear."

Mae was hunched over, she began to pick her nose, and then she said coarsely, "I suppose I'll have to sit through another one of these God-damned head-shrinking things again in another month, huh? Why the hell should I? Why should I? What's in it for me just to see your ugly face?"

I was moved; my professional facade had not been proof against this bursting forth of poetry. I was silent because I was moved and really didn't know what to say to this now transformed, profoundly distressed girl. I looked at her and said quietly: "You said to me before you read your poem that you thought it would show a change in you."

"Yeah, so what, Charlie?" Her face an icy mask.

I gave up; I couldn't bring it off. What the hell. I said, "Your poem has upset me. I'm so moved by it that I don't know what to say to you. I'm sorry. But I'm very impressed and I don't know very much about poetry. . . ." I turned off the machine, removed her microphone, and looked at her. "I hope that you'll bring more of your poetry next time, Mae. . . ."

Her features softened. "Thanks for the candy, Professor."

Sister Benedita was waiting in the hall when I emerged with my equipment. She asked me to come into her office. Mae called it a mini-skirt; I would have called it knee-length, but certainly these sisters wore feminine, secular garb. Her hair was bobbed, her face scrubbed clean. She had a small, oval face that seemed youthful, though I had known her when she pioneered in the drug rehabilitation movement many years before.

"Sit down, Frank Michael. You probably need it after that interview." She had a large laugh for so small a woman. "She came out like she was shot from a gun. What did you do to her? Ordinarily she shuffles along like a slug on a hot day."

"She's an amazing girl, Sister."

"She's a real problem girl. Do you know that she's assaulted no less than four people in the last two weeks. Every argument, every rumpus—there's Mae. Her lying, her boisterousness, her swearing, those are par for the course, but that fearful temper, those fists of hers. . . . We are not set up for her aggressiveness. Frank Michael, she's not like most of them. She's a tiger. My staff is more uptight over her. She swaggers or she sulks, she swears or tries to give them presents . . . she's always in hot water."

"Sister, she's a whore. All she knows is to sell herself to gain affection. That's what your people and the other girls resent . . . her giving herself so wantonly."

"Well, I don't know what we can do. . . . We just can't contain her in this setting. The first few days she was here, she exposed her breasts every time male staff was around." And Sister Benedita laughed. "It really was quite different for some of my fuddy-duddy young social workers. Quite different." Then, her face grave, she said: "The staff conferences on her are pretty grim affairs. Nobody gives her a chance. . . . They feel she's too far gone, too damaged."

"That's a pity, Sister. I think that should be turned around and looked at from the other end. I think Mae is living right on the surface, like a fruit close to the ground, ready to be picked. All of her defenses are right there on the surface; she's so eager to be helped. . . . Have you heard any of her poetry?"

"Mae writes poetry . . . ?"

"Yes, she does, and it's not quite like most inmate poetry. I don't think she herself understands how revealing it is."

"Well, I'll look into it. . . . Perhaps we'll find a handle to her. . . ."

"She'll probably deny it, and savagely, too. She'll feel that I've betrayed her."

I leaned forward and lighted her cigarette. She said: "Frank Michael, are you saying that she's very talented?"

I shrugged my shoulders. "That's really out of my field. I don't feel much competence about poetry, but I think that she is gifted. She's very powerful. She has tremendous energy. Now, that is different from most heroin users . . . energy. But she's so used to buying attention and favors. . . . I hope you won't get rid of her. She can only go one way if you let her go."

"She'll go back to court and be sentenced. . . ."

It was nearing my departure time. I had to get to the airport. "Well, you must do what you have to, Sister."

"Don't we always, Frank Michael?"

I stood in the doorway. "Have you had any breakouts?"

"That's the name of the game. . . . We always have them. You can't have women confined without constant scheming about breakouts."

"And Mae . . . how many times has she attempted to run away?"

Sister Benedita flicked ashes from her cigarette. "I'd have to look up her record. But I don't recall her name at all."

"And I'm certain that you would have, under the circumstances. . . . No, Sister, I think that you'll find that Mae hasn't run away. I'll bet you'll find that she hasn't even made an attempt."

4

There had been no word from Sister Benedita, so I kept my appointment. In due course Mae arrived, we listened to the tape we had made the month before and, in the silence that followed, Mae said: "I've got a miserable cold today." She snuffled. "You know, one cold gets started in a place like this and it's all over the place."

"Your face has changed. You look refreshed, Mae," I said. "You look young."

She snorted: "Tcha. . . . I don't know why—I'm miserable."

"I'll tell you that you look miserable and old and ugly, if that's the way you want it."

She smiled. "I believe you, but I don't understand why I look refreshed and young."

"Maybe it's because you've never looked at yourself in anything but a critical way. Why should I make up something that's not true?"

"Oh, I'm interested in what you see in me because I want to know what would make you feel this when I don't."

"You're very well dressed again. Your hair is getting positively long, your face has thinned, you sit very erectly in your chair. . . . I wish I could show you the change." I laughed. "I'll be very candid. I used to think that it would give me some protection to wear my glasses. I never quite knew whether you were going to take a poke out of me. You'd scowl so, and grunt your hostility. . . . I wonder if this outer change is any clue to something happening inside of Mae."

She listened carefully; she hesitated, her eyes moving. "I think I feel at peace inside of me. I'm at peace to the point where I'm going to accept me. I've given up guilt feelings. Some things I'll have to live with. Some things I'll have to cut off. Like, I've had an experience with a group of mine in which I got the feeling that they didn't accept me. So I went out on the floor, and one girl said she understood where I was coming from, this one girl, and I felt beautiful. . . . The relationship that I've had with my mother. Well, I had a letter from her and it stirred me up. But I analyzed it in my mind, and I knew what I was going to do. But I had to hear somebody else's opinion before I really made a move . . . and this girl she listened to me. And I've decided to just cut my mother loose. I'm not going to gain anything, and I have nothing to lose. I've never been that close to her and I never shall be. But I won't destroy whatever there was by telling her of my past experiences with my stepfather. And that's one big load off my mind."

"This girl you refer to, she gave you this advice?"

"See, I wasn't looking at things level. In my mind I was gliding over it because of the material values due to the fact that they send me money and that they can do something for my daughter. I ain't got nobody else . . . there's nobody out there. Until I can get out of here, I'm powerless to do anything. . . . I'd like a piece of candy once in a while, or money for smokes or some nice clothes. . . . See, they were the only ones who could shell it out. . . . So, like I say, it was a material kind of holding on. I didn't want to cut it loose; I couldn't afford to. But yet now I had to, I had to split. I have to stand on my own two feet. . . . I realized it myself, but yet I wanted to hear it from somebody else, too."

"Does this indicate that you feel more comfortable with your therapy group now?"

"I'm not exactly comfortable with them. There's a certain phoniness in people. I'm more comfortable with a few people now. See, most of those girls have no concern whatsoever. They're just rapping off the top of their heads. They're zonks. Entirely selfish, playing their games, spinning their webs. All their hangups they still got, and when they hit the streets they'll still have 'em. They keep holding on to them."

"So you don't give them much chance of staying off the stuff or staying out on the street?"

"Most of 'em don't have no chance in the world. I'll see most of 'em back here before I get discharged. . . ." She interrupted herself and leaned forward. She was very excited: "I see myself in them. I see myself in them. Keep everybody away by talking fast and never listening, by hitting out before you get hit, by hiding, always hiding in the center of your web. So I see only too plain what I'm like and what could happen in the future. You don't have to hit me with a pipe to make me see a warning. It's there, so I gotta stop."

"Can't you try to make them understand what they're doing?"

"Like, that's part of group, you know, that you help the others to see, but you can't pull their covers so easy. They're shrewd like they are outside. . . . Now, there's one kid, I've tried to talk to her—you know, outside of the group . . . on the floor or in recreation or at meals. . . . I tell her what she's doing; I point it out to her but she don't listen. So I tell you, it's gettin' me pretty damned pissed off her not listening to me, her spurning my good advice. I have made an effort with her and she rejected me. Now, I don't particularly like to be rejected, as you well know . . . especially when I know when I'm not rappin' off the top of my head. Now I could see if I was just gaming or rounding on this kid that she should be so hoity-toity, but I was coming out of a real bag . . . sincere. . . . She's just a kid, just seventeen. She's still a child, where I never was a child. I was born and then I jumped into womanhood, whooosh! I never really knew what being young really was. And, like, this stupid kid she's just groovin' on this one channel, she ain't furtherin' herself."

"How do you work with a youngster like this, Mae?"

"Jesus, I don't know . . . on account of I never coped with it before. . . . And I can't figger out how I even got started on it. . . . Who is she that rejects my good advice . . . ? What she needs is a coupla good knocks. Oh, I tell you, Professor, it wouldn't take me two seconds to knock her around. I'd bang some sense into her stupid, hollow head. Pretty, empty-headed little thing, like some kind of straw doll. She'll be swallowed up out there. Just wait till after she's been pawed by them. They're waiting. . . . She'll shoot all day and screw all night, and they'll find her in an alley, stiff. . . . God-dammit, how resentful it makes me that a stupid broad like that won't listen."

"Do you suppose that it would be of great value to you person-ally to really try to figure out some way of getting to this girl?"

She lighted a cigarette. "Leave that up to the mini-skirted Marys. I can't turn back the pages of life, look at one chapter after another of this loused-up broad's life, put together all of her torn valentines. I can't remake her—I can't. . . . Don't forget, Pro-fessor, we're all too busy looking at our own lives and our own problems to spend a helluva lot of time worryin' about somebody else. I don't really have time to worry about her. I don't. I got me. . . . And look, she feels the same way, don't you forget it. . . . She spits on my efforts to help her. She swears at me. She raises her hands at me. She acts like a God-damned whore. You know, no pride, no nothin'. I'm very selfish when it comes to that degree, very selfish. If you can't take an example from me trying to do my thing, then screw you because I ain't gonna be stopped, because I'm gonna make it while you stand there watchin' me. . . . Yes, sir, screw her, screw 'em all; this girl is gonna do it."

"I'm puzzled, Mae. . . . You've changed so greatly."

"I am, too . . . 'cause I don't know, neither. I get pretty cocky about me. I think I'm puttin' myself together."

"Are you . . . ?" I moved my microphone cable. "Do you sup-pose this girl rejected your help because she felt that you were trying to make her, trying to take her . . . ?"

The question didn't faze her; I had half-expected an explosion. "Make her . . . ? That skinny bitch . . . ? But you know, Pro-fessor, that mighta been it. That kind is scared from the day they get outside their mother's belly. She's probably been so pawed that she's sex-dry. . . . Yeah, maybe that's what she thought. Huh, I'll have to consider that. Maybe you got somethin', Professor. . . . I'll have to pluck my mind over that."

"Are you ready to leave here, Mae?"

She frowned as she lighted another cigarette. "Hummm. Well, I was never ready to come in here . . . which is a fact we both know, huh, Professor? Am I ready to go out? Like, Jeez, I think I should be given a trial, a chance to go out and try to make some moves."

"Do you think that anybody on the staff would agree with you?"

"You mean the mini-skirted Marys? I doubt it. . . . But you know, I'm gonna ask 'em. I'm gonna ask 'em. They get paid fer that. I'm gonna ask 'em."

"Suppose they ask you what makes you think you deserve this trial. . . . What then?"

"I'll tell 'em . . . I got a goal . . . I have a perspective. I didn't have it before. Then it was like I'd say, 'I wanna do this. I wanna do that.' But then I never had anything behind it. Now I want to do so much. I want to get a job. I want to get to know people. . . . Because I think I can understand 'em now. See, I want to look into them, to find out how they round on things, how they shift, lean offa things without goin' to the white lady. . . . Because they ain't got such a bed of roses just because they're squares. . . . I got to look into them. . . ."

"But what happens when life acts like this girl here, when it spurns you, when it scorns you. . . . What happens?"

"In the first place, I'm not goin' to come on so strong. I'm going to take time to lead up to things, to explain them. See, you got to think about things first. You gotta use your head to reason things out. Nothing is gonna make me blow my cool so that I end up in a looney crib like this again. . . . So that's how I'll cope with it. . . ."

"But you couldn't cope with the girl. What makes you think you'll do any better out there where things are really rough?"

"Look, Professor. I'm going to do my own thing. This stupid young broad here was just good practice. That's all a place like this is good for, practice. . . . See, I'm going to do it on my own."

"But what's in it for you, Mae? I mean, what's the percentage? What do you get out of it?"

"It's only part of human nature. It's somethin' called acceptin'. Acceptin'. I got to accept. . . ."

And to accompany these sentiments, Mae wore an expression of resignation that was reminiscent of those old-fashioned, garish religious plaques. "You know, Mae, you sound very much like somebody who's suddenly found salvation . . . or in this case, group therapy. Let me explain. You're taking everything that's been thrown out, and you're not thinking about it at all. Like that bag of candy that I gave you. You just grabbed a handful and stuffed it in your mouth. You didn't examine it. You just gobbled it up."

"There's certain things I need, Professor, and I don't stand on ceremony. . . ."

"It's not your hunger that should disturb you, it's the upset to your system that anything undigested causes. You just grab things and run. . . ."

"And why not . . . ? I don't need to stand around and hem and haw and be so picky that I end up doin' nothin'. Life moves fast, daddy. This little girl ain't about to be pushed to the side."

"But look, Mae. . . . There's never anything you do that you don't just jump into. . . . Take your relationships. They start and are full blown. Just as you described your development. You said you were born and then went straight into womanhood. You set yourself up every time. . . . Can you see that . . . ?"

"In a manner of speaking. . . ."

"You've said that you were gullible and suspicious. . . . True. . . . You give yourself completely to anything, recklessly, despairingly: 'Take me. Take me. I'm not worth anything. Please take me. . . .' "

She frowned, scowled. "You're raking over my feelings, Professor."

"Look at this girl you went and spoke to on your floor. What's going to happen there? What's going to happen? Next time I come are you going to be furious with her because she's disappointed you? Or the group? Are they going to be squashed because they didn't measure up . . . ? Look, Mae . . . I'm not trying to rake over your feelings. Listen to what you said just a few minutes ago." I rewound the reel until I located the place I wanted. I started the playback:

"In the first place, I'm not going to come on so strong. . . . I'm going to take time to lead up to things, to explain them. . . ."

Mae blurted out: "Jesus, I just finished saying that. You don't have to have that machine repeat them for me. I ain't no dope. I understand what I say."

"I don't think that you do, sometimes. You put so much out to people, Mae. What chance do you allow yourself?"

"Oh, Christ, now don't tell me that you're gonna lecture, Professor. Don't wind up and let go with that now. Don't get like the rest of these mini-skirted Marys. I don't need that. . . ."

I leaned forward and took her hands in mine. "Listen to me. . . . Do you recall what you said about always stuffing food in your face when you were a kid? You're hungry. . . . We know that. But you can't swallow everything whole. That's what gives you your trouble. These girls, the group therapy sessions, your stepfather, every one of your encounters, and your use of heroin . . . swallow them all whole to satisfy that desperate hunger of yours. Mae, you can't do it. . . ."

She snuffled loudly. "Ah, Professor, I feel lousy. . . . Just cool it, man, you're plucking my nerves too bad now. I got a cold. I feel miserable. . . ."

"I'm sorry, Mae. . . . But don't blow your chances here. . . ."

She blew her nose loudly: "You mean, blow my nose. I got no chance in this cat house. Bunch of hypocritical broads with a bunch of hypocritical nuns. Get this damned thing offa my neck." She tugged peevishly at the microphone. I removed it.

"I was looking forward to hearing another one of your poems. Last time I was here. . . ." Mae had opened the door halfway. She didn't want to appear too interested in what I was saying after her tirade; moreover, she was not well equipped to handle gratification. She hesitated there. I said swiftly: "I told Sister Benedita about your poetry writing. I wanted to get your permission to show her some of it."

It was just pure bad luck that made Sister Benedita pass that partly opened door at that moment. She said: "Someone taking my name in vain . . . ? Good morning, Mae."

"What's good about it?" she demanded thickly.

"Ah, you have a cold, too."

"What'dya expect in this disease-breedin' grounds . . . ?" And

Mae flounced off heavily, sullenly, her face scowling. Sister Benedita stared after her and slowly turned around and asked, "Did I
interrupt something? I didn't mean to, Frank Michael. . . ."

"No, we were finished."

"I thought for a minute there that I should have had the first
aid kit with me."

I laughed. "Everything she does is energetic. She has a cold dramatically, she has a temper dramatically, she has an infatuation
dramatically. . . . Everything is dramatic, so that she can hide her
feeling of not really understanding her own impulses. . . ."

"We decided to keep her for another three months. I think that
we'll have to give bonuses to the staff . . . you know, combat pay
for working with Mae."

5

"I was mad at you. . . . I get very mad sometimes. I just let fly.
. . . Besides, I had a cold. That don't improve your temper any.
. . . And then that mini-skirted Mary bargin' in like that. . . . I
can't stand the way they mouse around, as if they weren't broads
themselves. They're just a bunch of broads who couldn't make it
out on the street so they copped out here. That's all they are, a
bunch of messed-up broads. Insteada usin' junk, they used runnin'
away from the world. . . . Not me, Professor. What I am you see,"
and she took a deep breath, which made her ample bosom appear
to swell. "That's all me. . . ."

"You didn't use your fists. You didn't even threaten me."

"Why should I?"

"You said that you were mad. That was your judgment, not
mine. . . . So, is your anger now a hollow threat?"

She snorted and glared at me. "I wouldn't push that too far,
Professor. . . . Nowadays, instead of gettin' hostile with everybody,

I find myself too valuable to risk my feeling of anger. And that's wrong, too; it's wrong. I should risk it; if I want someone to know I'm angry, I should risk it. But then I get coy on it, I get defensive, and I don't want anybody to know how angry they make me. . . ."

"Can you recall what it was that I said to you that riled you so?" I watched the frown spread on her face. "We just heard it on the playback. . . . Why should that get you so furious?"

"Because what you said is true, and I know it, and I don't know how to handle it even though I try to tell myself every time that I'm fucking over my own feelin's. . . . That's why. . . ."

"But maybe you've also become so self-conscious now about your ways of dealing with stress that you have an additional reason for your being so short tempered. . . . Is that possible . . . ? Maybe you're on your way to control. . . ."

"I wouldn't bet on it." She shrugged her shoulders quickly, kicked at the microphone cable with her foot. "You got a cigarette, Professor?" She puffed on it deeply. "Lotta control I got. . . . Remember the girl I talked about in the last tape, the one I found who was sympathetic to me . . . ? I tried to smash in her stupid face, but they grabbed me so I couldn't get at her. . . ."

"Would you have hit her, or did you arrange things in such a way that there were people around to interfere and stop you?"

"Jesus, Professor, but you got a devious mind. . . . Of course not. . . ."

"This was in a group therapy session?"

"Yeah. They just held me off of her. . . . Sly broad, playin' on my feelin's in public, in front of all them. . . ."

"Isn't that the whole purpose of group therapy?"

"Not that," and she drew on the cigarette angrily. "She was playin' on my feelin's as an individual. She was openin' me up in front of all of them. Now, I ain't hid the fact that I'm gay. I told you right offa the bat that I was gay. Lotta these stupid broads are gay here. . . . That's the way it is in a joint. . . . That's the way it is when you come offa stuff anyway. . . . You get the yen again, but you been so messed over by dudes, you don't want a dude even if you coulda had one. So there they sit, those fat-assed broads,

holdin' their hands over their mouths like I got leprosy or somethin' when this other chick is throwin' in my face my own feelin's.
So I exploded and tried to get my hands on the zonk. I woulda fixed
her lyin' face for her. . . . See, Professor, if anybody'da looked, if
anybody'da cared they coulda seen my hurt. But they was too busy
being outrageous toward me. . . . You know, what the hell, there's
Mae, we can shift it all over on to her because sure as hell she's
gonna raise such a row that she'll break it all up. . . ." And all the
bluster went out of Mae; she seemed to shrink in the chair. "Now
I don't feel anything for that broad. She ain't valuable, she ain't
significant enough to hurt me. She can only get me angry, that's
the only feeling that I'm willing to risk with that broad any more.
She can't tamper with any other of my feelin's. . . . And I won't
lay a hand on her no more, no matter what. . . . I won't raise a
hand. She's not worth taking a crack out of. . . ." She sighed wea-
rily. "But I'm gonna be spared that, Professor, I'm afraid."

"What do you mean?"

"They're gonna ship me, I heard, you know, the grapevine. . . .
They're gonna ship me back to the court. But, to be entirely frank,
I'm not carryin' a bag of dry tears over it. Why should I? This
place is just one big cop-out. Just a big cop-out, and that Sister
Benedita with her mushroom face is the biggest gamer of all. . . .
It'll be good to get back to a joint, a real joint where they ain't got
this piss-poor attitude . . . you know, this holy, holy attitude that
ain't nothin' more than a cover for itchy-itchy. . . . Yeah, so in a
way I'm relieved. Livin' in this kinda atmosphere is very repressin'.
Makes you false. I'll be glad to be free to be myself again in a
joint. There you know exactly what is what. . . . No God-damned
mini-skirted Marys mousin' around, with their big eyes eatin' out
your heart to get some taste of the life you've lived for their sex-
starved gut."

"Are you sure you're going, Mae?"

"Well, you ever been in a hospital ward? Ever see how the word
gets around that somebody is dyin'? See the way the other patients
act? Oh yeah, the word is out. I can tell by the gentle way they've
got with me now . . . the word is out. . . . And I'm glad, too,
Professor, 'cause this ain't my place. Too false." She screwed up her

face. "I'm gonna miss this, though, Professor." She rubbed her hands together, and sighed. "What the hell. . . . There's somethin' to be said for goin' where you belong . . . ain't there, Professor?"

"And you belong in the joint, is that it?"

"Well, as far as that goes, I belong there more than here, don't you know. . . . I can be natural, not always have my feelin's raked over. . . . You know, Professor, one time when I was a little girl I was livin' with my grandmother—I don't know whether she was my for-real grandmother or not—anyway, she was an old woman and she had a coal stove which was all the heat which we had in this house we lived in, and I can remember her in the mornin's when I would get up real early, sittin' there going through the bucket of ashes looking for the pieces of coal that didn't burn up. . . . That's what this place has been for me. Now, who the hell needs to sit siftin' through her bucket of burned-out coals lookin' for somethin' worthwhile to be used again . . . ?" She snorted. "Especially when life has so many clinkers in the coal anyway?"

"You really haven't given them too much of a chance here, though, have you, Mae?"

"I gave them as much chance as they gave me."

"In what way?"

"I offered them my concern, my feelin's. . . . They fucked me over. . . . I didn't fuck them over. . . ."

"No, you just told them to go and screw themselves if they didn't take you on your terms."

There was something acrid, something bitter in the half-smile. "You could put it that way. . . ." She paused, reached for my pack of cigarettes, lighted one and shook out the match . . . and then, as if she had reached a decision, said: "I'll be glad to be out of the place."

"Before, I said that you didn't give them too much of a chance; I think that was inaccurate. What I should have said was that you couldn't give them much of a chance because you've never given yourself too much of a chance. . . . That is, until here lately."

She shook her head. "I'm just beginning to be aware that I can hurt a person just as much with my mouth, knowing what to say, and knowing what I say is true, as I can hurt him with my fists, with my punches."

"So you have at least discovered another way of handling situations. Who knows, in time you might have discovered any number of options. . . ."

"Yeah, Professor . . . I gotta agree. . . . Or it could be the other way, coming out of my scheming bag and be sneaky, you know, wait and then shaft them, not say anythin' beforehand to warn them. . . ."

"That's really not part of your style, though, Mae. Or at least it doesn't appear that way so far. Your impulse has always been to unload . . . jump into relationships full blown. You saturate with your affection, or you punch somebody in the nose. . . . So I think—and you can hear it yourself on the tape—I think Mae has somehow deepened. . . ."

"Oh, I don't know, Professor. . . . Life's too much fer me. Like, you know, going back to the joint. I should feel a lift, right now. Because I know there's got to be stuff running in there . . . I know that . . . and I know that I can get some. Now, bein' clean all these months, I know that first shot is gonna hit me like a hot flash of paradise. . . . But I'm scared, Professor. I'm scared of it. . . . Before, I needed it, I needed it to block out. I didn't want to face nothin', man. I was out on the streets. I didn't have any more reason to be out there than to get back at myself, to degrade me . . . to put it to me. . . ."

"But why?"

"Why not? Down at the bottom everythin' is dark.

"So you only felt comfortable at the very bottom of the barrel?"

"Sure. You sit around mumblin', pickin' at yourself. Everybody closed up in his own sack. You nod your head. 'Hey, man, like that's groovy. . . . You are significant. . . . You are so intellectually right!' Here you are, with all of them scabbed up, their pimples and sores running. . . . You sit among the elect."

"Did you ever say this to the group?"

"Yeah, once not long ago."

"And how did they respond?"

"They dug and dug at me. We hassled it around and around.

You know, I rounded on account of accordin' to them I was givin' an intellectual reason and not the real reason. And when we got down to the gut level, I told them what I told you long ago: I was enticed by a young man, and if I wanted to stay with him I had to pay. . . . And he ran that story to me that everything was going to be beautiful for us if I hustled for him, and so he psyched me. . . . What else did I have at that time to give but my body? So I was givin' him all I had for us. The only way I could have him was to use my body for him. Like, I had to turn tricks with every guy to get the money to support him and me . . . and provide money for him to buy his stuff. . . . See, Professor, I was usin' my body to develop love and concern, and I ended up in an empty sack. I didn't get either. . . . I'm not a dog. I'm not the lowest scum on earth. Everybody's done what I did, and more. . . . Every one of these broads here, and these mini-skirted Marys, if they ain't done what I've done, they've done it in their minds. . . . Only I came up with an empty sack. . . . I should feel valuable about myself. . . . I got some value, Professor. . . ." She took another cigarette. "Like, a coupla weeks ago we had job orientation. . . . So they asks me what I want to do. . . . Now, I know what they got to hear in order to keep their puny minds happy, so that they can mousie-mousie along the hall and say how Mae has seen the light. So I tell them I want to be a telephone operator. . . . Keeps them happy, makes me like the rest of the broads. Nothin' to make them bulge out their eyes so they can send me some more notes. . . . 'Listen to big ass, big teats, with her broad back. She wants to go to college, she wants to write poetry. . . . We know what she kin do. Only one thing . . . that broad back is just for holdin' up a man. . . .' So I'm gonna tell them about me and what I want for a job . . . ? Fat chance, Professor. . . . But I don't want your menial job. . . . You know, I'm writing constantly . . . that's my thing with me . . . like this:

> There she is, that frail with her masks.
> One for Sunday, and one for all the rest of the ashlike days of her week.
> Each mask stacked inside the other, each ready to cover that blank face.

A mask for that mother I never had, a mask for the men who
pawed me.
A mask for the whole emptiness the white lady filled with her
needle and high.
A mask for those women who used me like the men,
A mask for a mask for a mask.
Oh, what shall I do when the masks, all of them stacked one with
the other, drop away?
What mask will there then be, what real mask, frozen on my
features?
What naked stranger stands there now? Who are you, unmasked?
A mask for a mask for a mask.
Ah, my closet is full, each shelf spread with my mummer's array.
Wait, don't flee. I have a mask for any occasion.
Don't flee—tell me what you would have of me, I'm sure I can
find one to suit.
What would you have? My whore's mask of joy? My lesbian mask
for companionship? My junkie mask for peace?
Stay, don't flee—ask me, put it to me. What is it you would have?
I'll rummage my shelves, a mask I'll find . . . a mask I'll find for
thee.
Just wait, just wait. I'll find one you'll buy.
A mask for a mask for a mask. One for each of the ashlike days of
my life."

Mae looked at her hands. "You know, Professor, I'm glad I'm
going. . . . I couldn't tell these broads things like that. I couldn't
tell them that in order to please some of these men, what parts of
my body I had to use. . . . And to fix in order to do a torture
thing with myself, to get back to livin' with myself so that I
wouldn't scream out with my own shame. . . . Sure, I ended up
with a high contempt with men. . . . And a high contempt with
women, too. . . . But, Professor, I couldn't tell them. . . ."

"Would you consider showing your poems to Sister Benedita,
Mae?"

"Mushroom face. . . . She looks like she died two weeks ago.
Nah, I don't want those Marys for nothin', nothin'."

"I think you're selling her short."

"How refreshin' for a change to have me sellin' somebody else
short."

"Yeah, but you'll end up with the ashes, Mae."

"Your tape's done, Professor. . . . I gotta go. . . . So, like, if I don't see you again. . . ." She was at the door.

"Mae, would you let me play this tape for Sister Benedita? Would you give me permission to do that?"

"Sure. Play it for anybody you want, daddy. . . . You know me —out of sight, out of mind. I'll be long gone." There was an expression of desolation on her face, despite her bravado. "Good-bye, Professor. . . ."

I followed her to the door, but she was already starting down the corridor. Sister Benedita was coming from her office. . . . I saw her say something to Mae. I heard Mae, in that raucous, coarse, defense-mechanism manner of hers, say: "You ain't shippin' me? Jesus Christ, I'm doomed to die in this looney crib. I thought for sure that I'd be back in the freedom of a joint." But Mae's voice sounded triumphant.

I played the tape for Sister Benedita. After it was finished, there was a long silence. I looked at her. Tears were streaming down her face, and she said, "May God forgive my inability to see. . . ."

6

Whatever it was that I expected to find in Mae, it didn't turn out that way—but then it never does. She was listless, depressed, despondent, her face slack, her eyes lowered, that angry frown on her face. The butch image had returned. She had given the playback of the previous session a kind of derisive attention: snorting and yawning, or muttering, "Dig that broad." But the simple fact that she hadn't insisted that it be turned off encouraged me.

"Do you know what today is, Mae?"

"Humph," she snorted.

"This marks the sixth month that we've talked together."

"Oh, dear God, another nail in my coffin. . . . Six months." She hummed something under her breath. "What should I do, write a song about it . . . ? The golden six months of my life . . . I'm in the garbage of my years. . . . Tah-tah-de-tah. . . ."

"Well, however you put it, I think six months of anything is a big investment of an individual's life. . . . You know, whether you accept it or not, it's accountable. From where I sit I'd think that you'd be very gratified with what you've accomplished in these months. . . . A tremendous leap forward."

"You know Professor, I been readin' somethin'. . . . You know, one of those marvelous new books that our library gets from generous citizens, one of them that they had layin' in their cellar or attic, one they been just dyin' to get rid of. . . . It's called *Little Women* and it was put out five thousand years ago. . . . And the people in it talk just the same God-damned pea soup way that you do, see!" she snapped.

I grinned. "It's not the same, Mae. . . . It doesn't have that old grinding bite to it. . . . You don't even insult the way you used to. . . . You don't have the conviction. . . . You used to just lash out and the hell with the consequences. . . . I'm afraid that you've changed. . . . Yes, the six months have meant something."

She lifted her head, moved her lips, and then reached for my cigarettes. "Am I really different, Professor . . . ? I'm so God-damned hung up I can't tell anymore. . . . I'm so moody. I'll tell you somethin', Professor. I catch myself cryin'. Yes, God-dammit, cryin' for no reason at all. . . ."

"You're getting close to Mae."

She raised her voice: "That ain't it. Because I know myself. . . . I've been broken down as so I've become one of these loonies here . . . mini-skirted Marys and mousie-mousie social workers. That's what's happened to me—they got their teeth in me."

"You've changed, Mae. . . . I can play the tapes back from the very first one and prove it to you. . . ."

"You can play Napoleon if you want, but it don't prove not one God-damned thing to me. I ain't changed. I'm just makin' different moves. . . . I laugh and scheme and use my mouth. I know their tricks here. I'm just playin' their game."

"That's different, you must agree. . . ."

"Survival, daddy. That's all it is . . . survival. . . . I know every one of their little moves. So I'm stealin' a leaf outa their book."

"I insist that it's different, though. You're taking time to research their so-called moves. You're laying back. . . . You've changed. . . ."

"Like hell. Before, I was defeated . . . defeated and angry about bein' defeated. I got caught and what could I do? I had time to put in and I didn't know how much time, not like in the joint where you know how much sentence you got. And I used to say to myself, 'Oh, God, what am I gonna do . . . ? Why did I have to get caught?' So what could I do?" She sighed. "I don't know. . . . See, when I came in here this morning, Professor, I was not in a correct frame of mind. The Mushroom, she decided that I should see the psychiatrist. . . ."

"Sister Benedita arranged that?"

"Oh, yeah. . . . They didn't ship me like they was plannin'. . . . I don't know why. . . . I'm a good example for the rest of the girls, you know. Like I'm Miss Positive-Negative Personality for them, like their bug in a bottle. So, anyways, they got me seeing this shrinker for two times."

"Private therapy?"

"For him or for me?"

I laughed, "For both of you!"

"He told me I'm morbid. I told him he was sufferin' from the mini-skirt syndrome."

"Did he laugh?"

"No, he just wrote a little slower in his book. . . . But that only lasted twice. I guess he gave up on me. . . ." She looked at me archly. "I shoulda slipped my bra down maybe . . . that woulda speeded up his pencil. . . ."

"Aren't you morbid?"

"Sure, I'm morbid. . . . But who the hell has to be a Cincinnati lawyer to find that out about me? For Christ sakes. . . . I'm morbid. I been so low this last week, I been havin' all those old thoughts again. . . . Boy, if I coulda put my hand on a bag this week . . . oh, brother, would I have scored! Who needs a stupid ass like that to tell you what you already know . . . ?"

"What do you know, Mae? About yourself, I mean . . . ?"

"I'm uptight, man . . . I'm uptight. That's the only thing. And I can't explain it to me why. . . . Look, Professor, I ran this thing where I can blame the way I feel so bad on that woman, my mother. Lay everything to that damn woman. Like, there never was any love or concern there. Okay, I shift it on her. She had a man and he was gettin' what I felt I shoulda been getting, so I take him away from her. I didn't want her to have him if I couldn't have what she had to give. . . ." She looked at me with disgust on her face. "So I ran that and I ran right out of it. So I can't put my morbidness on that. It's not a valid enough reason. So then, as far as my hustlin' goes . . . sure I was psyched by this guy into prossing. . . . I was . . . I mean . . . I was suckered by this guy because I had a real yen for him. . . . But I see it was a game I was runnin'. . . ." She cocked her head and said defiantly: "Now, when I get out of here, if I want to peddle my tail I'll go out and do it for myself, and I won't feel a damn thing about its being degrading on account of I'll be doing it for myself and I'll be getting paid for it."

"So what you're saying is that you'll pocket the rewards yourself."

"You're damned right, Jack. Little old Mae, she never got anything for herself, she was always givin' the rewards to everybody else. But see, I went to women on accounta no man was worth it. . . . That was true—they were dirty, twistin', selfish bastards, using me like some dog. . . . But the women used me, too. . . . So that ain't a valid reason neither."

"Not a valid reason for shooting heroin?"

She was exasperated with me: "Well, what the hell else do you think I'm talkin' about? Perfume . . . ? Jesus, Professor, you ain't gettin' any brighter."

"But you see, I'm confused, Mae. . . . I thought you felt that you didn't go to heroin for any reason. It was just something you did."

"Ah, come on. Who in his right mind goes to junk? There's gotta be a reason. . . . See, I can't explain to myself why I got these dark thoughts, Professor. . . ."

"Isn't it curious the way you project yourself . . . ? How you'll get your rewards? As a whore—you'll go out and peddle and keep the profits. . . . That's where you project your image. . . ."

"Just a minute, just a minute. I said: *If I want. If I want.* Don't you forget that. . . ." She reached for another cigarette.

"Still, crack out of the barrel that's your first reference to yourself . . . a whore . . . I wonder why. This is you talking . . . not your mother, or stepfather, or the pimp, or the girl, or Sister Benedita. . . . You."

"Because, like I told you. The higher thoughts that I had for myself . . . well . . . forget it. I can be an operator . . . any kind. . . . I can grab men off like they was born to be bushed. It's no big thing. I can make it on my own. I don't need anybody or anything."

"You are consistent, I must say, Mae. Before anybody can point a finger at you, you jump the gun and tell them that you're the lowest of the low. . . . You're like a castle moated around, with the drawbridge up. . . . What are you defending?"

She breathed heavily. "I'm all screwed up. This place has gotten to me, Professor. . . . I'm really ripe for the looney crib. . . . I was a very healthy specimen, before I came in here with these God-damned mini-skirts. If that judge hadda sent me to the joint, I'd be out by now and flourishin'."

"Have you shared this feeling of being at sea with your therapy group?"

She snorted. "I just sit back and watch. . . . I don't participate unless I damn well feel like it."

"That's par for the course with you. You're either gullible or suspicious . . . that's your analysis."

"Those people have no concern for me. Why should I have any for them?"

"You weren't shipped. . . . That shows something like concern. . . ."

"My royal American ass it does. . . . They just keep me fer whippin'. . . ."

I played with the cigarette package. "No, Mae. You're foxing now. . . . What's bothering you is that no matter what you get involved in, it turns sour. That's what's chewing at you. You know, you said so before, that you can't lay off the responsibilities on anybody else. . . . So you're squirming because it puts you right on the point. . . . You're on the horn . . . you." And I said it softly, slowly, earnestly.

"It's always that way; I'm the bad guy, Professor. I do so much that's wrong. . . . They look at me, always expecting the wrong move from me. So why the hell do I need a bunch of slobbering junkies sitting around in their circle passing judgment on me? I been picked over by better."

"Poor, poor Mae. . . . Is that it?"

"You said it, not me."

"All right, then why are you so angry?"

"It could be, baby, that you'll make the rest of your tapes and I'll be just as God-damned angry on them . . . poor, poor Mae'll be just as angry."

"Tiptoe around me, world, on account of I'm dangerous. . . . Walk softly around me, world. . . . I bite." I raised my voice, my tone sharpened. "Before, you threw yourself at people and were hurt when they repulsed you; now you anger people so that they'll repulse you, and that makes you even more angry. . . . Attention grabber, you said. What are you afraid they'll discover about you . . . ? What're you afraid you'll discover about yourself . . . ?"

"Just let them make one wrong move. I'll be on them so fast. I'll fix 'em. I'll show 'em what it means to hurt."

"Yes, I'm sure you will." I talked down into my jacket, in a monotone. "Restrained, busted out of the program, put in prison. Mae, the born loser; Mae, the social outcast. . . . I know why you used heroin . . . and so do you. You're a lame. You're so totally dependent that you force people into proving it to yourself. . . . You just want to hang. You have no resources, you have no pride . . . you are just what you think so desperately about yourself. You're angry because people don't tell you that you are different from what you feel you are. . . . You make no attempt to change their opinion. . . . You just seek their confirmation of your own degraded self-evaluation."

All of a sudden she rose from her chair, jerked the microphone from her neck, her index finger pointing at me, her eyes blazing, her lips working.

Quietly I said, "It's no good, Mae, it's no good. . . . Maybe the first interview you could have assaulted me. . . . But I tell you, you've changed. . . . You can't do it, girl."

It must have been my gentle tone that made her collapse in her chair and sob. "I'm so screwed up, Professor. . . . See, I come together in one part and then in the other part I slack off. I can't do it all so it's in a whole. You know, I'm all in pieces. Must be this stupid place, like maybe I'm goin' through change of life. . . . I read about that." She raised her tear-blotched face.

"At your age? More like change of heart, Mae. . . ."

She blew her nose. "It's hopeless."

"So, when everything is opened up, yours is the junkie lament. Hopeless. No solutions, no effort, no motivation, no self. . . . Hopeless. A victim. . . ."

She said, tiredly: "You can't make me mad, Professor."

"That's because you're changed, Mae. . . . You've changed greatly. The old ways are not yours anymore. . . . But the scab will fall off. . . ."

"I'm going back upstairs, Professor. I ain't myself these days. . . . I'm not fit to be talking. . . . So long, Professor. . . ." At the door, she turned. "Oh, here's some poems I brought you." She dropped them onto the chair and left. I watched her walk down the hall, not shuffling, not walking erectly, somehow in-between. . . .

I opened the first poem, written with a curious blend of the Palmer method of penmanship and a childish scrawl. It was titled "Weathered."

> O rain, you dark dyer, staining the wind, blackening the gloom,
> Penetrating with your chill to my chambered heart.
> Locked in there I dwell, in the racing storm of me.
> Each gust, each flurry, each torrent pelts me with my past.
> In that tempest of remembrance I glimpse the child, that child of
>   inconvenience.
> In a cosmos of accident, of loss, of easy obliteration, where
>   brutality reigns,

Why did that child survive to raise echoes on lonely pavements,
    drum on empty streets?
Of those things known and sensed in that Spring of living,
I know but this: hate, pain, loss, strife, revenge, flight.
Oh, ravished child, Oh, despoiled Spring, so has my virginity been
    snatched,
Raped from me before I knew it's oneness with me.
O rain, you dark dyer, staining the wind, blackening the gloom.
Is there no April of love with soft shower, to glow 'round me with
    warmth?
Is there no Spring bloom to taunt my nose, fill my empty heart?
Who am I in this pretence of seasons, that I can be so trampled?
Is there no one who will accept my small bouquet of myself?
O Lord, why must each of my little offerings be ravished?
Why must I forever stand stormy-faced, trembling inside, locked
    in that chambered heart?
O Lord, am I not one destined to be fate's hostage?
To be used and despoiled and cast aside?
Isn't this it, Lord? Is that not my meaning? My future, the
    substance of my life?
Oh, great cruelty, oh, grinding ruthlessness, no little remorse left
    for this rabbit.
Lord, Lord, is there not for me even the mercy of forgetfulness?
    Not even the sparrow is brought so low.
O rain, you dark dyer, staining the wind, blackening the gloom.

7

It was her poem; I had recorded it by myself and attached it to our
last interview. I watched her as she listened to her own words
being read by another voice. She was unguarded, caught up in the
intoxication of hearing what she had created. In that instant I
caught on her face sensitivity, refinement, bewilderment,
spirituality—all the handiwork of defensiveness momentarily
fallen away. Truly—I realized with a pang the insight of her

own verse—she was made to be ravaged. When it came to an end and while I put on a fresh tape, she asked mildly, "You liked it?"

"I think it's wonderful. I only wish I knew how to talk to you on that level. . . . Isn't that, in your poetic world, where you really live? Even that I'm not saying right, Mae. I mean, you show so much of yourself through your poetry, I wonder if I haven't just botched up all these interviews because I didn't realize that."

She lighted a cigarette. "I let you read them. . . . That took time, you know. I had to trust you first. . . ."

"Mae, when you were on stuff . . . what about your poetry then . . . ? Do you understand what I'm asking you? Did you think poetry?"

"See, Professor, the addict lives fiction. He is fiction. He's like a perpetual dreamer, always shapin' his life to somethin' that ain't. . . . He's a fiction. Like, you sit around mumblin' with the rest. You hold a real rapping session, and the other hype'll nod his head and maybe mutter 'Yeah, man . . . like, too much. . . . Say it,' but he don't hear and know what you're sayin'. Chances are he's listenin' to another fiction spinnin' inside himself. . . ." She puffed on her cigarette and said slowly, "Sure, I used to say my poetry. It just kinda filled up inside. But I never put it down. . . . See, stuff makes you think that you wrote it down. It makes you think that it's all complete, all the job done, and you're entitled to the rewards. You and stuff set up for yourself what it is you want to feel—even though you know in your heart (and that secret place is always alive) that it's a fiction, a lie. Because you always know that somehow what you really want can't come so easy as stuff makes it seem."

"Did you ever once put down on paper what you thought about when you were high?"

"Every lame has. . . . It's lousy. It's lousy. It drives you back to junk on account of the contrast. It's broken-footed, crippled."

She was grave today, her face lean and pale. She flicked off some ash: "It's only since I been here, like, I listen to those footsteps and try and put it down on paper, Professor."

"You know, in that poem you wrote about masks . . . I get the feeling that the mask is necessary for you, not for protection against the world but protection against yourself."

She said thoughtfully, "Yeah. . . . It could be. . . . Because heroin is a mask. . . ."

"So then, at the heart of it, you either know so much about yourself that you dread, or you're so confused and fearful, or so damaged. . . ."

"Oh, I don't know, Professor. . . . Once you start to think, it's like a dog race, always after that rabbit that can't be caught up with while you chase after it. Then, when the race is over and the rabbit stops and you go over and sniff at it . . . you see what it is, a dummy. You been chasin' a dummy. Like, you know, addicts are everything you can say about them: lazy, stupid, damaged, bright, scheming, selfish, distrusting, scary. Like, take all the pieces of everything that's good and bad in everybody and mix 'em up, and what comes out is the addict. No rhyme or reason in the mixture. . . . We're just like everybody else except the mixture is so unstrained . . . and we know that. That's why we project an image."

"So then you're saying that what's needed is a place where the race can stop, a place where you can go over and sniff the rabbit and find it's really a dummy, a place where you can put off the masks."

"In a way . . . but, see, no addict wants to lay up, lose his freedom, wants to see himself. . . . Sure, he's always gonna put himself together, but like, 'Later, later, man . . . tomorra . . . or Sunday . . . or some day. . . .' " She put out the cigarette. "Right now, today, this minute. . . . I'm talking to you. . . . I don't know why I'm quiet inside. . . . Maybe because I heard you read that poem. It was outside of me. I can look at it. It tells me things that I thought about me. It's outside of me. . . ."

"Let me interrupt you. . . . What things does it tell you about you?"

"Oh, you know, stupid things. . . . Like, if somebody had only taken a second . . . you know, to see me . . . to stop me. . . . Now, I didn't make it easy. . . . I did wrong things. Even if I did right things, I tare-assed around so you wouldn't get to me, even though I was dyin' to hear the nice things you were going to say. . . . Like, I'm so destructive, and yet I don't want to be. I want you to take me and stop me, but I'll kick and bite and yell and swear so that you can't. . . . See, Mae is very confused and ashamed. My impressions are always so changeable. Like, lately I've had thoughts I never really had before. See, I been reading a lot. I been tryin' to understand my own psychology. Why am I so destructive, why do I want to hurt myself so? Sure, I know now that when they put me in that mental hospital when I was a kid there was nothin' wrong with me, but there was no other place to put me. See, it's taken me all this time to get over my fright that there was somethin' the matter with me. You ever lay in a bed, holding on to the bed bars, with your hands sweatin' for fear you were gonna do some horrible thing though you didn't know what it was, just that you had to tie yourself down so you didn't do it? That was me. To let go your hands was to spin off, away out of the world. . . . See now, there really ain't nothing wrong with me upstairs, Professor, and I'm listening to what I say to you while I say it, and I'm wondering if I'm really so God-damned sure, but I feel that there's nothin' wrong with me. I watch myself, every addict does. When I'm mad, and they call me the mad dog now and not the split-tailed whore . . . but I thank them for it . . . I do, Professor, on accounta I know when I want to hurt them I don't want to hurt myself. . . . But I been tryin' to intellectualize and rationalize my anger, to hold it back. I want to figger out what makes Mae tick. Three things I've gotten out of it: my motivation, my desires, my frustrations, and the conflict between them all. If I'm repressed in doing somethin' like knocking hell outa someone who's hurt me, and I don't even verbally let loose and show my anger, then I build it up within me and dwell on it, and I tear it apart and analyse it. . . . And I'm sore inside, I ache because of this anger that lays inside like a blind boil. . . . This is where my poetry enters, Professor. This is my therapy . . . my sickness comes out like a fever in my poetry."

"Do you characterize your poetry as 'sick,' Mae . . . ? Or is that an 'in' word that tickles your fancy?"

"All I know is that it gets out my feelin's that hurt me inside.

. . . There shouldn't be all that hate in me. . . . Professor, what kind of a world would this be, if there was as much hate out there as there is inside of me?"

"Be a lot better world if the hatred could be resolved into poetry."

She ignored what I said and continued. "My hatred runs so deep, I wash up things that happened to me way, way back in my life. . . . Look, Professor, when other girls were playin' with dolls, I was playin' with men. . . . I was playin' with men. . . . What do I know about the other world of dolls and little cups and saucers and little Band-Aids on a cut? What do I know . . . ? That's all a tinsel world for me. . . . Maybe it ain't even real. . . . Maybe nobody ever had it, but I don't know, so I build up this pity thing for myself. . . . I don't know what I'm supposed to feel. I don't know what's real—only that I hurt and I'm bitter about the things I never had. See, I'm jammed between what I've done that I know is wrong and the things I never had though I don't know if they ever existed. See how I'm jammed . . . ? So then I build up inside. I'm furious. I could claw you to pieces. . . . And then I'd take a shot, and it would slip away, and I'd float off and think my thoughts. . . . See, the acid I know, it cuts and eats away, but what else there is I don't know. . . . How do I get to this, to explain to anybody, Professor? Those other broads have their own hangups. They're like me, they don't want to hear somebody else's drum being beat. I'm tryin' to teach myself from the very beginning . . . like a language. . . . I'm tryin' to teach myself what it is to live, though I don't know what that means other than not to kill yourself with heroin or a gun or pills. . . . I'm tryin' to teach myself how you live, Professor." She had moved forward in her chair. Her eyes wide, her hands resting on her thighs, she said, almost reciting, "I watch time slip by me, and I have a sense that I'm going with it. Hope is a thin thing. I've jammed myself. But I'm scared to be in that corner. I want to break out of that cellblock. But you see, I have the fatal charm of driving off people because I'm so leary of being abused, of being rejected. See, I fight all of this battle inside of myself, every day. . . . I repulse everybody who even comes a little close to me. . . . I'll hurt you though you try to be friend to me, because what is a friend is unknown to me. But I want you to see through me. I must be that starved person in hell, with the food before me—great heaping trays of gorgeous food, turkeys and steaks and cakes and ice cream—and me with no mouth though my hunger consumes me. Do you see, Professor? Do I scare you?"

"You don't scare me, Mae. I wonder . . . if I spoke to Sister Benedita . . . I wonder if you'd read your poetry to her some time."

"Old Mushroom Face? She passes me like dirt in the hall. She'll kick me under the rug und look at me as if I shouldn't somehow be there."

"I think you're mistaken, Mae. . . . But you said you're learning life as if it were a language, right from the beginning. Take a chance on it. Let me speak to her."

She sat back, her brow furrowed. She reached nervously for the cigarettes and she yawned. It was the first sign of her own inadequacy that I had seen in some time. She said sloppily, "Ah, that stupid broad with her mini-skirted, mousie-mousie ways."

"Remember what you said: 'Not even a sparrow is brought so low.' You're not a sparrow. . . . You're not. . . ."

Suddenly she was defiant. "Why should I put myself out . . . ? I'm always havin' to pay out myself to be with people. Why do I always have to pay my way and only find that I'm stuck with a bunch of plastics. They don't accept me. . . . The mad dog. . . . They ain't offerin' me friendship. . . . I'm tired, Professor, I'm tired of it. They ain't got no concern. . . . I usta give without askin' fer anythin' just to be . . . like . . . just to be . . . like. . . ."

I offered: "To be accepted?"

"Like, to be accepted. No big deal; like, they should say to me: 'Here, Mae, take it. Use it. I hope it'll satisfy you. . . .' Not what I've learned to get: 'You whore. You stupid bitch. You dirty everythin' you touch. You won't get nothin' from me. Beat it, split-tail.' Professor, I don't want to go through that. . . . I don't ask 'em for nothing. I don't borrow nothin' from anybody."

"So what are you left with then, Mae?"

"Jammed . . . jammed. . . ."

"Right. You're jammed. You give yourself no options, no room to turn around in. You know, so many addicts do things like that. . . . You know: 'I'm going to get me a job, I'm going to get me a family, I'm going to make it in the square world. I'm going to . . . I'm going to. . . .' But when . . . ? You said it before: 'Like later, man, like later.' So here you are, come around full circle again, Mae. But now you can see it. You're jamming yourself. . . . Suppose you give me your sheaf of poems and let me give them to her. . . . How about that? What have you got to lose? Give them to me. . . . I'll show them to her. You won't have to see her. . . . Are you going to leave here just to go back out there jammed, so that you only have one way of handling your stresses . . . just that one way that has insulated you? Is that it, Mae . . . ? Is it just heroin that solves your conflicts . . . ? What will you do?"

She got up from her chair, removed the microphone, and left the room. Her sudden action baffled me. I turned off the machine, removed the reel, carefully marked it, and put it away. Perhaps five minutes passed as I broke down the equipment; Mae returned, breathing heavily, as if she had been running. She thrust a handful of sheets at me. She said harshly: "Let the bitch read the top one first. I only wrote it last night. . . . But remember, Professor, no mousie-mousie business about it. . . ." And with a grim nod of her head, she slammed the door as she left. "Read the top one first. . . ." Her little display of vanity brightened my day. I decided to read it first.

> My head against the pane, myself blended into the night. . . .
> "O night, my kinsman, I call to thee.
> It is I, your daughter, she who shares
> Your dark voyage, she who is diminished
> Like you by the waning hours, the nearing day.
> O night, my mother, in your sable embrace
> Whisper softly, cradle me warmly.
> O Black Mother, magician of gloom,
> Conjure, oh, conjure a spell for me!
> In the darkness who will know
> That I am your artful manufacture,
> Fresh, young, the dewy virgin,
> My mouth, my body, my soul wind-pure.
> Me wanted, me giving, me living. . . .

Who will know, kinsman, of your spell?
O night, my kinsman, I call to thee,
Ours is a short span, conjure for me."

Sister Benedita was not in her office, and my schedule would not allow me to wait. I put Mae's poetry in an envelope along with a note.

8

She appeared pedantic, with her index finger jabbing home her emphasis: "It's only what you do to me. It's what you churn up in me. If you hurt me physically, that could make me come out of my animal bag. But if you verbally come at me, abuse me, I can disdain you because in reality you are sick . . . sick, sick, sick, like sick, man."

I closed my eyes and listened to her. It was Mae's voice, that registration with its enormous emotional range, but I had to close my eyes to recall what she looked like so many months before. For as she sat there now she was demure, dogmatic, didactic; her dark dress with its high neckline made her seem thin, her hair tightly clasped in a severe style. . . . this was Mae now.

"Is it age that you're courting with those glasses, Mae?"

Slowly, with a tribute to an old Edward G. Robinson movie, she removed her wire-framed glasses.

"They rest my eyes. . . ."

"Rest your eyes? From all your reading . . . ? were they prescribed for you, is that it?"

"No. . . . My boyfriend, he brought them for me. . . ."

Since incredulity was not permitted to me, I asked perhaps more stolidly than usual: "Your boyfriend?"

"Yeah, you know, the guy who's the father of my daughter. . . ."

"Oh, yes, he was a schoolmate, you said. . . . Had you been corresponding with him?"

She smiled, but not like the Mae of the unexpected response; it was so studied. "This all happened very swiftly. He happened to run into my mother, and she told him where I was. This was about a month ago, and he came to visit me, and now we have an understanding. . . ."

I interrupted her: "I've forgotten—he wasn't a drug user, you said. . . ."

"Oh, no, not him. He was a very serious, virtuous fella."

"This understanding that you've reached, this indicates a renewal of relationship . . . ?"

"What else? We want our daughter to have a real home life. . . . We both feel guilty about what we've done to her, and to make up for it. . . ."

"So you'll take her from the foster home and set up a home of your own?"

She was so tolerant of me: "Yes, we will take her with us to share our way of life."

And the way she said it, you got the idea that they would be homesteading in Outer Mongolia. "And may I ask what that is?"

"Life in a religious community among the down-trodden . . . devoting our lives to others."

It was incredible; she had transformed her face into an alabaster mask of some ancient priestess. I felt almost sadistic as I passed my pack of cigarettes toward her. She brushed them away. "I'm not permitted."

"So a great deal has changed in the four weeks since we last talked, Mae. You've become betrothed to a man and to a religious community and to nonviolence."

"Well, I have always looked into religion . . . in my reading . . . and I have always rejected it, until my husband. . . ."

"You are married?"

"In the eyes of Him, my marriage is sacred. . . ."

"Without ceremony though."

"In the eyes of God, ceremony is like the drops of dew. . . ."

"You certainly must have gotten a lot talked out together in the space of four weeks. How many times have you seen this boy?"

"He comes every Sunday afternoon during visiting period, and we talk and meditate together. He's done more to make me see the light. . . . He's converted me. . . . He's helped me to look back on the sordidness of my life. . . ."

"His own life, too?"

"Oh, yes, his life has had its thorns, too."

"I'm sorry, Mae, I'm so obtuse. He's a minister, is that it?"

"Yes, he was called to our faith. . . ."

"And you haven't seen him in, what, five years . . . ?"

Dreamily, she murmured, "Something like that. . . ."

"What made him suddenly become aware of this responsibility toward you?"

"He's always felt it. . . . He just couldn't find me. He's been atoning for what he did to me all these years. . . ."

"I see now. So together you will make up for your sins by doing good works, is that it?"

"Exactly."

"You'll live together, though, as husband and wife?"

Oh, the expression of disgust, of pain, on her face as she said for-givingly: "We shall be of one flesh but not of the flesh. We are to live as brother and sister."

I searched for a cigarette. "So there'll be no more physicality in your life . . . no fists, no agressiveness, no carnality . . . ?"

"I have just implied that to you, Mr. Cortina."

I was dashed. It was the first time in eight months that she had ever called me by my name. I might have laughed at the absurdity of it all, but her face, her posture, her tone daunted me. She was transformed.

She leaned forward slightly. "I cannot hurt you or anyone else any more. I cannot and will not."

"You'll have to be patient with me, Mae, but this is such a con-trast with the girl we listened to on that tape that I'm sort of left gasping. . . . What about your poetry?"

She flicked her hand. "Gross and self-pitying. Self-indulgent, false, worldly, ungodly. I now have found something that gives me peace and makes me alive to everyone around me. . . . I do understand people now. . . . I follow the Prophet. I am not allowed to argue. I'm always to be at peace; nothing is to penetrate this peace."

I blurted out: "Sounds like you're back on heroin again, blocking out everything but being on the nod."

The silence that greeted my remark was devastating. She was demonstrating her new role of meek acceptance. "Drugs blinded me to Him. They cut me off from living. Drugs will always be the works of the dark world. I am now studying the holy booklets, preparing myself to go forth. . . ."

"You're being released from the program?"

"Yes, shortly. I have had word. I want to use my days in preparation."

I asked self-consciously: "May I smoke?" She nodded her head. "This religious faith that you've espoused, it's pretty rigorous, isn't it? You've had your troubles with discipline in the past. . . ."

"I have faith in this discipline. It will rule my life. It will be my staff and rod, it will support me in those dark hours. . . ."

"So you do expect some rough times ahead?"

"Of course, for that is the human condition. . . . But I'm prepared. . . . You see, Mr. Cortina, before, I was not ready to do what I was told but now I am. . . . I embrace the discipline. I'm not allowed to smoke, to eat white bread or butter or pork or sugar or alcohol or drugs of any kind. My clothes shall be simple and somber. . . . I must be accepting."

"Sounds pretty exacting to me, Mae."

"It's simple and sustainin'."

I brushed some ash from my pants. "Does it strike you as being terribly different from what your style was before?"

"Oh, yes, but what is a conversion but a terrible difference? It's really very simple if you have strong belief in it."

I shook my head: "And all this came about because this young man came in to see you four weeks ago . . . ? Astonishing."

"But can't you understand that I had been preparing for this all along . . . underneath . . . underneath?"

"Must have been underneath all right."

"It was silently fertile; like the seed swaddled in the sleep of snow, so am I now. And when the breath of Spring kindles the warmth, I ache with the joy of birth. . . . I am reborn. Can't you share belief, Mr. Cortina? Listen to me. I never believed in anything before. . . . I now believe in a here-and-now and a hereafter. You come from dust and you go back to dust, but your soul is a golden chalice of redemption. I now know that I am an instrument, His instrument. . . . Through me will He work his ways. I am total submission."

"You've surrendered yourself . . . given yourself . . . to this young man . . ."

"In a certain sense. . . . I must be submissive to him and, because of that, to Him who is above both of us. . . . I follow Raymond, that's my baby's father, I follow Raymond where he goes. As he sees truth, so do I . . . together. . . . Truth and purity."

I lighted another cigarette and leaned back in my chair. I studied her face. She caught the incredulity on my features. She said submissively: "You cannot believe, Mr. Cortina. You see how faith confuses the sophisticated? You cannot with your worldliness accept my spirit of reconciliation . . . my humbleness . . . my docility."

"Well, maybe that's it. . . . But let's agree that it's not whether I accept it or not but whether you do. Isn't that it?"

"Of course, but I would like you to see it, too. . . . Because you have spent a lot of time with me . . . I would like you to share in my joy. . . ."

"Look, Mae. . . . If this is your way . . . what the hell, if it can keep you off heroin or pills, fine. . . . But you said long ago that you were gullible and suspicious. Remember that? If I played you back every tape that we've made together, each one would testify to that, each one would demonstrate your own perception of that gullibility and suspiciousness. . . . How else should I react now, after all that you've related these last eight months . . . ? You try on things like coats on a rack . . . heroin, pills, prostitution, lesbianism, maternity, religion. Why? Why do you continuously have to give yourself away to something or somebody? Why? What's wrong with you that it is so necessary that you fling yourself at something? You have value as a person. You have gifts. . . . Your poetry is beautiful. You have worth, Mae. . . ."

She puzzled out what I said and then remarked with defensiveness though in a quiet voice: "I am not throwing myself at anything. If Raymond falters, I will still have Him. . . . I am not throwing myself away at anything any more."

"Mae," I reached out and tried to touch her hand; she withdrew it quickly. "Mae, do you think that you tried to give yourself away to things before?"

"Cool it, daddy. . . . Of course I did . . . in my ignorance. I was a seeker. . . . But them guilt feelings came from that. . . . My mother and stepfather, my prossing, junk, lesbianism . . . nothing wanted me. . . . But now I have Him. . . . Don't you see, man?" Somehow, despite her enforced calm, her voice had coarsened.

"Why are you so hard on Mae? How can you be so down on her . . . ? What makes you throw up your hands and stuff everything about Mae and run to the cooker? That's what you're doing. . . . You're stuffing it again. . . . You'll be out there a week and you'll be back on your bent spoon."

Her face had hardened, her pupils were large, her lips thin: "Drugs are not it, daddy, not drugs. . . . But what chews me up, makes me run, puts me all down between my legs? That was my life . . . down between my legs. Is that my life . . . ? All that hunger that never gets still . . . ? A lot you know about my life. . . ."

"Drugs let you down. You gave yourself to something that took you and let you down. Just what you're doing now."

She shook her head grimly: "You can't make me lose faith, daddy. I can only get strong by listening to your tongue of darkness. . . ."

"Mae, you know about drugs. You know that pills or junk will give you peace. That's the only way you have of handling things, the only choice you permit yourself. . . . What happens if this new religious awakening turns sour . . . ? What happens . . . where can you go? You know only one alternative. You have no choices.

Your memory will recall to you that rush, that euphoria. . . . Mae. . . ."

She interrupted me. "I have Him. . . . I have my faith. . . ." She rose, removed the microphone, and passed it to me. She said with great dignity: "We'll probably not see each other again, Mr. Cortina. Next time I'll probably be out in my mission work with my husband. . . . I have enjoyed talking with you. . . . Between us has passed the breath of the spirit. Good-bye." And she left quietly; all I could think of was that dowdy girl whose breast hung out of her dress.

"Yes, it was impressive, but how many have you had to do with over the years who showed exactly the same kind of intermittent talent, Frank Michael?"

"Sure, but it was less the poetry than the dazzling insight into herself that was significant. She could put it down on paper but apparently couldn't perceive what it was that she revealed about herself. . . . You spoke to her?"

"Yes, I spent almost half an hour with her. Didn't she tell you? I told her how much I got from her poetry and that I knew someone on a magazine. I could tell she was pleased, by her gruffness."

"And how close is she to getting out, Sister?"

"Perhaps the end of next week. . . . We're terribly overcrowded, Frank Michael. We have some girls sleeping in the recreation room on cots. We're bursting at the seams. We've got to move them. . . . Don't you think she's ready?"

"No, she's not ready. . . . She's on this religion kick now, just the way she was on her other kicks. . . ."

She looked at me and smiled. "Frank Michael, I've known you a long time, and I often wondered whether deep down inside you didn't have just a slightly grudging sort of uneasiness about a religious approach to drug rehabilitation. Why can't religion be a therapeutic tool? Why should you rule it out?"

I looked at the floor; the tiles gleamed. "I don't think that's so. Perhaps I'm just suspicious of it, Sister. It offers such a rich opportunity for the drug-dependent to hide at a certain stage in their putting themselves together. . . ."

"Doesn't that apply to just about everything? How many addicts have you heard talking about how they were going into youth work or into community work . . . several thousand? What else do they have left to them but to use their drug experience in a positive way . . . ? And you know how they make for themselves some great charismatic role. . . . So why should Mae's 'conversion' disturb you?"

I had to smile. "Because I don't think it's conversion."

"And if it's not . . . ?"

"Yes, that's it."

"She'll go back to drugs? Don't most of them, and isn't that your pet theory, that they have to go back in order to finally purge themselves?" She reached over and took one of my cigarettes. I lighted it for her. "You know that I'm not being cynical. . . . You know what the percentages are. How many girls that you have interviewed here in the last ten years have finally and totally given up drugs? Certain things happen . . . factors we still don't know much about. . . . Things like maturation, or that other idea of yours of drug addicts becoming eccentrics to the drug culture. . . . What makes you think that Mae is so different?"

"Because for me they always have to be different."

"Yes, and you know why that's so, because, unless you believed that, you couldn't work with them. And what is that but faith . . . and isn't faith exactly what you are objecting to seeing in Mae now?"

"But it's so grotesque in her case. She's denying everything in her own life. . . . She's doing the same old arithmetic that will add up to failure. . . . It's such a denial."

"And what about your denial? You deny how damaged she is, how little she has going for her, you deny all the omission and neglect of her life. What about your denial? Don't scoff at her chances. . . . You shouldn't, of all people, because you had faith that we didn't have. We would have shipped her out as unmanageable months ago if you hadn't spoken to me. I think she'll surprise you. Perhaps the sting would be taken out of it if you could change religious conversion to self-maturation, huh?" and she laughed.

I rose. "We'll certainly find out. But meanwhile, will you get her telephone number and address for me, just in case?"

"I'll give it to you next month. . . . Now could we talk about the other girls you're interviewing? We have a few others here in this facility."

Yes, her point was well taken. There were some three hundred other girls in residence.

9

It had taken six weeks for me to manage an appointment, Mae was so peripatetic, and there was no assurance that she would appear now. But the place she had chosen was attractive; from where I sat I could see the muddy Potomac, swollen by the Spring runoff. And near me, though he kept himself protected from my view, a brown thrasher uttered his antic cry: "Hey you, hey you, hey you. Who me? Who me? Who me? yes, you; yes, you; yes, you." Somehow, this bird with his jauntiness, his sauciness, was the perfect prelude to Mae. While he cried "Drop it, drop it, drop it," I saw Mae approach from the far end of the path. The swagger, the roll of the hips, the suit, the fur piece, the made-up face with the eyes of the eighteen-year-old girl peering out uncertainly. Yes, it was Mae.

"You certainly pick elegant spots for meetings, Mae."

"The damned city is so full of creeps. . . . No place is safe any more. You know, they got the highest nighttime crime rate in the country. Ain't that somethin'? Some of my old friends . . . workin' girls . . . beat up, taken for everything they have. . . . Dangerous city. . . . Nice out here, though. . . ."

We shook hands. She was not as thin as she had been the last time, but she was obviously nervous. "I'm glad to see you, Mae."

"You know, I been wondering how you were going to tape this meeting out here. . . ."

I opened my topcoat and showed her the small recorder that was draped from my shoulder. It was recording.

"Oh, Professor, you are the God-damnedest bird. . . ."

We walked along the path. "I didn't know that you would come, Mae. . . ."

"You know somethin'? I didn't either."

"What's it like, being out, Mae?"

"Shitty. . . . Like you got a sunburn and everything keeps slapping you." She stopped and looked toward the river. "Ain't you going to offer me a smoke?"

I laughed. "I'm sorry. Here."

She looked into my face as I lighted her cigarette. "I'll tell you the truth, Professor. I was going to duck you. . . . But I remembered that candy that you brought me that time. . . ."

"I'm glad that you came. . . . How long have you been out?"

"Seven weeks out of the mousie-mousie factory."

"You haven't been back at all?"

"Listen, I had enough of those mini-skirted Marys to last a lifetime. . . ."

We were walking slowly and I could tell that, for all the attempts to sound like the old china-smashing girl, Mae was extremely nervous and ill at ease. "Does this get-together sear you?" I asked.

"I won't tell you a lie. . . ."

"Because of me . . . or you . . . ?"

"Just because of . . . of. . . . Like I said, I'm sunburned, Professor."

"Quite a contrast from our last session, Mae. It didn't work out?"

"For him it did, I guess, but not for me," she said cryptically.

"You mean, you found you couldn't be that submissive?"

She said sharply: "I mean I could be anythin' I had to be, if you just didn't try to game me. . . . See, I been so fucked over so many times, Professor, that I don't want any more games. . . . He wasn't interested in anything but getting me. . . . A God-damned creep, though he is the father of my child. He's still standing back

twenty years waiting for a trolley car. A liar, playing a game, projecting an image. . . . he needs a mother."

"And your daughter?"

Her hand shook, but she flicked her cigarette away with an air
of bravura. "I saw her. . . . Thank God, she don't look like me.
. . . You know what I mean? She's not going to be big in any of
the places her old lady is. . . ."

We got to a bench, and I took her arm and pulled her down
next to me. "Mae. . . . You don't have to work so hard with me."

She bridled as she shook off my hand. She sighed and then
shook her head. "What's the matter with me, Professor? I'm all
screwed up nowadays . . . like I'm going through my change at
my age. . . ."

"You said that months ago. . . ."

"Yeah, but I was inside then. I ain't no better, Professor, just
more screwed up than ever. . . ."

"Are you using?"

She laughed: "Wouldn't that be the cat's ass if I could only answer you 'Yes.' No, I'm not usin', and that's the trouble. . . . I'm
not using, and everybody else is. I oughta spit right in your eye,
you and those mini-skirted Marys. You guys made me into a lame.
You didn't tell me about this junkie world out here. Everybody
runnin' a game, projecting an image, always tryin' to run you
through changes. . . . Oh, Professor, you guys have done a good
job on me all right. . . . Took a perfectly good whore and turned
her into a zonk."

"Have you seen your mother?"

"From a distance. . . . She looked the same . . . same old shit.
. . . 'What've I done? My poor daughter.' And her breath like
paint thinner. . . . She couldn't even see that I didn't have no
makeup on and my body was clean of sores. . . . She couldn't even
see that, Professor. She still had that old reel of me in her mind.
She couldn't see the difference. I squashed that. . . . Screw her.
. . . Wanted to come live with me. . . . Can you imagine . . . ?
Wanted to come live with me. . . . Where, in a freight car?"

"And your stepfather?"

"Oh, he's made it. . . . Yeah, he's really made it. He's in jail, the son of a bitch. He got busted for molesting a kid. . . . Yes, Professor, it's been merry, merry, merry."

"Had you expected it to be merry?"

"Why not? Huh? Why not?" she demanded and reached for my cigarettes. "You and the mousie-mousies working on me, making me a God-damned lame. I ain't square and I ain't a hype. I'm nothin'—like that damned twig out there floating on the water. . . ."

The sun had slipped down, and the rays slanted off the trees. "Are you working, Mae?"

"Sure, I'm an executive . . . big office, heavy salary, great responsibility, two cars. . . ." She heaved her shoulders up and then let them droop. "Come off it. You still sound like somebody in *Little Women*. . . . You get a chicken-shit job. They want your life for four cents. The guys lean over you to explain, their hands like tools. . . . Not honest like a guy who wants to buy you for fifteen minutes. . . . And then, this should kill you, I got a job on a community drug-coordinating program. You know, a charity job, for junkies like me. Would you like me to spin you a beautiful web about how I'm saving kids from using shit? Lecturing to them, telling them about the horrible world of drugs . . . ?"

"I can't think of anything more suitable for you, Mae. You could do such a job. You're so expressive, you've got all the talents to help."

She sawed an imaginary bow across an imaginary violin and hummed 'Hearts and Flowers.' "You're a pistol, Professor. . . . You're dead square. You're institutionalized, that's what you are. You've spent so much of your life 'inside,' talking to fuck-ups, that your whole idea of the world is ass-backwards. Let me tell you about the world. I'm the one who should tell people about the world and not you, because you are screwed up."

"You're right, Mae. You should tell people about the world. I agree with you. . . . That's just why I say that you would be invaluable as a narcotic-abuse counselor."

"Well, I tried it. There's drugs all over the place. All over, Professor. . . . And where there's no drugs, there's talk about drugs.

It's a whole drug bag. . . . There's only one thing wrong, Professor. The problem ain't drugs."

"We know that. . . . But we've always known that, Mae."

"Yeah? Then we're in a God-damned small minority. You go to a school and you talk to the kids. . . . Same old shit as always. . . . I can remember it, same as when I was in school. . . . Kids are foolin' around with pot or pills or junk. Or they say they are, just to be in. And the principals and teachers and parents are screaming about the drug problem . . . and taking their excedrins, and gin, and broads and guys to bed. . . . And they're sure their kids are usin'. And then they get to pickin' nits from each other's scalps. . . . The kids say: 'You're usin' alcohol; that's worse than pot.' And the parents are sayin': 'But we know what we're doin'; we're your parents. . . . And pot'll lead on to heroin.' And you got a million guys like you, doin' studies on the drug situation. We must have the whole God-damned warehouse space in the whole country filled up with books and studies on drugs. . . . And the problem gets worse and worse. Drug problem, my ass. . . . My royal American ass."

"But you must admit this is the problem, Mae. The whole thorny problem. . . . How do we zero in on it?"

"Write another book, Professor. Not me. . . . You know, people don't want to listen. They want to talk, to get in their two cents, to run their fears. Like a bunch of God-damned junkies, they're all copping out by yelling about the drug problem and poppin' pills at the same time. I don't even look at television any more because of some smart-assed writer puttin' together a show on drugs. . . . The junkies have finally taken over the world. You know how? Because they gamed everybody into yellin', and they can hide and use. Everybody in the whole stinkin' world is hidin' and usin' his stuff. . . . That's the pretty world that you and them damned mousie-mousies fitted me for. . . . Bunch of copping-out liars. Everybody running his game, from the top to the bottom. Well, I am a junkie, Professor, and don't you ever forget it. I've had it in my arm, and I've booted the blood in and out of the dropper. I know it. I know the pus in the sores and how it stinks on a hot day and how it squirts out in all of its yellow-greenness, but it's a helluva lot sweeter than the fuckin' lies of your square world. From the top to the bottom, they're liars. Everybody out for what he can get. . . . Humph," she snorted. "Drug problem. . . . Jesus, that's easy. If it only was a drug problem. . . . But it ain't, it ain't, Professor, it's much worse. . . . It's a people problem . . . a people problem. . . . And there ain't no methadone for that!"

A lovely purple haze settled over the Potomac, and the thrasher called: "Hey you, hey you. . . . Come here, come here." A warmish wind stirred the tops of the trees. I offered her a cigarette. "Do you have any friends, Mae?"

"Tons of them."

"Any good ones?"

"They're all good . . . I don't know what for. . . ." She blew out a cloud of smoke. "They take you out. You run along the beach at twilight, and they tell you all about themselves. . . . And then they say how wonderful you are. What they could do if they had somebody like you at their side. You're so refreshingly different. They try to lay you, and you find they got a wife and four kids and so many hangups that you think you're in a checkroom. . . . Yeah, like I say, I got tons of friends. . . ."

"What're you doing now?"

"Sitting on my big ass, watching the river."

"Pretty rough. . . ."

She sighed. "See, Professor, you guys did me a disservice. You told me that heroin screwed me up. . . . Honest to Christ, you guys did me a disservice. You told me that stuff put me in an unreal world. What you didn't tell me is that most people have to have an unreal world to cushion them from the real world. You got to fantasize in order to be healthy, in order to take the whole screw-upness of livin'. . . . But I'm so raw, I'm so open. . . . I'm so clean I'm afraid to take a shot for fear it'll kill me; I'm afraid to talk to anybody because they're gonna try to take me. So I sit in that God-damned room and stare out at a pot of some waxy flowers on the fire escape across the way. You guys have done it for sure. I'm a lame, I'm damaged . . . damaged. . . ."

"Are you going to try to get your daughter back?"

"You mean give her a break, allow her to have me around her

to guide her tiny feet? I'm screwed up but I ain't so screwed up that I'll do that."

"I wonder if that's the way your mother reasoned. I wonder if that's why you were passed from relative to relative in your childhood."

Mae snorted: "Could be. It figgers. . . . So maybe I'm a little more hep than my old lady. . . . Good for me."

I rubbed my hands together. "Well, Mae, you've blasted the world. . . . You've certainly been exploited. You've been victimized. So what's the next step? The cop-man and that first shot . . . ?"

The twilight had deepened; she looked at me and smiled grimly. "Sure sounds like it, don't it, Professor . . . ? I ran it for you, though. . . . I coulda ducked you. . . . But I gotta go . . . I gotta get back to look at them damned waxy flowers, they mighta changed. . . ." She got up suddenly. "So long, Professor. . . . I got to beat it."

"Is there anything I can do for you, Mae?"

She laughed. "Yeah. . . . Stop the world so I can get off."

"Do you need any money?"

"Money? Me? Oh, you got to be kidding."

I gave her a twenty-dollar bill. She looked at it. She whispered: "That could buy me four five-dollar bags, Professor. . . . Don't you feel guilty . . . ?" She stared hard at me and put her finger on my lips. And she turned away. I heard her heels on the gravel long after the darkness had swallowed up her swift departure.

10

The contract my company had with Sister Bendita's organization ran out and, what with other assignments, almost two years passed before I found myself in Washington once again. It was late after-

noon as I walked those streets, those very special streets, where my
acquaintances lolled in the sunlight or nodded in the hallways. I
nearly always recognized someone, or rather they recognized me
and swiftly turned their backs or scuttled away at my approach.
After dinner, I called Sister Benedita. We chatted away. I asked
about her program.

"Well, we've got plenty of girls, Frank Michael, but no
money. . . ."

"Yes, that's true all over the country, Sister. . . . No money for
programs. . . ."

"Are you busy these days, Frank Michael?"

"We keep going. . . ."

And then with that archness I knew so well, Sister Benedita
quipped: "Why don't you drop in at the Pentagon while you're
here, Frank Michael? I understand they have a problem with heroin. I think you might arrange some interviewing. . . . But no, on
second thought, they probably don't have the money to afford your
services. . . . They'll wait until the problem hits the communities. . . ."

"Sister, you sound just as charming as ever. . . ." I hesitated.
"Have you ever heard from Mae?"

There was a pause. . . . "Mae?" And there was silence. I could
understand. She'd had thousands of girls in the two years. "Oh,
Mae? That Mae. . . . Yes, I've heard about her. . . ."

I couldn't tell from her tone. I asked: "She came back?"

"Why don't you come over, and we'll have a smoke together.
. . . Come over around eight o'clock."

There was an unfamiliar receptionist in the foyer. She called to
find out if I was expected.

"Mr. Cortina, Sister Benedita was called away unexpectedly . . .
but she'd like you to see her assistant. You know the way?"

Through the corridors, the rock-and-roll strains echoing, the
laughter, the swearing, the oceans of female voices. Yes, it was familiar now. I entered the office. No one was at the outer desk. . . .
I called: "Anybody here?"

And from Sister Benedita's office came: "Just us cats. . . . Come in, whoever you are. . . ."

She had her back to me, but she was clad like the rest of the sisters. I said: "Hello, I'm Cortina. I was supposed to see Sister Benedita. . . ."

"Well, sit down. . . ." And she turned around.

"*My God!*" And I began to laugh. I laughed and laughed. "A mini-skirted Mary, by Jesus Christ!"

"Professor. . . . Professor, you keep the wrong company."

"Mae. . . . My God. . . . Mae. . . ."

"Correction: I am Sister Caritas . . . or I will be in a couple of months when I take my finals. . . . Don't it beat hell, Professor?"

I held her hands and looked at her. I was speechless.

"Fooled you, huh . . . ? Really stopped you. And brother, that's got to be something when you can't rap. I know that. Sit down. . . . Where are your cigarettes . . . ?"

"How come, Mae . . . Sister Caritas . . . ?"

"How come, he says. . . . How come . . . ? I don't ask. I'm here. I'm happy. . . ."

"For how long, Mae?"

"Going on two years, Professor. . . . I guess it was always this." She searched my face. "You asked because you wondered if it was another image I was projecting?"

I laughed. "Well, you were using roles up pretty fast at one time, Mae. . . ."

"I can't use this one up . . . though I must be the worst nun who ever lived."

"I can't believe it, Mae. . . . You. . . ."

"You mean my being here with drug addicts or my being a nun?"

"Yes, your being a nun. . . . The rest of the world turning away from a kind of medieval form and you. . . ."

"But it figures, doesn't it, Professor? I don't care about it being out of style. When I was a kid, somebody threw away a pair of what was to them a pair of worn-out shoes. I got them out of the garbage can and wore them for almost three years. . . . They fitted

me perfectly, they were comfortable, and they were all broken in.
. . . So I don't care about that. . . ."

"I just can't get over it. . . ."

"You better believe it," she said, giving her hips a wiggle.
"These junkies can't get over it in here either. They can't game me
with their sorry-sorriness. . . . I can play all their games, all their
changes, all their projections, and there I am. . . . Oh, Professor,
I'm glad to see you. . . . I really am. . . ."

"And it was Sister Benedita who helped you . . . ?"

"Oh, that one. Benny is what we call her. Not to her face. . . .
She's a great woman. . . ." Suddenly she sat down and leaned forward across the desk. "Do you have your recording equipment with
you here in Washington?"

"Back at the hotel. . . ."

"Would you do an old friend a favor?"

"Sure. . . ."

"Well, look, we got one fresh young broad who came in off the
street just a few weeks ago . . . a real outrageous character . . .
stubborn, playing the game, real defended, kinda frail. . . . You
know, all armament on the outside but a mouse inside. I want you
to talk to her, like you used to talk to me. . . . Will you do it, Professor . . . ? Because this broad is gonna be saved. . . . Talk to
her, will you, and then we'll let her hear herself played back. . . .
Because that's it . . . to hear yourself played back, as if you were
somebody outside . . . that's it, Professor."

I walked back toward my hotel. The white dome of the Capitol
illuminated in the darkness. . . . I recalled one of Mae's early
poems:

> On my beat, along those lonesome streets,
> My hips sway to some music I cannot hear,
> Some voice calls, some hungry eyes seek,
> I pause, and then the hoarse invitation,
> And I hear the footfall next to me,
> That silence that precedes my moment of intimacy.
> Oh, if he be young and not bruised, with trembling
> He'll come to me, unlearned and clumsy.
> And in his bought moment a great light
> Will burst between us, banishing gloom,

Giving to each full measure of insight
Into the other, into ourselves, into life.
For me he'll be less damaged than I, less
Knowing, less untrusting, less demanding.
I'll see me reflected in his face as a mirror.
I'll see me clean and free and unashamed.
I'll see me quiet and in repose, no gnawing hunger.
That hunger whose sharp teeth drive the body,
That filthifies the image, that sullies the mind,
That breaks the dream, that curls the soul. . . .
He'll strike and the rock of the sepulcher that
Hides the dead girl will roll away, will roll away,
And she will arise like some unexpected bride,
Blushing to face him who called her forth.
On my beat along those lonesome streets,
My hips sway to some music I cannot hear,
To some music I cannot hear, music I cannot hear.

Simple. Simple. . . . I just hadn't been perceptive enough to
capitalize the pronouns.

THE
BETRAYAL

1

There was one very simple but essential condition that my organization insisted upon in these assignments: the subject must be picked at random. It's inherent in the very nature of institutions of any kind—prisons, rehabilitation facilities, hospitals, etc.— that there is an official version of "random" and an unofficial or informal version (and this is just as binding, perhaps more binding, than the formal one). So, as I looked at Gerard, blond, short, chunky, sitting very still, his face a study in effacement, I wondered which side had elected him to be the candidate.

"And you're how old, please?"

"Sixteen." It was offered coldly, stiffly, with an implied "sir."

"How long have you been here?"

"Three days."

"Did you come in on a petition or were you busted?"

"Busted."

"How come you weren't sent to a juvenile institution?"

Gerard didn't move, gave no indication that he heard what I asked. He just watched me with that studied blank stare.

"So what you're implying is that when you were brought before the judge he offered you a choice? Either a correctional setting or a rehabilitation program . . . is that it?"

"Yes."

"I see. . . . And why were you brought before the judge?"

"Heroin."

"How long had you been using heroin?"

"Two years."

"You were addicted?"

"Yes."

"Did you start using heroin by snorting?"

"Skinning."

"Skin-popping? Sometimes it's called taking G. shots, isn't it?"

"Yeah."

"Then after a time you began to mainline?"

"Yeah."

"How long did it take from your first skin-pop to your starting to shoot into your veins?"

"I skinned for two months and then went to mainlinin'."

The voice registration had no color, no presence, no warmth, no rhythm. He stared straight forward. "Had you a habit from skin-popping?"

"From mainlinin'."

"How long before you developed a habit after you began to mainline?"

"Month."

"So you must have been using pretty heavily. How much were you using a day?"

"Every day."

"Uh-huh. But how much were you using every day?"

"Two, three, four, five bags."

"That was when you were mainlining? How much did you use as a skin-popper?"

"Bag and a half."

"You'd divided that bag and a half up, is that it?" I asked, but he sat motionlessly, no hint of response. "When you're skinning, do you fix at regular times? Do you understand what I'm asking?"

"When I got the money."

"I'm sorry. . . . When you got the money . . . ?"

"Soon as I got some money, I go cop again."

"I see. It wasn't a case of sickness driving you. When you could get some money, then you'd score? You never got strung out on G. shots?"

"Didn't skin-pop all . . . every day." He glanced at the reels turning on the recorder. "Used to skin-pop on the weekends in the beginnin'."

"Can you get a habit from skin popping?"

"Yes."

"You knew people who developed a habit from G. shots?"

"Yes."

"What made you switch from that to mainlining?" I asked. "Did someone suggest it to you?"

"Curiosity."

"Curiosity? But you knew what the high was from skin-popping. Or is it different?"

"It come on faster and stronger."

"I see. . . ."

He offered: "Instant high."

"How long does it take to get high on a skin-pop?"

"Minute and a half."

"Well, a minute and a half isn't a very long time, really, is it?" I watched him consider, his face unrevealing. "Or is a minute and a half too long for you to wait?"

"You don't like to wait that long, most time. You go out there like that, you can get beat, you know, go buy stuff that ain't that good, and you skin it and you got to wait. When you main it, you just got to go get it, cook it up, and shoot it in, and you know right away if it's bad."

There was a hint of animation in his reply. "So that minute and a half is critical. Did you ever get beat by getting poor stuff?"

"Yeah."

"What did you do?"

"Didn't cook up. Went back to him. Told him it didn't cook up."

"What did he say?"

"Said he was sellin' good stuff. I told him he wasn't. I told him I wanted good stuff or my money back. So he gave me some more. This time it was stuff."

"Why would he do that? Were you such a good customer of his that he wanted to keep you happy?"

"No. My regular got run out so I used this lame."

"I understand. But lots of pushers are cutting stuff all the time . . . meat tenderizer, talcum powder. . . ."

He volunteered: "Quinine, bonita. . . ."

"Right. So why should he give you a replacement bag? Was he afraid that you might turn him in? Did you threaten him?"

"I came with a rough attitude."

"Ah. . . . He was afraid of you. Had he reason to be?"

"What?"

"Had he reason to be afraid of you? Are you a tough guy . . . ?"

"Okay. I'm no sucker."

"How do you really know when you're getting good stuff, Gerard, except when you start to shoot?"

"You don't."

"So you could be shooting battery acid or anything into your vein . . . ?"

"Sure. You looks at it, you cooks it, and if it does that, you shoots. . . ."

"So it's always a gamble. . . ."

"You takes a chance," he said, glancing again at the recorder. It was as if he had just become conscious of it.

"You risk your life perhaps?"

"Right."

"Did that ever occur to you while you were cooking up, that you might die?"

"Sometimes."

"Did that worry you?"

"Once in a while. When you gets into it, you never thinks about it too much."

I brought out my cigarettes and offered him one. He drew back slightly; he wasn't having any part of it. Was I trying to bribe him? I lighted up and placed the cigarettes on the floor next to my chair. "Straight heroin, not cut right, stuff that's too good will kill you, too, won't it . . . ?"

"O.D."

"Yes, overdose. I wonder why you weren't concerned about that?"

"You just don't think about it."

"Or perhaps you just don't care. . . . Life might not be worth living anyway."

"Life is. . . ."

"Is it?" He was still very uptight. I wondered at his control; he sat so quietly. Just his eyes moved, and they watched carefully, sharply. His was not a prepossessing appearance. His one eye seemed slightly out of focus. "You must have gotten pretty well tracked up?"

He held out his arms. "Got tracks."

"Yes, you have. Do they mean something to you?"

"How?"

"You know, like a tattoo. . . . You belong to a group. . . . Perhaps you're proud of them . . . the tracks?"

"No. I wasn't."

"You weren't. . . . How come you started to use dope in the first place?"

"Because, my cousin . . . because of my cousin, you know, he said it was nice. So he kept on, so later I tried it. And I liked-ed. And I kep' on."

"And you still like it?"

"I don't like what it can do to you," he said, in that flat rhythm that I had begun to grow accustomed to.

"You didn't like the high, is that what you're saying . . . ?"

"Didn't like what it can do to you," he said stolidly. "Make you steal, you know, from your house. You always on the run. You don't have time for this, that. You always on the run, always on the go. It's adventure life . . . adventure life, that's what it is, takin' chances every day. . . ."

"What was it costing you a day to use dope, Gerard?"

"Thirty dollars."

"That's a lot of money for anybody. How could a fella your age get that kind of money?"

"Steal."

"What do you mean, steal?"

"Shoplifting. Muggin'. Workin'."

"Did you do a great deal of mugging?"

"Some. Worked, too."

"What kind of work?"

"Give out samples . . . packages . . . telephone books."

"So you do any kind of work that you could, is that what you're saying . . . ?"

"Not any kind of work, just the one that would pay by the end of the day."

"I get you . . . so that you would be paid immediately so that you could go out and buy your stuff at the end of the day. . . . A job on a weekly basis wouldn't have worked because you wouldn't be able to supply your daily dosage. . . ."

"Ummmmm."

"Does that kind of hit-or-miss job pay thirty dollars a day?"

"Told you I shoplift and I had them little jobs. . . ."

"Gerard, how much would you have to shoplift or steal in order to come up with thirty dollars at the end of the day . . . you know, to clear thirty dollars?"

"Get as much as you can, as much as you think you can get. . . . Sometimes steal a hundred dollars to get ten or twenty dollars out of it. Steal much as you can if you think you can git it. Then you got no worry about tomorrow."

"You shoplifted every day?"

"Just about."

"What would you take?"

"Particular things. . . ."

The odd word that cropped up every now and again— particular. "Particular things . . . such as?"

"Like pants, you know. I'd ask certain people, you know, like what they was needin'. Pants and dresses and stuff like that stuff. . . . Yeah, shirts and shorts. I say, 'Lady, what size dress you want, you know, certain price you pay? I'll get it. I'll go down and get it.' "

"So you'd steal to order, as it were. You had your customer's size and everything before you'd shoplift. Now, did you shoplift from mostly little stores selling cheap goods . . . ?"

"Nope."

"Then how would you go about it?"

"Look for a pretty dress. Shop for it. I picture the people in my mind, and I shop for somethin' they look good in."

"And how much might this dress be selling for in the store?"

"Maybe twenty-three dollars or twenty-five."

"Then what would you sell it for after you had shoplifted it?"

"Eight, nine dollars."

"Less than half. Tell me, did you always have a customer?"

"Not always. Sometimes fence." He looked at me keenly and repeated to see if I understood: "Fence."

"Gotcha," I said smiling. "You'd sell the fence one article at a time."

"If you got one piece or a lot. Take what you got. Had to watch him. He was crooked. TV sets . . . portable; radio; took a refrigerator one time, suits, tennis paddle . . . car batteries. . . ."

"How the devil would you walk out of a store with a refrigerator?"

"Burglarize. . . ."

"I see, you wouldn't shoplift that. Heavy appliances you burglarized. . . ."

"Had to. Too big to put under your jacket."

"You must have had a very active day, Gerard, what with shoplifting, working, burglarizing. . . . And all of it to come up with thirty dollars to pay for your junk. I understand what you mean when you said before that you always had to be on the move."

"Yeah, burglarized . . . every day. . . ."

"Do you mean at night?"

"Broad daylight. . . ."

"And you never got caught?"

"Never."

"How many burglaries did you commit, do you know?"

"Better'n a hundred."

"You must have been very clever."

"Nope."

"Ever nearly get caught?"

"Nope."

"Were you lucky, then, or did you have a good partner?"

"Took a chance. . . . Had a crime brother."

"A crime brother. . . . Was he your age or older?"

"Year younger. . . . Them days I just turned fifteen. He was fourteen. He was fourteen."

"Was he your shooting partner as well? You took off together?"

"Yeah. We wus shootin' brothers. We come up in the same block. We wus friends."

"Is he in a drug program now?"

"Dead."

"Dead?"

"Blood went bad."

"Oh, blood poisoning from a needle . . . ?"

"Dead. . . ."

"But not you. . . . Lucky. . . ."

"Ran right up his arm. Showed me the red line. . . . Up his arm, jumped across his neck. Dead."

I pushed the cigarette pack toward him. He saw the move, reached down, and handed them to me. I said, "Thank you. Don't you smoke?"

"I do."

"Have one."

He shook his head.

"You know, Gerard, these are just preliminary questions. We'll be seeing each other for quite a while."

"How long?"

"I have no idea. . . . I have nothing to do with how long you're kept here. And because we talk together doesn't mean that you'll have to stay here just because we're talking together. I'll follow you wherever you go."

He didn't answer, but his look was sufficient. He wasn't borrowing anything from the future.

"You lived with your mother and father?"

"Yeap."

"These were your real parents?"

"Yeap."

"You had sisters and brothers?"

"Yeap."

"How many brothers?"

"Three brothers."

"And sisters?"

"Three sisters, one died . . . died."

"So, including you, there were seven children in the family. And where were you in the group . . . oldest, in the middle, or . . . ?"

"Baby."

"So that means that some of the others were away from home, married or on their own."

"All of them."

"How much younger are you from the next child?"

He stared at me, he moved his lips. . . . I understood. He was counting. "Six years."

"So your father must be in his fifties?"

"Sixty-five. . . . Retired."

"Well, that's the age we get retired at these days. . . ."

"Been retired seven years. He has Parker's."

"Parker's? Parkinson's disease . . . that's what your father suffers from?"

"Parkinson's disease."

"Who supports the family?"

"Got a pension . . . he got one."

"And there are just the three of you, so you can make ends meet, is that it?"

"Not it. . . . Said before, my sister died. She had five kids, one's two months old, so they lives with us and we got welfare. . . . On welfare. . . ."

"Your mother works, too?"

He permitted himself to show disgust at my obtuseness. "She's gotta take care of the kids. Can't work. Got them five kids and my old man."

"Pardon me."

"Yeap."

"Is your apartment or house large enough to accommodate five children, your ailing father . . . ?"

"Nope. Crowded. . . ."

"I guess you preferred to be out on the street."

"I liked home."

"With all of your activity, you couldn't have spent too much time at home."

"Every night. . . . Home every night."

"You came home every night . . . even though you were high?"

"Every night."

"Your family knew that you were an addict?"

"Found out."

"How long did it take?"

"Eight months."

"Was it your mother?"

"Yeap. . . . She found a set of works. . . ."

"And she recognized what they were for?"

"She probably had the idea of what they wus. . . ."

"Did she confront you?"

"Nope. She investigated, I guesses."

"She never spoke to you about it?"

"Yeah, she told me why don't I stop."

"Just like that?"

"Sure. She told me why I don't stop usin' drugs, you know, but I was high then, and when drugs got you, you know, you don't wan' to hear nothin'. You don't have time to listen to a whole lot of lec-turin', you know, you want to get out there. So it went in one ear and out the other, you know, an' I was back out on the streets again. . . . Yeap. Outside."

That was quite a spiel for him. I smiled, but again he was not buying any overtures. This was an interrogation, he understood what that meant, he would put up with it, and that was the extent of it. "You're not a very talkative fellow."

"Talk. . . ."

"This crime brother of yours who died . . . he was a real close friend . . . ?"

"Yeap."

"Your only friend?"

"Got friends."

"Many?"

"Who needs 'em?"

"Do you have a girl friend?"

"Some. . . ."

"Oh, you play the field. You have several girl friends?"

"I tip around . . . tipping."

"Do you talk to these girls?"

"I talks to 'em."

"What'd you talk about?"

"Things. You know, a lot of times just look at television. . . ."

"Would you tell them that you were using heroin?"

"Yeap. Tell 'em. They lived right there. They could see."

"You weren't trying to impress your girl friends with the fact that you were a dope addict?"

"Impress?" He seemed to ground himself on that.

"Did you think that it might make you appear to be somebody important to tell the girls that you used heroin?"

"I knows what you said before."

"I beg your pardon, Gerard."

"Nope. . . . The girls they could see what was happenin', on account they was there on the streets themselves. . . ."

His voice with exactly the same dull, mechanical registration, his face expressionless, his posture unchanged—Gerard might have been a fixture, except he awakened caution in me; by his very immobility, he seemed menacing. It was something I would have to mull over, for he was not the obvious punk type. Perhaps my thinking along these lines prompted my next questions: "Gerard, before, you said that you had never been caught committing one of your many burglaries. . . . But you are here, and you did go to court. . . . What was the charge?"

"My mother ratted me out. Said I was sellin'."

"Was she trying to help you?"

He ignored it. "They grabs me. I had three bags on me, I always buy ahead so I got it for my next, and they says on the sheet I'm a cop-man. . . ."

"You got a bum rap?"

"I'm in now."

"And this is your first institutional experience? You never had a delinquency probation or anything like that?"

"Once'd-a I got picked up . . . hooky. . . . Didn't amount to nothin'. . . . My mother said I wus sick. . . ."

"You played a lot of hooky?"

"Just didn't go."

He stirred in his chair. It seemed a major movement, as if he had reached some great decision, but in a second he had relapsed into his old pose. I asked: "How old were you when you first used anything?"

"Drank wine-er . . . when I wus eleven."

"How long did that last, drinking wine . . . ?"

"Long time . . . still drinks it sometimes."

"You smoked reefer, too?"

"Yeah. Once in a while."

"You didn't like marijuana?"

"It was okay. . . . But my cousin, you see, kept shootin' stuff . . . so I wanted it. . . . Didn't need reefer, no more. . . ."

"I suppose you never used pills?"

"Yeah, I used pills. I didn't like 'em. I felt tall as the room. . . . I didn't like 'em. . . . Never took 'em no more."

"How did you get any of these things, the wine, or reefers, or pills? Was this your cousin?"

"Tried one of my father's pills. . . . You kin buy pills. . . ."

"You'd try one of the pills prescribed for your father's disease . . . ?" What was it I caught in his eyes? Contempt? Impatience with my repetition? Instinctive resentment? "Were you a pusher ever?"

"Nope."

"You never sold pot or anything?" I pressed. "You can make a fast buck that way."

"Didn't want to sell. Wouldn't be here today if I wus a pusher."

"What does that mean?"

"Because they woulda kilt me because I woulda messed up the money. . . ."

"You would have gotten greedy with all that dope and shot it up yourself? Then you would have been short in your receipts . . . ?"

"Short in my receipts," he echoed. "Then they'da kilt me."

I jiggled a cigarette from the package and deliberately ignored him. "Have you ever been curious about why Gerard had to drink wine, smoke reefers, try pills, shoot heroin? Have you ever thought about that?"

"Nope. Didn't have to do it."

"Ah, you didn't have to, you say?"

"I liked-ed it. Jest fer the feelin', jest fer the high. Made me feel good, like at a party."

"And you couldn't feel that way without some kind of help? Life wasn't comfortable without drugs . . . ? You didn't like it so much?"

"I liked life. I wus comfortable. . . ."

"All right. . . . What was there about your life that you liked? What were you happy about?"

"It wusn't so happy. . . . I wusn't down about life. Didn't feel nothin' against it. . . . Reefer made me talk and laugh. . . . Junk made me high. . . ."

"Did you ever talk very much to your parents?"

"Yeap. I guesses so."

"You guesses so? When you were ten and eleven were you out on the block a great deal?"

"Nope. I was on the stoop. . . . Had to be home. In the summertime I could stay right on the stoop, and my mother she could see me from the winda. In the wintertime I wus home by eight o'clock."

"You had your own room?"

"Yeap. . . ."

"Did anyone share it with you?"

"My sister's four kids. . . ."

"So there were five of you in your room? By the way, where was your sister's husband?"

Just his eyes shifted; one of them seemed not quite right, as if it were sluggish. "She ain't got none. . . . She's dead."

"Was she a drug user?"

"Nope. I'm the only dope fiend. Died of a heart . . . heart. . . ."

"Attack? Seizure . . . ?"

"Fail-eee-your."

"Your father is confined to the house. I mean, he can't get up and move about or go outside on the block?"

"Jest sits there."

"Parkinson's disease, you said?"

"Don't walk so good. Shakes. Then the cops beat him up. Said he was a drunk. When we wus at the clinic . . . the doctor he said to the cops he wusn't drunk. He had Parkerson's disease. . . . So we found out. . . . He was layin' on the floor."

"And the police beat him up because they thought he was drunk . . . ?"

"They didn't know. . . . We didn't neither. . . ."

I lighted a cigarette. Gerard said: "Didn't talk so good . . . sit there . . . shake . . . quiet. . . . Very quiet, exceptin' when he shakes. . . . Cops didn't know. . . . We didn't know. . . . My mother she told them cops. . . . We took him home. . . ."

"Cigarette?"

"Nope."

"Gerard, what happened to you when you had a really good fix? How were you different?"

"Different. . . ." And when he repeated the word it wasn't with the rising inflection of a question. It was his prelude to a further statement. "Felt nice. Gave me a good feelin'. I'd walk aroun', git me a soda, watch 'em shoot pool, rap with a broad. . . . Talked to her a little, not much. . . . She don't know what you's talkin' 'bout. Cause you's mumblin', mumblin'. . . . Anyhow, you ain't wantin' to talk none. . . . You wants to be with your own kind."

"To be with other users?"

"I guess, you know, all of us together, then to make some money and go out and get high again."

"But do junkies talk much among themselves?"

"Talk 'bout what we did. . . . We'd laugh and have fun an' shit like that."

"Was it always fun and talk?"

"Yeap. . . . And mumble. . . ."

"This cousin of yours, who introduced you to heroin. . . . Is he in jail or is he still out there using?"

"He didn't have no habit. He wus chippyin'. He didn't have no habit. . . ."

"But you got one. . . . Doesn't seem fair, does it?"

"Fair. . . . He liked-ed it. An' he kept tellin' me 'bout the rush when we wus gettin' high blowin' reefer, tellin' me 'bout the rush. He kep' sayin' it wus nice, I should try it. . . . I could see he wusn't smokin' reefer too tough no more. So I say: 'Damn, it must be nice' so I went over there and trys it. . . ."

"What did this cousin say when he discovered that you had gotten hooked?"

"Nothin'. . . ."

"Did he avoid you?"

"Avoid. . . . Why should he . . . ?"

"Did you hit him up for money . . . ?"

"Sure. . . . I lended him money, he lended me money. . . ."

"Gerard, drugs did something for you. You liked heroin. . . ."

"Yeap. I liked-ed it. It was nice. . . ."

"Were you high when you were picked up?"

"Nope. No time. Them fuzz just grabbed me. My mother cool-catted it. They jest grabbed me. . . ."

"You got sick . . . withdrawal?"

"Yeap. . . ."

"Did they give you anything to help . . . ?"

"Didn't want no help. I wus tellin' I wusn't a dope fiend . . . they had the wrong guy. . . . But my tracks . . . couldn't fool them."

"Perhaps your mother did you a favor. . . ."

"Favor? How you mean, favor . . . ?"

"Maybe you would have killed yourself if you'd stayed out there. . . ."

"Humph. . . ."

"Perhaps they'll help you here."

"Help! Don't need no help. . . . Wan' go home."

"But you'd be right back on heroin."

"I can try like hell. . . . Move outa the block, git different friends. . . . Try like hell. . . ."

"Chances are that you'll have to stay here for a while, Gerard."

"I knows. . . ."

"It may do something for you?"

"Yeap."

"You can see that it might?"

"Yeap. . . ."

"What do you think it'll do?"

"Keep me confined-ed. . . ." He stared right into my eyes, an expression of implacable hatred on his face.

When I finished for the day, I dropped by the director's office. He hadn't had the job very long. He had come out of the California system. Stoner was a young, dedicated man, patient, compassionate, perceptive, and highly trained. We had known each other in California. We sat chatting in general for a while, and then Stoner said: "What do you think, Frank Michael?"

"It's a breakthrough. What else can you call it? Here's a city of almost a million, never had any kind of drug program, now it's got one. . . . Seems to me that's a tremendous leap forward. . . . Besides, they have you, Darrell."

He gave me a crooked grin: "They got me all right. They got me coming and going. They insisted upon those walls and the barbed wire on the top as well. I griped about that. . . . You know, the place is an abandoned hospital and grim enough, but putting that wall around. . . . Somehow, they always have the same old sense of walling in. They talk about therapy and treatment, but they think in terms of maximum security . . . a kind of typical corrections' mentality."

"That's why you're here. . . . You'll educate them."

"I don't know. . . . Now that they know we're here, those judges just automatically send the addicts in. We've got beds for two hundred, and we have a house population. . . ." He riffled through some papers. "As of today, we have three hundred and twenty-seven bodies. . . ."

"All ages . . . ?"

"All ages from fifteen to seventy-one."

"That should make life interesting."

"Grim, Frank Michael, grim."

"You've only been going a year. Things will change, Darrell. . . ."

"It's staffing that's the problem. You can't get trained people. . . . Let me take that back. You can get them by raiding. You know, raid New York or California. But I don't have that kind of salary scale. . . . So most of my people are fresh out of college. . . . Never worked with addicts before. . . ."

"The addicts are young, too, Darrell. They get younger every year. . . ."

He lighted a slender cigar. He looked at the glowing tip. "That's for damned sure. How many young ones have you got?"

"Just two young ones, who should be in a special facility. . . ."

"That's just it. . . . These kids shouldn't be mixed in with the old-timers. . . . You see, the powers that be haven't the foggiest notion of how long a time is involved when you work with drug abusers. Though they yack with all the therapy terms, they have a sneaking suspicion in the back of their minds that all that's involved in giving up drugs is determination, and a willingness to assume middle-class values. You can see as soon as there's a runaway or an abscondence. The newspapers rave, the neighborhood gets up in arms, and the first thing you know you're hearing about imprisonment, citizens defending themselves with arms. 'Lock him up, put him away. . . .' I think the city-wide prayer here is: 'O Lord, there's got to be some great panacea for drug addiction. Send it to us.' " He puffed nervously on his cigar.

"You'll educate them, Darrell. . . ."

"How do you prove to them that methadone freely dispensed is not the answer? How do you make them understand that drug abuse is not a police problem . . . ?"

"That's your job. . . . Let's face it—for the public, the addict is a criminal, and he is. . . . And they're scared, and they should be scared. . . . But it can't stop there. . . . That's where you come in."

"Hot dog, that's the old Frank Michael spirit. All I need along with that is more staff, more facilities, more money, more official support. . . ."

After my interview with Gerard, I hesitated to think of what the dimensions of the problem really were. Time perhaps would offer a less discouraging picture. Besides, Stoner had just needed someone he could trust so that he could unbend a little.

2

It had to be called an ability, his power to sit so quietly, like some species of predator, blending into the surroundings, doubly danger-ous. That's the quality that Gerard created. We were hearing the tape we had made together four weeks earlier, and Gerard was lis-tening, although, through this rare gift of motionlessness, you might not think so; it was his one eye that betrayed his involve-ment. He seemed unable to control it.

The tail flapped against the tape deck; the tape had played itself through. I turned it off, reloaded the machine, and put it on Re-cord. All this while I knew that he watched me, peering from his fastness, as it were. I sat back and waited. In the quiet that lay upon us there was no silence, for the institution had its voice, a voice that sounded through the baffles of corridor, radiator, public address system, and schedule requirements. I had to smile; he would not talk if we sat there for hours. With no pretense at sub-tlety, I pulled out my cigarettes and offered him one. He ignored the gesture. Perhaps, just perhaps, I detected a trace of hate in his face, that expression I had seen last time at the end of our inter-view. I said, "What did you think of that voice you just heard?"

"Voice . . . that I heard?"

"Yes. On that tape . . . the one we made together."

"Nothin'."

"It was interesting to me to hear how well he knew himself." I smoked my cigarette.

After a moment he said: "Whatcha mean?"

"I said that I was impressed by how well you knew yourself. . . ."

"Yeah. . . . Why?"

"You said you wouldn't be a dope peddler . . . because you would have been murdered. . . . You would have been too greedy. You would have shot up the stuff yourself."

"True. . . . That's right."

"Another thing. You kept holding back even when you were talking. Your voice betrayed you. You made it flat and hard and unrevealing. . . ."

"Whatcha mean . . . ?"

"I mean you were trying to make your voice play a game, make it do your rounding for you, project an image. . . . I could hear that. . . ."

"How you know that? I never said that. . . ."

"Are you sure? Are you sure, Gerard . . . ?"

"I never said that. I heard what I said. . . ."

"Well then, obviously, if you heard the tape, then I must be mistaken. I must have read something into it that wasn't there. So I'm wrong about that. I wonder what else I'm wrong about?"

"How should I know?"

"Gerard is really very angry . . . really angry. . . . I'll bet you, when you left me the last time, you were kicking yourself . . . you were very upset. . . ."

"Upset. . . . Kicking myself. . . ."

"Yes. . . . I'll bet you plucked your nerves like mad. . . ."

"Yeah. . . . Why . . . ? Huh?"

"Because you were scared . . . scared. . . ."

"Scared, man. . . . Why I'm scared . . . ?"

"Because maybe you said too much about your burglarizing, your shoplifting, your habit, your mother, yourself. . . . Maybe I was going to rat you out like your mother. . . . Maybe I was going to rat you out to the Man downstairs, and he'd find out about you and keep you here longer. . . ."

"Didn't sound like me. . . . Not my voice."

"Whose voice was it then?"

"Didn't sound like me."

"Had you ever heard your own voice before . . . ?"

"Oncet."

"Where did you hear it before?"

"In a tunnel . . . in a tunnel. . . ."

"Tunnel?" I asked, puzzled.

"You stands inside of a tunnel and you yells out: 'Gerard . . . Gerard. . . .' And you hears your voice come back to you. . . ."

"The echo. . . . That's where you heard your voice. . . ."

"I heard it. . . . Didn't sound like this."

"Of course not. But come on, you remember we sat here and talked together. Who the devil's voice would it be that could talk so knowingly about things that only you could know . . . ? No point in trying to round on that. . . ."

"Not tryin' to round. How you know about my bein' mad?"

"That's no great mystery. You could hear it on the tape. . . . And I'm sure you felt that you'd been too honest in talking about what you had done. . . ."

"Yeah, when I went downstairs las' time . . . I think: 'Oh, Jesus. . . . Oh, Jesus. . . . Kee' my mouth shut.' "

"Okay. . . . It's done. . . . It's over. What do you think now?"

"That's my voice . . . my voice."

"It didn't impress you?"

He stared at the recorder. I primed the pump again: "What didn't you like about that voice?"

"Didn't sound like me."

"How do you sound to yourself, Gerard?"

"How do I sound to myself? I know . . . like me . . . me."

"Do you recall in the tape where you spoke of what you had to do in order to get your money for heroin? Do you recall when you said that you were a mugger?"

"Yeap."

"Who would you mug?"

"Who?"

"Yes, what kind of victim would you pick out? Me, for example? Would I be a likely victim . . . ?"

He uttered some kind of sound in his throat, one he had not used before: "You too big; look like cop. . . ."

"So you carefully size up your intended victim. It's not just a spontaneous thing. You don't just pick anybody."

"You crazy, man? Pick 'em out. . . ."

"But not me . . . not somebody like me?"

"Old man or woman, drunk . . . or small guy. . . ."

"You do it alone . . . ? You mug alone?"

"Me an' this kid who got the blood poisonin'. . . ."

"Would you assault the victim?"

"Assault . . . knock him out. . . . Has to, otherwise yell, an' get caught. . . ."

"You might have killed someone that way, Gerard—an older person with a bad heart or just scared to death by the attack. . . . You might have been guilty of murder."

"Mighta been caught. . . . Coulda got caught. . . ."

"You knew that at the time . . . ?"

"Every time . . . every time. . . . You break into a place, you boostin' in the store. . . . You ain't sure but what they's waitin' there with a gun to shoot you, or waitin' with a knife. . . . You ain't knowin' that maybe las' week they wus knocked over by somebody else an' now they's waitin' fer you. . . ."

"But that never stopped you, that fear?"

"Fear, what you mean . . . ? You gotta use your head, otherwise you gets swung. . . ."

"The violence never bothered you . . . beating or whipping . . . blood . . . pain . . . ?"

"Whatcha sayin' . . . ?"

"Did you ever get hurt as a result of one of these muggings?"

"Me hurt by a muggin' . . . ? Got kicked in the head. . . . Old guy but wus rough. . . ."

"Did you knock him out finally . . . ?"

"Run away. . . . He's too tough. . . . Little guy, and ol' too. . . ."

"Why would you take such chances, Gerard? You wanted to get busted . . . you wanted to get killed?"

"Didn't wanna get sick. . . ."

"And you had been sick so much . . . that you knew you had to feed your habit . . . ?"

"I been sick. . . . Didn't wanna get sick. . . ."

"But how sick were you that you would be able to conquer your fear of arrest or injury . . . ?"

"Get sick. . . ."

"How sick were you at your worst?"

"Threw up dry. . . . Back hurts and nose runs and my ear hurts . . . an' your head . . . and you aches and aches. . . ."

"And that's enough to make you go out and knock down an elderly person, perhaps cripple them or kill them . . . ?"

"Don't wanna get sick. . . ."

"But you never got that sick. . . ."

His anger poured out unchecked: "How in fuckin' hell you know, man? You ever strung out?"

I looked at him and waited. . . . I could see him withdraw, the anger vanish, the imperturbable mask return. . . . If he had been swallowed up by some impenetrable undergrowth, he could not have disappeared more completely.

"Gerard, I'll bet that you were mostly afraid of getting sick, not because you had ever really been that sick, but because you had heard about the sickness and you had in your mind a fear of it. . . . In your mind. . . ."

After a long pause he said: "It's there. . . . You worries about it. . . ."

"Heroin changes everything, doesn't it . . . ? It lies about everything. . . . It makes you different than you really are as a person. . . . It even makes you think that you're different than you really are."

"Whatcha talkin' about . . . ? How it makes me different . . . ?"

"Most addicts will admit that the sickness is mostly in their minds. Those times that they have been sick haven't been all that bad. . . . What they want is the high, the detachment, that feeling of being at peace with themselves. You want the heroin to block other things that you feel about yourself. And it gets harder and harder to feel that high the longer you use. It gets harder and harder to feel that old euphoria. . . . So you keep increasing your dosage all the time. . . . Heroin is a liar. . . ."

"Don't wanna git sick. . . . Nobody wants to git sick. . . ."

"So it's better to take a chance on killing or being killed than to get sick?"

"The things I wus doin' . . . I guesses so. . . ." And he suddenly stopped. I waited quietly. After a time he resumed: "Yeah, you wants to git high, but you don't wants to git sick, neither. . . ."

"So you're really reckless about yourself. You'd do anything to get the high and avoid the sickness?"

"Wouldn't shoot nobody. . . ."

"You draw the line there. . . . Why?"

"Cops got guns. . . . You one guy. . . . In two seconds they's ten cops, ten guns, six rounds, sixty bullets. I seen them cut a guy up. . . . Blow his head right off. Like a water fountain in the park the blood come out. . . ."

"You never used a gun?"

"No, man. . . . I had a gun . . . twenty-two, fixed up. . . ."

"It was altered so that you could fire a heavier bullet . . . ?"

He glared at me suspiciously and then looked at the machine. There was silence.

"Boy, you know, your mother did you a real favor by ratting you out, by passing you over to the cops. And you were right last time when you said that you would be killed. . . . Yeah, you might have been dead by now. You're a real uptight guy. . . . Did your mother know that you were mugging?"

"Nope."

"You don't know. . . . You're just saying that. She knew that you were swiping things from the house to buy junk. . . ."

"How you know that?"

"You said so. . . ."

"Me . . . me . . . ?"

"Just a minute, I'll put last month's tape on and let you hear yourself tell it. . . ."

"Shit."

"Are you a liar . . . ? Were you rounding on me? Is that it . . . ? So you never swiped from your house. . . . You were putting on an image with me . . . ? Playin' the game . . . ?"

He cut right across what I said. He understood immediately. "It was true. . . . I swiped from the house. . . ."

"Would you have beaten them out of their welfare check?"

"Whatcha mean?"

I dropped it. "The police beat up your father, you said."

"They did. . . . Beat him good. Dropped him on the stones. . . . In the hospital, he left blood all over. . . ."

"That didn't bother you . . . ?"

"Whatcha mean?"

"I mean you were accustomed to that. . . . Right? You selected old men and women to mug. You knocked them down or kicked them or opened them up. . . . Your father would have been an ideal victim for you. He had all the qualifications: old, sick, help-less."

He didn't stir. It was his glance that was savage. It escaped from him. He could have killed me in that moment. That was his response. That one eye was way out of focus. He rose from his chair. "Whatcha doin' to me?"

I said softly: "How many bags did you need just before you came in, to keep you from getting sick?" No answer. "I'll bet you were using five or six at a time. I bet your habit was growing by leaps and bounds." Still no answer. He stood over by the window with its fine, steel-meshed screen. "You know, you're very different from most addicts I've known, Gerard. . . . Most of them are not violent people. Oh, they beat you out of every dollar, or they'll game you out of everything you own, but they shy away from vio-lence. . . . They always puff themselves up. . . . They always have to give you a story. Their mother or father or wife or husband or school experience. . . . That's why they shoot dope. . . . Now you're different. You're honest . . . and you're violent. . . . Maybe . . . just consider it for a minute . . . maybe, Gerard, you went to heroin not because of the high, not because of the sickness, but be-cause you knew that you were violent, and you knew that you were too honest. . . ."

He turned around and came back to his seat, his brow furrowed. "Whatcha sayin' . . . ?"

"Perhaps you used heroin to overcome your problems. Problems of violence and honesty. . . ."

"I got no problems."

"Would you like a smoke?" No response. I lighted mine. "Are you having group therapy these days?"

By now he had seated himself again. The same old air of watchful menace.

"I'm sure that in group therapy they ask you questions, try to pull your cover. What do you tell them?"

"Nothin'."

"Well, that tells them something. . . ."

"What?"

"Tells them that you can't talk, or won't talk, or you have too much to hide, or you're ashamed of the way you talk, or you're too mad to talk. . . . It tells them a lot when you won't talk. It just proves what I said about your honesty. Have you tried to take a poke out of anybody yet?"

"Whatcha sayin'?"

"Haven't you had a fight with anybody yet?"

"Nah. . . . I ain't fightin' here."

"So they don't really know what you're like yet, do they? Have you learned anything about them from the sessions . . . ?"

"Learn about them . . . ?" It was odd the way he repeated. "Bunch a liars. . . ."

"What do they lie about?"

"Everythin'."

"That's a sweeping accusation. Everything? So you won't tell them about yourself and your problems because you can't trust them, that it?"

"Not talkin' to them 'bout nothin'. I got no problems."

"What's your group leader like?"

"Group leader . . . mean the staff . . . ? It's a girl. . . ."

"Ah, it's a woman group leader. . . ."

"No, it's a girl . . . young girl, big mouth . . . Mrs. Chalmers. . . . Big mouth. She's a liar. . . ."

"Because she told you something about yourself? Or she indicated that you couldn't get out of this program until you began to participate in group therapy . . . ?"

"All of 'em tells stories . . . lies. . . . They bounces things offa you. . . . They cries and yells. . . . Like a bunch of faggots. . . . Liars. . . ."

"Not going to bounce anything off you, are they? You'll show them they can't game you. You'll bust them in the mouth. . . . Her, too, if they try. . . ."

"Whatcha talkin' about . . . ?"

"Have you heard from your folks since you've been here?"

"Saw 'em last week. Visitin' day."

"Your mother and father? I should think it's hard for your father to get around. . . . Must mean that you're very important to them if they come and visit you."

"Father shakes, like he's drunk. . . . Should stay home."

"Please you that they came?"

"Talks about the baby and the other kids. . . . Baby wus sick. . . ."

"What do you feel about their visiting you? Does it prove to you that they really care about you . . . ? That your mother had you arrested because she wanted you to be helped?"

"I wanna go home."

"So you can go back to heroin?"

"Ain't gonna. . . . Gonna try to stay off. . . ."

"But you haven't changed any. What chance would you have of staying off stuff? You don't know why you went on so you can hardly stay off it. Nothing new in your life. You've just been out of circulation for a few weeks. You been laying up. . . . Your first bag when you go out will give you a beautiful high. . . . That's what you're thinking of."

"Whatcha sayin?"

"You know, you're not as talkative this time as you were the first time. And I think that's because you're really letting your anger show now. . . . I think you're really letting your hostility show. . . ."

"I don't talk. . . ."

"So what's that prove? Your face talks, your eyes, your body, the way you got your feet planted. . . . You talk but you don't realize it. . . . And I'll tell you something: after a while you're going to be surprised and proud to discover how well you can really talk. . . ."

"Pfuhhh."

"You may even admit that this place can do something for you."

"Make me mad. . . ."

"That's because it's getting to you and you're too honest to disguise it. . . ."

"Got no problems. . . ."

"Why did you use heroin?"

"Problems didn't make me use dope. Me an' my cousin wus hangin' together and he had some, and it was new, so I tried it on and he skinned me and. . . ."

"And you enjoyed it."

"Whatcha say?"

"You liked what the high did for you because you felt like you never felt before. Why was that? Because you never felt good about yourself without wine or reefer or junk. So why should this be . . . ? Because you have some ideas about yourself or some experience with yourself that makes you down-rate yourself or something. You're mad at yourself first, and then at me, and then at everybody else. . . . You're just like a raccoon in the spring: hungry, grouchy, willing to bite at a broom handle because you feel so damned miserable inside. . . ."

"Whatcha saying, raccoon . . . ?"

I lighted a cigarette slowly. "Yes, I see great changes on the horizon for you. This program is definitely going to help you. . . ."

"Shit."

"All this is on the tape, you know." I watched the subtle but almost imperceptible change on his face as he understood what I said. "So even if you don't come next time . . . I have two pieces of you. . . . Two pieces of you—this tape and the one last time. . . . Outside yourself. . . . Two pieces of you." The tape ran off the reel. "I'll see you next time."

His jawbone twitched; that eye was unfocused; his chunky

figure moved slowly toward the door. He stood there for a moment, his hand going through his blond hair. "I got nothin' the matter with me. . . . This program ain't gonna do nothin' for me. . . ."

"Thank you. . . . I'll see you next time."

Downstairs, I stopped in Stoner's office but he was at a meeting. I left him a note: "Darrell, check Gerard's file. See if there's anything in it about hearing problems. Also check for record of eye damage. Suggest he have a thorough eye and ear examination. Thanks."

When I got to the airport, I learned that my flight had been canceled because of mechanical problems with the ship. It had been re-posted for departure in three hours. I checked my baggage and equipment and grabbed a cab back to town. I had Gerard's address.

I walked those streets in the full sunlight of a midwestern autumn. The air was clear. Nature had played every enchantment, but she could not soften the excrescence, the abomination. I observed a policeman, his uniform unpressed, his shirt less than clean, his air demoralized—another captive of the culture. I had seen Dresden in the days when it was torched; I had seen London under the same circumstances. But this city had not been under bombardment. . . .

3

He was wearing glasses. You could see that he was not used to them yet by the way his hands periodically wandered to the bows. Typical of most institutional issue, to ignore anything of an individual nature: since Gerard was fair, the frames of the glasses were dark and massive. With his short blond hair and broad face, he looked like some precocious genius. But behind the glasses his anger simmered. . . . It had become obvious; no one could mistake it now. It was an accepted part of him, like the color of his eyes, the shape of his head, the line of his nose.

"You look very distinguished this morning, Gerard."

"Distinguished? How dya mean?"

"Those glasses."

"Don't like 'em. They pulls my head down."

"Well, I guess you haven't gotten used to them yet. They change your appearance."

"Change my appearance. . . . My eye is weak. . . . They 'xamined-ed it. . . . Pulls other way. . . ."

"You have to wear them all the time?"

"Yeap. . . ."

"Do you read any more now than you used to?"

"Nope. . . . The same. . . . Use two eyes now . . . 'sonly difference. . . ."

"What do you like to read?"

"Space comics . . . other stuff. . . ."

"Other stuff, huh?"

"Likes to read . . . read everythin'. . . ."

"Well, I think the glasses look great on you."

He dismissed that with a snort and glared at the tape machine. "Do you suppose that you didn't like school maybe because you couldn't see properly?"

"Whatcha say? Couldn't see school. . . . Didn't go."

"I know you said that you were a truant. . . . Don't be so alarmed. You said that yourself in the course of our interview. . . ." I selected a cigarette with studied deliberation. He was watching my hands. He wanted a smoke so badly. But I didn't offer. Instead, I placed the pack on top of the recorder; all he had to do was to reach. Suddenly he began to fiddle with his glasses.

"Do you suppose that you do things and say that you do them for reasons that are not so . . . ?"

His brow furrowed. . . . He had followed what I said. . . . After a while he muttered, with that flat tonelessness: "Ain't no liar. . . ."

"Of course not. I didn't say you were. I wasn't trying to insult you. Do you remember last time, we just heard it repeated on the tape a moment ago, last time you said that you didn't think that it was your voice . . . you didn't recognize it. . . ."

"Rekanize it? My voice. . . ."

"Now, it was your voice, so you just weren't familiar with it, you never had a reason to become aware of it. I wonder if there are not other things that you do that you are not familiar with, or things that you do that you assign reasons to that are not accurate. . . . Like your reason for not going to school. . . . Is it possible that you played hooky from school because you had trouble with your eyes?"

He clenched his teeth and shook his head incredulously. "I don't even know why I comes up here, why I keeps comin' up here. . . ."

Very pedantically I said: "It's possible that Gerard is almost a total stranger to himself. For instance, I think that you'll discover as you go on listening to yourself talk on these tapes that your speech will change, your words, your attitude . . . many things will change. I'll bet you, when I play you back the first tape we made together, you'll be astonished at the contrast."

"Why, huh?"

"Because of the tremendous difference that will be apparent to you. . . . To you. . . . You're no dumbbell, Gerard. You're a real bright guy, but you don't want anybody to know that. . . . So I'm just throwing this out. . . . I don't care if you credit it or if you scoff at it. I'll bet you that so much of what you've done in your sixteen years just happened, like a reflex, just a reaction, like a guy pulling his hand away from a hot stove. . . ."

"Hot stove. . . . Whatcha mean?"

"You just react, you don't catch what you're doing. Remember, you said that you were always running? What is that but reacting . . . ? No, I think that you're going to be very surprised about what you learn about yourself. . . . Really, I do. I think the glasses are a great beginning. . . ."

"Look like a faggot. . . ."

I ignored the remark. "For instance: You're madder than hell right now. Before, you used to hide it pretty well. . . . But now you don't try and hide it. . . . You're madder than hell at me, I guess. . . . Why . . . ? What have I said . . . ? Just for your own sake . . . why should you be so mad at me . . . ?"

"I don't like you. . . ."

"I see. . . . My face. . . ."

With animation, he pointed toward the spinning reels on the machine: "I don't like that. . . . Why everythin' got to be put on tape . . . huh?"

"To remember what we say."

"For why?"

"Because we find it convenient to forget most times."

"I jus' don't like comin' up here. Gotta go to group, gotta come here. Why I gotta go to both?"

"So you're getting a double dose, is that it . . . ? Have you told them in the group that you'd like to split from them?"

"Split from them. . . . I can't. . . . I gotta go there. . . . Gotta do it. . . ."

"And you don't know why? Really, you know, that's somehow in keeping with your whole life. Most everything about you is unknown. . . . For once, that machine is capturing some of what you say, revealing the way you say it, suggesting certain clues. . . . And you're scared of that."

"Scared. . . ." His eyes behind those glasses narrowed with hatred. "Why I got to do this?"

"You've been hiding and running all of your life. And you say that you don't lie . . . you say that you're honest. . . . But like everything else about you, maybe that's not so. . . . What do you know for sure about yourself . . . absolutely for sure?"

"I don't lie."

"What will that tape do to you?"

"Why I gotta have this an' group?"

"You talking these days in group therapy?"

"Nope."

"So you can lay back? Really, Gerard, look at it in this way. You tell me you have no problems. . . ."

"Didn't say that. . . . Didn't use drugs on accounta I gotta problem. . . ."

"Yes, that's exactly what you said. You used drugs because you liked them. . . . Heroin made you feel good."

"Ain't gonna use it no more."

"But why not . . . ?"

"Don't like the changes makes me go through."

"Like being busted, like stealing from your house, like having to talk."

"Ain't gonna use 'em."

"How can you say that?"

"I don't lie. You want me to say I ain't, but I don't know until I gets out on the street. . . ."

"Can't you say that you don't know . . . ? Because that's the whole purpose in your mother having you committed to this program . . . so that you can find out why you went to drugs so that you'll be able to stay off them."

"I got no problems. . . . My mother . . . she don't know. . . ."

"She doesn't . . . know you?"

He considered that. "She knows me. . . ."

"Of course she does. . . . She wanted to get you help."

"Why . . . ? Why she put me here, huh?"

"Why did you get glasses?"

"This place ain't gonna do nothin' for me."

"It's done something for you already. . . ." I said casually.

"Whatcha say? Made me mad. . . ."

"Made you mad, got you a pair of glasses, made you hear your own voice, made you stop for a while, made you clean up. . . . Big changes I'd say."

"Yeap. . . . You'd say. . . ."

"In the three months that we've been talking together, I've seen you change visibly."

"How?"

"Your face. It's gotten longer. The skin seems clearer; before, it was puffy and all broken out. You hold your head up now. . . ."

"Hah. . . ." I can't capture the guttural quality of his utterance, but there was no mistaking his derision.

"Yes, you've changed, Gerard. . . ."

"Lot you know. . . ."

"And you'll change even more. . . . I said *you* will change . . . because it's going to be *you* that does it. . . . For example, I'm sure that you're hung up right now trying to understand why you should be feeling two ways about the same thing when before you never thought about it at all. Take heroin, for instance. . . . Your cousin introduced you to it. You burglarized and shoplifted and stole from your home to support your habit. . . . You did these things for what reason? You liked the high. That was it. Everything else you had to do to gain that feeling was secondary. . . . But now what's happened? You can remember the high. . . . You still enjoy that in your mind. . . . But something else has happened. You've discovered what you have to do in order to get high: steal, burglarize, mug, shoplift, maybe get busted, lose your freedom. . . . You've learned that yourself. So you have a choice now. To go back out and start all over again with the cooker. . . . That means, no matter how clever you are, you'll be caught sometime or killed or locked away for years. . . . Not so simple now. You've been tainted with thinking. . . . You've had to think. . . . No matter how you slice it now, no matter what you say to me . . . you have yourself to think about now. You went to heroin out of curiosity. Okay. But now you are left with the sneaking suspicion that there's something very curious about you for having that kind of curiosity. That's why you dread that machine, because it echoes you, it throws you back at you. . . . No, you've changed, Gerard, you've changed. . . . You're even thinking at this very moment about how to defend yourself against what I've said. . . . Don't bother. . . . You'll have it playing back in your head tonight on the ward as you lie there trying to get to sleep."

I lighted a cigarette.

"All my life I'm gonna like stuff . . . not that I'm gonna use it. . . . But all my life I'm gonna like stuff."

"Most exaddicts say the same thing."

"They's liars, them junkies."

"But you're not."

"I ain't."

"You broke into places, and you were scared doing it. You stole from your own family, and you were troubled by it. . . . That's coming from two ways at the same time. . . . Now you know that. . . . Can a guy come from two ways at the same time for very long, Gerard? And still say just what you've said, that you're not a liar?"

"All dependeds on the fella . . . I guesses. . . ."

"Not sure, though? Now, I suppose, another thing you could say is that drugs were all through your neighborhood."

"True. . . ."

"But you were using wine before pot or pills or junk. . . . That was because of the neighborhood, too. . . ."

"They wus there. . . ."

"So, no matter what was in the neighborhood, purple pictures or golden bells or pink garbage cans, whatever was there, Gerard would have used?"

"Whatcha say . . . ?"

"I'm saying that, no matter what, Gerard had to have something. . . . By himself he was nothing, so he had to have something . . . ?"

"Shit. . . . You's tryin' to bounce me offa them walls. . . ."

"Am I?"

"I try drugs and I liked-ed 'em."

"I believe you."

"Liked-ed 'em. But I didn't like them changes they put me through. . . ."

"What changes?"

He glared at me. "You jus' said 'em. . . ."

I brushed some ashes from my shirt. "Now you have glasses. . . . You see better, differently. . . ."

He interrupted: "I got glasses. . . ."

"I wonder, if you'd had glasses, if you would have stayed in school. . . ."

"Nope. . . . Too borin'. . . ."

"Stupid stuff, huh? Or were you stupid?"

That was beneath his contempt. He turned away ever so slightly; he didn't want to give the impression that he was yielding. "I could do the things. . . ."

"But you couldn't see well. . . . So how could you read well?"

"I read better with one eye 'n you with two. . . . Could read. . . ."

"And hear what was being said . . . ?"

"Hear. . . . Hear. . . . Jerky teachers. . . ."

"And not talk when you were called on?"

"Why talk . . . ? Stupid stuff. . . . Too borin'. . . ."

"I agree with you. . . . But these are the things that made you drop out. . . ."

"Why not . . . ? Get a job. . . ."

"Sure. . . . You got a job. . . . You had a number of them, right? You had to. . . . You had a thirty-dollar-a-day habit to feed. . . . You had to have jobs. . . ."

"I always work hard, even when I wus a kid. . . ."

"Is that so?"

"I wus a good worker. . . ."

I stirred in my chair. He watched me very alertly and then said, as if he hadn't been interrupted: "I like to work. . . . I works here. . . ."

"But you don't talk. . . ."

"I talks. . . ."

"To whom?"

"Whom. . . . Whom I talks?"

"Yeah. Have you any friends?"

"Sure. . . ."

"How many?"

"Five, six."

"And you've told them about yourself, the way you've told me . . . ?"

"Didn't ask me. . . ."

"I see. They haven't asked you the right questions, otherwise you would have told them about yourself. . . ."

"They didn't asked-ed. . . ."

"Did your mother or father ever ask you questions . . . ?"

"Sure. . . . Whatcha think?"

"Questions like what? About school, or your eyes, or what you were doing . . . ?"

"All kindsa questions. . . ."

"I'll bet you had a lot of fights in school. . . ."

"Yeap."

"With the teachers, too. . . ."

"Yeap."

"Those would be fist fights, right?"

"Yeap. . . ."

"Why would you have to fight with a teacher . . . ?"

"They wus stupid. . . . Put you on the enda the line. . . . Makin' up things . . . liars. . . ."

"So your mother would have to come to school a lot and listen to the complaints about you. . . . Must have been embarrassing. . . . Especially with all your friends knowing about it. . . ."

"She had all 'em kids to take care-a. Make her come to school. . . . Make her come down and see 'em creeps. . . ."

"Would she believe the teachers when they complained about you?"

"Sure. . . . I didn't lie. I punch 'em. . . . I didn't lie. . . ."

"What would happen . . . then?"

"Git hit. . . ."

"By your mother or your father?"

"Father can't . . . shakes too much. She hit me. . . . Her face get all red, and she yell and cry and puff. . . ."

There was a pause. I asked, "What's going to happen to you, Gerard?"

"Goin' home, get a job, go to school, get married."

"Is that so? Now, you continually remind me that you're honest. . . . May I ask if what you've just said is not something that you've picked up from therapy groups you've been going to?"

"I heard it . . . there . . . but I thought 'bout it on my own. . . . They jus' talk about problems. . . ."

"And that doesn't apply to you because you have no problems . . . ?"

"I don't got that kinda problem. . . ."

"Oh. . . . Now I'm confused. . . . Maybe I don't understand what you mean by problem. Maybe it's the meaning of that word that's got me hung up. What do you mean by problem?"

"That's a word they uses here. Problem. . . ."

"Yeah, I get you. But what does it mean to them when they use it?"

"Somethin' that's botherin' you."

"And that's not what problem means to you?"

"Somethin' that's in a math book."

"A problem is something you find in a math book. . . . And it is something that can be solved or has an answer, is that it?"

"Yeap. Somethin' that can be solved. . . ."

"So, if this is your meaning of problem, what do you call what they're talking about . . . ?"

"Means somethin' botherin' you . . . like mental. . . ."

"So, since you say that you didn't go to drugs because anything was bothering you. . . ."

"I didn't have no problem. . . ."

"Does the group agree with your point of view, that you don't have a problem . . . ?"

His shoulders lifted; it was almost a shrug. "I don't talk. . . ."

"Well, in that case, they for sure feel that you have a problem. . . ."

"Whatcha say . . . ? How . . . ?"

"If a guy doesn't talk . . . why not? What's he hiding, is he scared, is he gaming, is he laying up? Oh sure, they've got you figured as a guy with a problem. . . . You're meat to them."

He gave me a keen, searching look.

"Though you don't talk in group therapy, I guess you must listen to what others say. Do you think any of those guys have problems . . . in the way they use the word?"

"Yeap. Plenty."

"For instance. . . ."

"They's all different. . . ."

"Like what?"

"Trouble. They's havin' trouble at home. The wives and the kids. . . . Or with they mothers. . . . Or with the schools or the cops. . . . Hangups. . . ."

"Do they ever mention anything that rings a bell with you?"

"Whatcha say, rings a bell . . . ?"

"Do they say things that mean anything to you . . . seem familiar . . . ?"

"You mean, relate?"

I nearly fell off my chair. I had all I could do to repress my smile. "Yes, that's the precise word that I was looking for, relate. Thank you. Do you find yourself relating to anything that they say?"

"Can relate to a helluva lotta things. . . ."

"Such as?"

"Can relate to a lotta dudes and what they's sayin'. Like girl problems and mother problems. She don't got no time. . . . I can't bring it out right now 'xactly. . . ."

"You'd rather not."

"Can't remember."

"But you never lie, so it must be that it wasn't important enough for you to remember?"

"Yeap."

"Or perhaps it made you so uncomfortable that you've just blocked it out . . . the way heroin would block out things for you so that you could rap with girls or look at television or go to the pool hall. . . ."

"Jus' the whole thing. Bein' here. . . . Goin' to group. Confined. Talkin' to that . . ." and he pointed, "machine." He let his hand down. "Why I gotta come to two places . . . jus' me, huh?"

"Do you talk to your counselor? She's a girl, you said the last time."

"Woman. . . . I talks to her. . . ."

"What do you say?"

" 'Hello' and 'So long.' "

"You don't talk to her the way you do here?"

"She don't asked-ed the questions. . . ."

"And you wouldn't bring anything up yourself . . . ? You don't have any hesitation in correcting me or telling me that you don't like me. . . . Why don't you tell her what you feel? What's the difference?"

"Whatcha sayin'? Difference. Don't understand you. . . ."

"Why do you hold back so?"

"Hold back?"

"Yeah, what're you ashamed of? You're a bright guy. You've got ideas, opinions. . . . Why are you hanging back in group therapy? What have you got to lose?"

"Hang back?"

"You complain about having to go to group therapy and coming here to talk as well. What difference does it make? You're here in this facility. You're not going to lose anything if you have to go to three extra appointments. You can't leave. I mean, are you losing something by talking to a person? What's it costing you?"

"Ain't costin' me nothin'. I jus' don't like the idea. . . ."

"What's the idea that you don't like?"

"I jus' don't like it."

"As a guy, you just don't like to talk . . . or to be talked with?"

"One of the things is I don't like to have everythin', you know, goin' on that there tape . . . I don' jus' dig it no matter what you says. . . ."

"But they don't have a tape recorder in group therapy session, do they? You don't participate there either. . . . Puzzling, isn't it?" Somewhere outside someone was being paged over the loudspeaker system. "You listened to the tape being played back a little while ago. What did you think about that guy?"

"It wus me. . . ."

"Right, it was you. But it was outside of you. You could hear yourself as you sounded and thought a month ago. What did you think of him . . . ? Listening to that voice, you got ideas about that guy? For example: Did you feel he was a very suspicious man?"

"Suspicious . . . like I shouldn't trus' him?"

"Right. . . ."

"I trusteds myself. . . ."

"Then why are you so suspicious of talking and having your words recorded?"

"I jus' don' like the idea. . . ."

"What idea?"

"I don't know. . . ."

"You don't lie, you say. But you do cop out, and are you copping out right now . . . ? You're scared that in some way what you say is going to be used against you."

"Why you should talk to me, huh? Why you should talk to me? Why, man? What's it to you, why you should listen to me, huh?"

"Perhaps I'm interested in you. . . . Perhaps I feel that you should be interested in yourself and that maybe the only way to get you interested in yourself is to make you hear yourself. . . ."

"Yeah. . . . Why, man . . . ? Whatcha say . . . ?"

"I say that you were given glasses so that you could see better. Maybe you need glasses inside yourself to see better, too. Maybe you don't see things as they really are. . . ."

"Huh, glasses inside myself. . . . What's that? How . . . ?"

"Is it possible that your ideas about school, about your neighborhood, or your family . . . are not quite accurate? I mean your father was. . . ."

"He wus a porter . . . 'fore he got Parkinson's disease. . . ."

"That's exactly what I mean. . . . I could put on that tape we made together weeks ago and let you listen to how you pronounced your father's sickness. You said 'Parker's,' and just this second you said 'Parkinson's disease.' How many other things about you are you mispronouncing, misreading . . . ?"

Gerard shifted in his chair, cleared his throat, didn't say anything, but his eyes betrayed his evident absorption.

"Did your cousin have things that bothered him?" The sudden shift renewed his suspiciousness. "You know, things like family . . . girls, school . . . ?"

"Some troubles . . . I guesses. Didn't go to school neither. . . . But it come in the neighborhood, and he tried it and he liked-ed it, and he brought it to me. He tol' me it wus nice. So I tried it. . . . But same as me, he jus' fell into it . . . jus' like me. . . ."

"And he was mugging and burglarizing and shoplifting?"

"No. Not him. . . ."

"Why not?"

"He had a allowance. . . ."

"An allowance from his parents, is that it? That wasn't like you. Perhaps he wasn't like you in many ways."

"Nah, he wasn't like me. Had a room. . . . Went to school."

"Where is he now?"

"Out on the street."

"He has a habit?"

"Nope. . . . He stopped. . . ."

"Lousy break. He introduced you to heroin, and now he's stopped and you're in here. . . . You got the stick. . . . He had a lot of influence on you?"

"Whatcha say, influence . . . ?"

"He could make you do things. . . ."

"Nah, only if I wanna do 'em. . . . We went our separate ways."

"You went your separate ways?"

"We had to do our thing. . . ."

"I understand, and doing your thing was mugging, breaking into places, shoplifting, getting a heroin habit, and ending up here having to talk to me. . . . What a terrible punishment. . . . Me and that machine. . . ."

He frowned, glowered at me . . . and almost seemed to be repeating to himself what I just finished saying to him. I smiled at him. He smiled back—if I hadn't been watching, I would have missed it. But he had smiled. Two of his front teeth were missing.

"They couldn't find anything wrong with his hearing, Frank Michael."

"There's something the matter with that kid's hearing, I tell you, Darrell." I smoked my cigarette. "Talk to him for a minute . . . it's obvious. He's always straining to catch. . . ."

"I don't have time for private consultations. . . . I'm happy to keep the city fathers off my back for two minutes. I have to save all of my energy and listening for them. . . ." He reached over and nervously grabbed my cigarettes. His hand shook as he lighted one. "What a bunch of nervous nellies. It's all political. They're so God-damned scared to have these addicts in one place. Always scared that they'll break out. Never occurs to them what a menace they are out on the street." He exhaled a cloud of smoke. "You were right about the glasses, though. The left eye was pretty damaged."

"What's he like in program?"

He dug through a pyramid of papers. "I don't know where the damned evaluation sheets are. Next time, I'll have it for you. . . ." He got up and looked at a chart pasted on the wall. "Gerard, Gerard, Gerard," he repeated under his breath. "Yeah, he's got Ursula for a counselor. Maybe she's twenty-one, right out of school, wears mini-mini's. . . . How do you make her understand that she'll get raped one of these days, dangling that ass of hers around in front of these guys . . . ?" He sat down, puffing on the cigarette. "I got a meeting, Frank Michael. . . . Next month, I'll check it out for you."

"All right, Darrell."

"That is, I will if I'm still here. . . ."

"I wish you could have his hearing checked again. . . ."

"So long, Frank Michael . . . so long. . . ."

"And while you're at it, could you have his teeth looked at . . . ? Okay, I'm on my way. . . ."

"Why don't you ask me to get Jesus Christ to work with him?"

4

His mouth appeared less pinched, especially the upper lip; this took away the ravening look from his face, that lean and hungry ferocity. Slowly, as if his tongue were timid, he licked his lips.

"Does your mouth hurt you?"

"Yeap."

"Been punched there?"

"Punched. Why I should be punched . . . ?"

The flatness in his speech was altered by an almost imperceptible variation.

"I beg your pardon for saying that. What happened to your
mouth to make it sore?"

"They's fixin' my teeth. . . ." Gerard grimaced to prove his
point. "They's put three of them in there."

"I tell you, what with your glasses. . . . Brother, when you start
to smile . . . watch out, world. . . ." And I laughed. "Why are
they doing all this, Gerard?"

He frowned, deliberated, and then said: "I don't know yet. . . .
Must be some reason they got."

"Your teeth are beautiful. . . . Besides, they're more than deco-
ration, it means you can chew better. And you can see better. Why
aren't you growling at me this morning?"

"Whatcha say?"

"You don't seem mad at me this morning . . . or you're conceal-
ing it. . . ."

"I ain't mad today. . . ."

"You were last month and the month before and the month before that. . . . Have you taken some pills?"

"Pills. . . . Whatcha say, pills . . . ?"

"Pills, nice pills, pills you take to become good humored.
Forgive me, I'm teasing you. . . ."

"Teasing me. . . . Kidding me. . . ." He smiled. "Used to have
a attitude. . . ."

"Yes, you mentioned that before. . . . So that's gone now or
changed . . . ?"

He shrugged, his face grave. "I guesses, I jus' accepts it. . . ."

"This program. . . . What they're trying to do for you and others who depend on drugs. . . ."

"I ain't looked into that too tough. . . . But no point in fightin'
a losin' battle. . . . It's a losin' battle. . . ." He peered at me, his
glasses giving his face a studious expression.

"In the four months that you've been here, you've been thrown together with a number of other guys. Now, I know that there's very little that goes on around you that you don't see and recall. . . . Have they changed much?"

"Works like this. . . . Some do it, like, change, 'cause lot of 'em has done time before. . . . All of 'em been busted before. Me, I ain't never been busted before. . . . They's used to, you know, bein' locked up. . . . It ain't the bein' locked up, neither. . . . It's the idea of bein' locked up. . . . You know. . . . You goes to the door, like, you ain't thinkin' none . . . and the door, it don't open. . . . Locked. . . . You can't move it. . . . And when you tries, the staff they looks at you. . . . They thinks you want to bust out. . . . It's the idea. . . . The lock-up by itself ain't nothing. . . ."

"So it seems more and more as if your mother did you a great service by turning you in. . . ."

He grunted and stared at the floor: "Hummmmm. . . . Don't know 'bout that. . . ."

"You wouldn't even have dignified my comment with a response a month ago. . . . You would have stared bullets at me. What're you doing these days?"

"Whatcha say? Doing . . . ?"

"You go to group. . . . Are you going to school?"

"They's got school. I go. . . ."

"Boring?"

"Ain't boring. . . . I liked-ed school. . . . Too noisy. . . ."

"You mean here, or when you were going to school at home it was too noisy . . . ?"

"Here. These damned guys jus' fool aroun'. They's smart when they talks but they's stupid when it comes to books. So they figgers, by makin' hosses' asses outta theirselves, then you won't catch that they can't read no good. . . . I catches them. They puts on a image . . . but they's stupid. . . . I tells 'em."

"That should make you popular. . . ."

"Whatcha say . . . popular . . . ?" He snorted. "They can't say it ain't so. I don't lie. . . . See, they's old. I'm sixteen, so I'm okay to go to school, but them guys they's eighteen, one guy is even twenty-eight. . . . Like, you know, they ain't got no call to go to school. . . ."

"So you're enjoying school?"

"I likes it . . . passes the time. . . . But I likes the problems . . . I likes to work on them problems. Big book with a blue cover, an' it's got like a big bird on the front. I likes them problems. . . . Teacher can't see how I can figger 'em out. . . . I does it in my head, real quick. Zing, I get the answer, then I looks at the back of the book. I gets the answer but I didn't do it like they say. . . . Teacher says I gotta learn their way, otherwise I don't understan'. I don't gets that but I'll learn it. . . ." He shrugged.

"Have some guys been going home, Gerard?"

"Yeap."

"For good?"

"Some fer good, some on passes. I could get a pass."

"You mean for a couple of days, to visit your home?"

"To visit your home," he repeated. "Right. . . . I cou' get that kind of thing."

For some reason, the public address system that linked all the rooms and corridors together was incredibly loud this day. The room we recorded in rang with the call. . . . It boomed out again. . . .

Gerald offered: "I kin axe 'em to let me go out on a pass."

"You mean you just have to ask . . . ? You mean, the staff?" I brought out my cigarettes . . . but I didn't offer them to him. I watched him observing my hands. He made no attempt to conceal his open scrutiny. "Or are you saying that you ask your group therapy session . . . ?"

"Group, you axe. . . . There's that woman there, Ursula. The leader. . . ."

"Gee, they don't hand out passes to go home just for the asking, do they . . . ?"

"You gotta learn how to deal wit' your problems. . . . You gotta accept 'em, accept reality. . . . When they see's or when they think you is dealin' wit' 'em and accepts reality. . . . You axe and they. . . . You gotta rap wi' 'em and makes 'em see. Then they axe you some questions, axe you what you wanna accomplish, you tells 'em, and you is ready."

"Why would they believe you? They must be being told all the time. . . ."

"I don't never lie and they knows that," he said, drawn erectly in his chair.

"I didn't mean you, I meant the other guys that you accused of lying and cheating."

"I tells 'em, too . . . now. I tells 'em. . . . I jus' says, 'Stuff it. . . . You ain't fer real.' "

"Aren't you afraid they'll gang up on you . . . ?"

"Whatcha say, gang up. . . ." That old malevolence was on his face: cunning, ruthless, savage . . . feral. "You is supposed to talk up. . . . I even tells the leader, she ain't tellin' the truth. . . ."

I leaned back and lighted my cigarette. Again he followed my hands. He wanted a cigarette badly. "You've changed greatly, Gerard. In every way. . . ."

"Look-ed in the mirror to see like you said 'bout my face gettin' longer. Don' seem no different to me . . . except my glasses. . . . Look all right."

"I'm afraid that you're just going to have to accept that . . . your changing. . . . We all change. It's inevitable."

"Inevitable. . . . Whatcha say?"

"Look. . . . You smiled at me today. . . . You smiled at me last month. You talk now. You haven't once glared at the recorder, you've almost forgotten it." As I said it, almost as if he suddenly were aware of its menace, he glared at it. "You have glasses on, you have teeth. . . . You'll just have to accept the fact that you've changed. . . ." He watched me puff on my cigarette. I really couldn't put him in the position of making him ask. And if I offered it to him. . . . I rose from my seat. "Somebody is in the hall out there making noise. I'll be right back. . . ." I unhooked my microphone. I tossed the cigarette package onto the chair. "Help yourself. . . ." And I went out. There was no one in the corridor, just a squeak from the loudspeaker. "I must be hearing sounds in my head," I said, fixing my microphone when I came back. Gerard was smoking contentedly. "Now where were we before we were interrupted?"

"You wus tellin' me how I changed. I has changed."

"So you see that?"

"I put on another attitude. I jus' started acceptin'. I stopped, you know, but I ain't stopped completely. I'm still curious, but I ain't so curious as to make me afraid. . . . You know what I mean?"

"You're not scared about finding out about things, things about yourself, now . . . ?"

It was a marvelous smile, as if man had been given for the first time this fresh, freely given ability to express what words could never convey. He smiled openly. "Yeap. I didn't, I didn't want no part of anythin', didn't wanna hear it. . . . Didn't wanna hear it. . . ." And he said with gravity, "Like, I hated you . . . not you but that . . . machine. . . . I didn't wanna come here. . . . But I had ta. . . . Like, I wus gonna go to isolation . . . go to isolation . . . no smokes, no books, no nothin', jus' them four see-ment walls. . . . I wus gonna go there insteada comin' up here to talk to you . . . and nobody wus gonna make me come up an' talk to you. . . . But I thought it out. . . . I thought it out, you know, and decided to come right on up here. . . . This's supposed to help me, too, one of my problems, you know, keepin' quiet, not talkin', not speakin' out. So, you know, this is the thin' that can help me, you know, talkin', even though, you know, all these chairs ain't filled up with people, like they is in group therapy. . . . I jus' never talked nowhere. . . . 'Cept when I started to talk with you. . . . I jus' started to talk in the group . . . this week. . . . Took me nearly four months to say somethin' in group." He nodded his head and with great delicacy removed the long ash from his cigarette. He smoked it as if it were fragile, precious to him. "I cou' never talk to people, you know, in front of 'em all, 'fraid I might say somethin' stupid, somethin' like that, or they wouldn't accept it, might axe me somethin', or they wouldn't accept me. . . . I might lose my friends, you know, all kinds of shit like that, you know. . . ." He lifted his cigarette, took a final, graceful puff and then deftly put it out. "Now it don' bother me no more. I can go in there and talk. If they accepts it, good. If not, then like later, man, later. But I gotta come up here, man. I gotta because I gotta deal with that quietness, 'cause if I don't keep talkin' I jus' fall right back into that bag I wus in before. . . . So that's why I decided to keep comin' here. . . . 'Cause I talk here. . . . Like, you don't think so because I ain't said, like, much, but man, you know, I really raps with you. . . . Deep talkin', deep, man. . . . I talks with you. Like, the group they nearly shit their pants when I up and spoke to 'em. They nearly shit their pants on accounta I talked. Ursula, her face got red, when I says to her that she wus a liar. . . . She never heard me talk." He paused and looked at the machine. . . . And suddenly he began to speak again: "See, the reason I didn't like to come here with that machine is like it makes me feel that I ain't right up here." And he tapped his head. " 'Cause I feel that you's a psychiatrist and this machine is your accomplish. . . . He catches what I'm sayin', to prove to 'em that I'm sick in the head . . . mental. . . . Like, I'm a guinea pig that you is gonna analyze. . . . That's why I didn't dig it. . . ."

"Mental? Analyze?"

"Got 'em outta a book they got downstairs. . . ."

"What do you think now?"

"I gots my doubts but it'll always be in my mind, but I gotta talk. . . . I gotta deal with my quietness. . . . That's all, I gotta deal with that. . . . Even with the doubt in my mind. . . ."

"For the record . . . I'm not a psychiatrist. . . ."

"You tol' me that three times. . . . Don't make no difference; I gotta keep outta my quietness bag. . . ."

"As you'll never forget the heroin high, so you'll always nurse a suspicion that I'm a psychiatrist. Or perhaps more accurately, you have a suspicion that people feel that you're not all there?" And I touched my head.

"Whatcha say . . . ? Not all there . . . ? Right, right, man."

"Someone once led you to think that you were not right upstairs?"

"Like, sometimes, the ways people looks at me. . . . They's scared or somethin'. They holds back. I sees them. . . . Like in

school. . . . You know, you sees these things. . . . On the street.
. . . Like this Miss Ursula, I knows she pulls back. . . ."

"The really important thing here is that you've been fearful
yourself that there was something wrong with you; that's what's
been bugging you. . . ."

"Yeap. . . ."

"I'll bet you were sent to the psychiatrist here?"

"Yeap."

"And that tore it. Because you felt somehow that your worst
fears were being realized. That you really were 'mental' and that
everybody here knew it."

"I figgered him and you were accomplishes. He'd sit there mumblin' to soften me up, and then I'd git sent up here to be talked to
death by you. . . . I figgered him and you for accomplishes. . . ."

"Honest to God, I never knew about it. . . . How many times
have you seen him in the four months?"

"Jus' twice. . . . I never said nothin' to him. Jus' gave him my
name. . . . That's all. . . ."

I smiled at him. "Rough, kiddo, rough. . . . I understand."

"Whatcha say . . . understand . . . ?"

I ripped off some more of the paper around the cigarette package, picked one out and then, as if I were preoccupied, I extended
the pack towards him. He looked up, hesitated and then selected
one. I lighted my own first; I didn't want him to feel "special."

"Must be that you heard stories about psychiatrists, Gerard. . . .
A doctor examined your eyes for glasses, a dentist for your
teeth. . . ."

"One's been at my ears. . . . Figger I can't hear no good. . . ."

"Psychiatrist is just a doctor, too. . . ."

" 'Sokay when you goes on your own, jus' the idea. . . . Then
when you comes outta a quietness bag . . . you gits all chewed
up. . . ."

"Dreading the feeling that you're perhaps mentally ill, is that
it . . . ?"

"Yeap."

"Do you still feel that . . . ?"

He said, solemnly puffing away: "I don't guess so . . . I don't guesses so. . . . But like, you know, I still has it a little piece in my mind. . . ."

"I see. . . . Just a remnant of that fear. . . ."

"Remnant," he repeated. "Like, a little bit. . . ." He held the cigarette with that elegance you see in advertisements. "See, you puts yourself in a box. . . . You's in that quietness bag, you's thinkin' inside. . . . You's always watchin', watchin' people, you puts together what you thinks they is thinkin'. . . . You gets yourself into a hellified box. . . ."

"You're an extremely perceptive fellow, Gerard. It seems to me that you're at the place now where you'll have to re-evaluate all your ideas and opinions about yourself. You're probably going to make all kinds of discoveries. . . ."

"Whatcha say . . . re-evaluate . . . ? About myself . . . ? Shit, man, I thinks all the time. . . . Like, I hears what I says from that tape. I hears it and I takes it back downstairs. . . . And I thinks, 'When I know that dude,' and he pointed his cigarette end at me, 'I'll really tell 'im. . . . Like, I'll show 'im I'm cool. . . .' But right offa the bat I can't say nothin'. But I'm thinkin' all the time. . . ."

"But that's changed now with the group, and your ward mates, and that machine. . . ."

"An' you. . . . It's still in the *process.*"

"I see. . . . Still in the process."

"See, I guesses I wus born with this quietness bag. Didn' like fer people to know . . . 'bout me and my business. . . . Like I wus scared I might say somethin' wrong. . . . Like I couldn't always come up fast with what they axed me in school. . . . Like I would stan' there an' stare back at the teacher like I wus mad at her. . . . See, I wus thinkin' all right, but I couldn't speak right away, and then she'd come swoopin' down at me . . . like I wus mouthin' off or somethin', and first thing you know I wus down in the office. . . . So, shit . . . I got pretty pissed off at 'em. . . . I musta been born with that quietness bag. . . . My mother, she never bothered 'bout it. . . . She knowed me. . . . She never bothered. She figgered I wus in my quietness bag. . . . She never nudged me atall. She knowed. . . . Beside, she had my sister's kids. . . . They talked enough fer ten of me. . . . My father he knowed, too. . . . So I wus born that way. . . ."

"It's possible, since you do so much thinking, it's possible that you developed this quietness bag as a defense. You know what I mean? For instance, you felt that you couldn't give an answer quickly, and you felt that people expected a quick answer or they would suspect that you were unprepared, so maybe you began to frown and look tough, just to protect yourself. . . . Do you dig me . . . defensiveness?"

"Whatcha say . . . defensiveness . . . ? I supposes so. . . . Could be. I gotta figger. . . . See, my brothers and sisters wus all growed up. . . . Then these little kids come into the house. . . . Now, when theys little like that and their mother is dead, they gotta hellified problem. I usta talk to my one brother, but he got married and went away. . . ."

"It's also possible that you're shy and thoughtful and maybe that's not very acceptable where you come from. . . . You know, maybe where you come from you have to be quick in response. . . ."

"Quick in response," he repeated. "Hummmm. . . ."

"Now, where I live . . . everything is slow. Like, on the island where I live, everything is much slower than here. The way people walk and talk and do things. . . . It's the rhythm. . . . You know, the weather is warm, you sweat easily, the air is softer, less noise, the whole life style is different. . . . You know, how does an addict say it . . . ? Different strokes for different folks. . . ."

He smiled. "Right, right. Like, I sees where you're coming from. . . . Different strokes fer different folks. . . . Like maybe I wus. Like, one time I was asked to go up in front o' the class to do a math problem on the blackboard. I wus good in math. I could do the problem. . . . But when I gets there with all them faces, I freezes up. . . . I didn't have no shield, I didn't even have a cigarette in my hand, nothin' to round with, jus' me standin' there, you know. . . . Couldn't face that. . . . So I goes back to get the book . . . like I didn't know the answer, an' the teacher she jus' lets go with: 'Whatcha doin', gettin' that book? You cheatin'. . . . You sit down this instant. . . . An' you write fer me one hundred

times: I will learn my lessons. . . .' " I can remember that. . . . It
happen when I wus a kid. . . . That kinda thing. Where I had the
answer but I freezes up . . . you know. . . . That happened. I used
to think and think 'bout it. . . . An' the more I thought about it,
the slower it would come . . . an' the more pissed off I'd get. . . .
Finally, hell, man, I wus fightin'." He stared off into space. "They
passes you by. And you know, like, you slows up . . . I slowed up
a lot. I started to drop behind in the work, everythin', the readin'
and the history, and even in the math which I could do good, I
jus' slowed up. . . . More you slows up, more you can't catch up.
. . . Till you finally says: 'What the hell, they is way the Christ
and gone around the corner . . . can't catch 'em no more. Don't
wanta catch. . . . What the hell's so good 'bout it anyways . . . ?
Ain't worth it. . . .' Kin I have one of your butts?"

I passed the package and the matches to him.

"You never had any fears about your ability to do the work?"

"I couldn't do it when I slowed up, that's for certain sure. . . .
Couldn't, on accounta I chucked it . . . stuffed it, you know, like
by slowin' up. But before that I could so do it. . . . I jus' wouldn't
let myself do it. Then, you know, man, I get all uptight, thinkin'
she's gonna call on me. So I makes a face. I gets tough. 'Fuck you,'
I says. . . . I'm down in the office. My mother comes. . . . Helli-
fyin' bad. . . ." He sighed. "I don't rightly knows what happened. . . ."

"You drank wine . . . took pot . . . and then heroin . . . that's
what happened. . . . What did they do in relation to what happened to you in school . . . ?"

He grinned. "The wine upset my stomach. I liked-ed the high
but I usta throw up. . . . See, I needed a lot o' it. . . . Then the
pot, it wus all right 'cause I did a helluva lot of laughin' on it. I
wus heavy with it. Funny thing, it made my one eye work by itself
alone." He pointed to his left eye. "Whatever it wus, that eye, it
wouldn't work right. . . . Might not even-a been the pot, but it got
to me. . . . Besides, the pot made people look at me, like they
didn't dig me as bein' Gerard. . . ."

"Made you appear out of character. . . ."

"Whatcha say . . . out of character . . . ? Yeap. My mother

and the other kids. . . . So when my cousin, he says, try this . . .
you know, with junk . . . that was it. . . . Junk let me talk just
right. Not too much, not too little. Jus' right. . . . Like, when I'd
be in the stores, lookin' fer them dresses or clothes the people ordered from me . . . I really liked-ed that. . . . Not bein' scared I
was gonna be snaggled, but see them pretty colors, and how the
cloth felt in your fingers. . . . And I got so I always picked the
best things out. . . . My customers would say: 'You got good taste,
Gerard. . . .' And they wus right in that. . . . If it coulda stayed
like that, no more, no less. . . . But it couldn't, you know, I knows
that. . . . The sickness, the runnin'. . . . Jesus, you gits so run
down, all run out so your legs is short. Then, you know, all them
changes. . . ."

"How many of your boyhood friends used stuff?"

He snorted: "Most of 'em. Wus all over."

"Did they have problems too, is that why they went to it?"

He shrugged: "Musta . . . I guesses so. . . . Some of them
stopped though. . . . Like, one time I was fixin' an' a kid says to
me: 'Whatcha doin' with that stickin' in your arm . . . ?' He wus
scared shitless. . . . I wus, in the beginnin' when I first started. I
held on to the leg of a chair. . . . I wus so scared when I got
hit. . . ."

"Would you say that your sister's kids, the ones being raised by
your mother, will have to go on dope, too?"

He looked at me in astonishment, puffed thoughtfully on his
cigarette. "I hopes not. . . . Maybe, me . . . what happened to me.
. . . An' my mother, she's different with them. . . . They don't
never come outta that quiet bag. . . ."

"So maybe they won't have to go your way . . . ?"

"Whatcha say . . . go my way?"

Darrell couldn't sit still. The office reeked of his cheap cigars.
His glance kept darting from my face to the mountain of papers
on his desk. "All right, Frank Michael. He's got glasses, he's got
teeth. They can't find anything wrong with his hearing. . . ."

"I think perhaps he's hearing better, Darrell."

"Hum. . . . Now, his evaluation. . . . Well, that's different.

. . . Here. . . ." He started to hand it over to me and then thought better of it. "Catch the words: 'Sullen, combative, suspicious, noncommunicative, uncooperative—Suggest transfer to psychiatric unit. Possible paranoia. Wrong setting. Needs specialized care.' That's what she filed last week. Ursula Chalmers, Mrs. Chalmers. . . . I arranged for you to see her. . . . Don't ask for anything else, Frank Michael. They got me running like a rabbit. God-damned city fathers. I didn't create their drug problem. . . . All they know is: keep them quiet in there. Make sure they don't break out. . . . Cure them, the bastards. . . . But most of all, Stoner, keep them quiet. We've given you a million dollars. You gotta be able to cure them for that amount of money. Frank Michael, ever feel that your head is coming off . . . ?" He picked up the phone: "Ursula, I'm sending Cortina to your office. . . . Cortina. . . . I told you. . . . Gerard. . . . Cortina. . . ." He hung up. "She's only twenty-one. . . . Go see her. Good-bye, Frank Michael. . . ."

"Darrell. . . . Have dinner with me tonight. We'll talk. . . ."

"Are you kidding . . . ? They got me signed around the clock. I got to go see the head of the city council. Hold his hand, reassure him that his children won't be raped by these sex maniacs when they break loose. *They* need psychiatric care. . . . They're the ones. . . . They're gonna drive me right up the wall. . . ."

She was very busy and very young. Her glasses frames were of golden metal, and they were exaggeratedly large; the lenses were tinted. Her tunic, or shirtwaist or whatever it was, was form fitting, and her breasts appeared small and very high. She was standing, her cigarette hanging from her lips, talking into the telephone. She nodded at me brusquely.

I said as she put down the phone: "Miss Chalmers, I'm—"

"Mrs. Chalmers. . . ."

"I beg your par—"

"You wanted to tell me about Gerard Onslow?"

"I wanted to talk to you ab—"

"What's there to say? Fairly obvious, isn't it?"

"No, I think it's anything but obvious. . . . One could easily mistake surface manifestations in his case. . . ."

"Please, Mr. Cortina. . . . Don't try to shape my responses. . . . My only value is my insightful response. . . ."

"He frightens you. . . ."

"Frightens . . . ? That's too subjective. . . . He's alienated, unpredictable, remote, and badly damaged. . . ."

I felt sorry for her. She was rattled. "Mrs. Chalmers, I wonder if you could find the time to listen to just a part of this tape that I made today. It reveals a very interesting. . . ."

"I resent, Mr. Cortina, very much, your obtruding yourself. These people know one thing supremely well, how to manipulate others. They are supreme manipulaters. They will *con you out of your life.*" She looked at me; perhaps she hoped that she had added twenty years to her age in the glance. "Now what are your qualifications that they will permit . . . ?"

I rose slowly. "Obviously, I don't have them. . . . I'm sorry I bothered you. Sometimes, you know, a kid wears a certain kind of exterior that dooms him to being a criminal all his life. . . . Good-bye, Mrs. Chalmers. Thank you for your time."

5

It was apparent that, in the month since I had seen him, Gerard had been trying to cultivate a beard; a blonde cluster of silky hair like an overlooked patch of dirt covered his chin. I watched his hands steal to it, touch it, as if by this he would encourage a richer, lusher growth. There was nothing relaxed about him this morning—that old monumental stillness had vanished. . . . "Something important pressing on you?" I asked, turning off the machine, interrupting the playback halfway through.

"I gets very bored these days."

"Bored? With the tape? Hearing your own voice?"

"Gets bored with everythin'. . . . Gets bored in the group, gets bored in the ward, gets bored with the whole thing."

"Is that because you don't invest anything of yourself in what you do?"

"Whatcha say . . . ? That ain't it. . . . I puts somethin' in . . . I participate. . . . Jus' everythin' is slow, like, dragsville. . . ." He felt his beard, the bows of his glasses. He was fidgety. "I wan' to get out among 'em. . . . It's out there. . . ."

"Ah, it's that you feel you're ready to go. . . . That's the reason for the restlessness. . . ."

"Next week, I got a birthday. . . . I'm gonna be seventeen. Can't lay up forever. . . ."

"Has anyone indicated that they agree with you . . . ? That they feel you're ready to go?"

"Around here they don't 'gree with nothin'. They jus' yells and complains. . . ."

"What about Mrs. Chalmers . . . Ursula . . . ?"

He snorted. "She jus' sits there movin' her legs. . . . Lamb with all of 'em wolves aroun'. She plays the game; she likes to feel scared of us. . . . Me she don't like 'cause I don't lie. . . . She don't like me . . . always gotta put me down."

I felt a twinge of conscience. I wondered if her attitude came about because of my intervention. "Perhaps you ought to make the effort to win her over. . . ."

"Win her over . . . for what? I don't want no part of that broad. . . . She's too nervous."

I laughed out loud. "Too nervous. . . ."

"She's sittin' there and twitchin' and shiftin' and pushin' against the chair. . . . She ain't got no business bein' here. She's too young, man, you know. . . . Like, got but two speeds. Trying to be like them. Like, no matter what they done she done worse, or she so sure what they oughta do on accounta it would nice fer them to do it her way."

"For a guy we just heard saying on that tape that he came out

of a quietness bag . . . you've become quite a conversationalist
. . . with ideas and opinions. . . ."

A momentary, charged silence fell. He studied my face. You
could feel him relaxing. "I goes in and out, you know. . . . But I
talks now. I don't believe she likes that. When I was in my bag
she could have somethin' to say 'bout me. . . . Now I goes right
back at her and tells her . . . and them guys, too."

"Since they can influence when you get discharged or when you
get a home leave . . . perhaps it might be well not to antagonize
them. . . ."

"Antagonize . . . antagonize . . . them. . . . Shit. I got my
thing to do, man, like, you know. . . . They's gonna be here
playin' their little games, while Gerard he's out there movin'. Let
'em get antagonized. . . ."

"Don't you think that you should be conscious of it? Isn't it part
of the whole picture to be able to get along with others . . . ? I
mean, you know, you can be talkative and not get along with people just as easily, maybe more easily, than to be silent and not get
along. . . . When you talk you're out in the open . . . they can
point a finger at you more easily. . . ."

"Whatcha say . . . ? Get at me for talkin'. . . ." His eyes
looked cold, as if they were shuttered and had no depth. "I kin
take care of myself. . . . That broad, she ain't got but one place to
go . . . on the floor. . . . They'll take her one day. . . . Then you'll
hear the yellin'. . . ."

"Perhaps you don't give her enough credit, Gerard. Is it possible
that Mrs. Chalmers knows exactly what she's doing? After all,
she's a trained worker. Perhaps all of this is part of a design."

"Design . . . design. . . . Ain't no design when she gets so mad
when they asks about her husband and herself and she busts out
cryin'. . . . What in hell kinda design is that when she gets up
and runs out and claims we is all beastes. . . . Then she comes
back with some kinda jive about testing us. . . . I ain't got no time
for that. She wants me to like her on account of her needin' everybody to like her and she's gonna help me. . . . She's gotta play her
own game. . . . I ain't jive. I got my own thing. . . ."

"And what is that thing . . . ?"

"What is that . . . ? When I get out of here? Get a job, go to school, stay offa stuff."

"Can you do that?"

"Whatcha say . . . ? Can I do it? Who's gonna stop me . . . ?"

"Who's going to help you? That's more important than who's going to stop you. . . ."

"Helps myself. . . ."

The glasses softened his face, his new teeth restored his youthfulness, but even so there was revealed such an expression of hostility. . . . In the way of things, rehabilitation in his case was not the key. It had to be habilitation, and he was the one who had to perform that miracle. That unprepossessing face would be his downfall unless he could somehow recast its way of responding. . . . This passed through my mind with a searing cogency. "How are you going to stay off stuff?"

"Stay offa stuff? Stay offa it!" he said flatly.

"But how?"

"Whatcha mean . . . ? You stays offa it, like, you does, man."

"But maybe you just can't do it that simply. . . . Maybe it's conditioned you . . . do you know?"

"Conditioned . . . conditioned. . . ."

"Yeah, look. . . ." I lifted the cigarette package. "We both smoke. That makes us very different from the person who has never smoked. It's done things not only to our body but to our pattern of behavior, the way we look at things. Remember, you told about being up at the blackboard with the math problem and you froze; you said you didn't even have a cigarette in your hand to help you . . . ? Now, if smoking has that much influence on us, what about something so powerful as heroin . . . ? It's more than just a physically addictive substance. . . . It's a way of life, it's a way of response to stress, to almost everything. . . ."

"Conditioned. . . ." He was with me, his eyes alive with the challenge. "I'm cuttin' it. Hung it up. . . ."

"Okay. . . . But what's in its place? What has it done to you that's still there? What did you use it for?"

His brow was crinkled.

"Look at heroin by itself. The physical part is dropped a thousand times a week. . . . Any time a guy gets busted, he's dried up, right? He can't get it so he's clean. You've kicked; you know that. . . . Usually, though, that guy goes right back to it as soon as he gets out. Why?"

He said quietly: "Why does he goes back to it? Because he likes it. He wants to. . . . He. . . ." And he paused, feeling around inside of himself, at last coming to grips with the nettle.

"You're off heroin. You say you're through with it. You're out of your quietness bag. . . . But what else has changed? How do you handle things? What's taken its place?"

"Me . . . I . . . I has taken its place. . . ."

"I wish I had a mirror with me. I wish I could show you your face at this very minute. . . . Your face looks as if you wanted to knock me down and stomp my face in." He pulled back, aghast. "Please, Gerard, don't choke up on that. That's nothing. . . . But think for a second, you're a real bright guy. You think about things. . . . Remember, in the math book . . . you could dope out the answer to a problem . . . and then you'd look in the back and find out that you were right but you hadn't done the problem in the way it was done in the book? Remember that? Something like that has happened to your life. You've changed . . . you say. . . . But what have you added to that change. . . . You've got the answer, but the steps in between, how you arrived at the answer . . . this you don't know. . . . When you're out there, it's going to be different. There will be no Mrs. Chalmerses who are put off by your manners, your way of talking, your way of reacting. They won't have patiences, or tolerance, or empathy. . . ."

"Empathy . . . empathy. . . ."

"You have got to make for yourself certain safeguards. You know, escape valves . . . protective devices . . . not defenses so much as cushions. . . ."

He asked sharply, with irritation: "Whatcha sayin' . . . ? I ain't changed . . . ? My attitude . . . ? Comin' out of my quiet bag?"

"Yes, all those things. True. . . . True. . . . But I'll bet you . . .

if somebody brings you up real close and lets you have it . . . you have no way to turn but to hit back, and if you can't hit back you'll run for the cop-man. . . ."

For the first time in all the months, his voice was high and shrill: "Whatcha sayin', man, you know . . . ?"

I lighted a cigarette and looked at him. "Have one. . . ." I thrust it at him, but he drew back, anger on his face. "Look. . . . I'm not down-rating you. . . . You have changed. . . . But now the work really begins. . . . If you go out this way. . . ." I bit my tongue, I caught myself. I was about to say that he would be killed in the environment that he would return to, because his new values were barely paper-thin, they would not suffice. "Things haven't changed out there, Gerard. Your home, your mother, your father, the street. . . . But you have changed." Was it hurt on his face? I had never seen that expression before. I couldn't tell. But the curtain that fell between us was palpable.

I said quietly: "When we do anything for a long time, certain practices grow up around that thing. . . . Do you see that?" He had withdrawn. "Don't act like a junkie. You're not one of them any more. You're not a junkie any more, beating your breast and wailing that you're a victim. That's not you, Gerard. . . . It never was you. . . . You're a smart guy. You know from experience that you had to have something to get into an apartment. A key to the lock or a piece of wire or a file or a rod to open the window. . . . You need that now . . . to get out there and stay out. . . . Things to replace heroin. . . . Before, what the hell, no matter what went wrong there was always that one solution . . . heroin. . . . Now, what do you have in its place, now that you say you're through with it?" I said almost angrily: "Don't just sit there and cop out with your quietness bag. . . ." I paused and stared at him. "Or am I blind . . . ? Is it that now you sit there quietly, and before you would have struck me and run?" I waited, his eyes fixed upon me. "You see, I know some things about you. You're thoughtful, you're able to talk, you're energetic, you're intelligent, you're honest. . . ."

It just burst forth from him, like a cistern overflowing:

"Whatcha sayin' to me, man? Like, I gotta stay here for years and years . . . ? Whatcha sayin' to me, man . . . ?"

"I am saying to you that you have made remarkable advances. I am saying to you that you have done the most amazing kind of analysis of yourself. I am saying that you have demonstrated a depth of insight and perception about yourself that is remarkable. I am saying to you not to throw this all away now. . . . The job is not completed, the job you have to do." I observed him mulling over what I had said. He reached for a cigarette; I gave him the matches.

How gracefully he handled that smoke. "I has changed, you know, man. I thinks on what people says to me. I think I knows why I shot dope now, why I drunk the wine and smoked the reefer. . . . I didn't see it then. . . . I was under a lotta strain, man, a lotta strain. . . . Like, my father, him bein' so sick all the time, and them kids sayin' he was always drunk, and me, too, feelin' he was always drunk, and them neighbors catchin' me out an' talkin' about my father. . . . But he wasn't drunk, man, you know, he had Parkinson's disease but nobody believed that. . . . And my sister, anybody could drag her into the hallway. . . . I seen her myself, her face all red and her gruntin' behind the cellar-way—gruntin' and catchin' her breath, like it was her heart bein' squeezed. . . . And the kids tellin' me 'bout my sister with her pants down and her cunt showin'. And then with them five little kids, not one of them havin' no father. And my mother, thin like a strap . . . coughin'. . . . I couldn't never get up and talk. . . . I knowed what I wanted to say, but I couldn't git it out. . . . Man, I was under a strain. . . . I was so God-damned strung out, and it wasn't from no dope. . . . It was strain . . . and the marks and the hooky and my cousin. . . . He had such a nice house, and a allow-ance, and he was fuckin' around with horse. . . . So I figgered he ain't no God-damn bit better'n me, usin' that shit, he ain't no God-damn bit better'n me. . . ." He smoked. "I sees all that now, man, but you know, I didn't sees it then. I jus' wanted to get out . . . get out . . . move . . . move . . . go. I'd get high. . . . Now, I'd think when I was floatin'. . . . You don't jest go off your cap.

. . . You thinks when you is on the stuff. . . . Like, I'd sit there on the side, on a loadin' platform at night, and think 'bout my brothers and sisters. . . . They wus gone, all 'cept the one who up and died. How come they could do it and get out . . . ? I wus always hearin' how good they wus in school. They has jobs way off in another city. They's so successful. Come to find out they wusn't all that high and mighty. But it wus true they never made my ma come down to the school. Seems like the more I didn't want to get in no trouble, the more I got into it. . . . More got into more. . . . Strain, man . . . strain. . . . It gets into you. . . ." He felt his fuzzy patch. "Everythin' I did, after a while, come out wrong. . . . I looks at somebody, and they throws a punch at me. I looks at the teacher, and she yells somethin' about bein' impersonent. I goes to the church to the social, and they raps my knuckles fer puttin' my fists up on accounta a kid shoves me into a girl. . . . Like, nothin' I do never works out, man, but inside I sees that somethin' is wrong. . . . Like the cop who hits me on the side of the head with his club because I gotta come along when he's cleaning out a crap game and I sees him puttin' the money in his pocket. . . . He raps me . . . with that club. . . . I wus under a strain, man . . . strain. . . . Horse, it put me down. . . . Too far, I sees that. . . . Too far, I sees that. . . . Too hellified far. . . ." He smoked silently. We smoked together. He said after a while, "I thinks they's gonna give me a three-day pass for my birthday. . . ."

"Are you up to it?"

"Whatcha say . . . ? Up to it . . . ? Gotta do it out there, man, you know. Out on the street. . . ." It was a strained smile, but it was a smile. "I sees you next month, you know, man, like next month. . . . You was sayin' 'bout my face before. What I looks like when I says somethin'. . . . I'm gonna look in a mirror when I talks. . . . I'm gonna check it out. . . ."

"Why not . . . ? You know, you can get away with murder if you have the right expression on your face. . . ."

"Smile an' you kin tell 'em to go shove it?"

6

A bone-chilling gray day; the winter wind, a ring master, eddied the snow flurries. I felt cold, and the equipment seemed extraordinarily heavy as I trudged toward the facility. I couldn't understand why I had not been able to park my car any closer. In that gray light I saw the detention wagons lined up at the curb, the prowl cars on the sidewalk, the cordon of policemen barring the way— and they stood as policemen do the world over—waiting to learn what role it was their community would thrust upon them. There was laughter; some talked quietly; a few young ones seemed pinched by the cold and perhaps pinched by inexperience and frightened by what was to come. I was stopped by a good-natured, middle-aged cop, his face florid from the wintry blasts: "You don't want to go in there, young fellow."

"But I have to go in there, officer."

He looked at me with mock seriousness. "But you don't look the type, now, you don't. . . ." He glanced at my identification, the wind whipping at the corners of his heavy overcoat. "How do you stand them, sir? And what is the answer to the problem? I have kids myself now. . . . What is the answer to dope?" And he was very grave, the vapor of his breath torn away by the wind. . . . " 'Tis a problem. . . ."

"What's going on this morning, officer . . . ?"

"Oh, 'tis somethin' 'bout transfers or somethin' about a mass runaway. . . . Or somethin' comin' out of the mayor's office. After I see the afternoon papers, we'll both know. Come along. . . . I'll lead you in."

Inside, the place was pandemonium. The foyer was crowded with policemen; they ringed a cluster of rehabilitants still dressed in municipally issued pajamas and light-weight dressing gowns, their hair disheveled, their eyes stuck with sleep. Obviously they had been hustled straight out of bed. . . . Behind the desk Darrell Stoner, tall and lean, a chewed-up cigar in his mouth, was talking into the telephone. He was like a general on the front lines. He saw me, cupped his hands over the phone. He grimaced; I knew what was going through his mind: "Oh, you, Cortina. Today of all days!" Instead he called: "Go to my office and wait."

How he could ever find anything in that chaos of paper and folders. . . . His desk was a battlefield. I cleared off a chair and sat smoking; a shaft of cold rushed into the room; the front door was open. The shouts of: "Inside, boys. One at a time. There's seats for all. Don't shove. . . ." Footsteps on the stone floor . . . laughter here and there. . . . The public address system blaring: "All residents except those whose names were called are to remain on their floors." It was repeated and then followed by: "All classes, therapy sessions and other activities are canceled. . . . Repeat: . . . ."

A sudden thought, colder than my feet from the draft along the floor, made me go back outside and search the faces of the men being loaded into the detention wagons. The snowflakes drifted down when the wind abated for a moment and then swiftly slanted when it blew again. But I couldn't see Gerard. . . . Nor could I imagine him as trying to escape; it was not his style. But did I know his style? I went back to Darrell's office; I was cold and my teeth felt sensitive. . . . The clamor diminished; the pipes clanged with heat; the cold draft along the floor lessened. The front door had closed. . . . A truck motor throbbed off and died. . . . I heard the hissing of the radiator. It was an old building, the paint peeling, peeling from the acid of the human condition.

"What the hell's happened, Darrell?"

He closed the door and shivered. He folded up in his chair rather than sat down. His face was as gray as the outdoors. His lips were purple: "Oh, Jesus Christ. I'm going into ecology, Frank Michael . . . I'm going into ecology. . . . I been here all night. . . . Some of the rest of the staff, too. . . . We shifted a hundred and forty men. . . . What a senseless, stupid mess. . . . All political. . . . All political. . . . Rousing those poor bastards out so that the mayor will look good. . . . You know, part of the program is the issuance of short passes, twenty-four hours or forty-eight or seventy-two hours, periodically. . . ."

"Part of all treatment programs," I murmured.

"Sure, it's therapeutic. . . . Well, I've told you how overcrowded we are. . . . Anybody who goes before a judge, if he's only taken aspirin, is certified as a narcotic user. . . . You know, that wonderful, flexible classification of 'narcotics-related offense.' Two weeks ago we got up to four hundred in here. Now that was just plain insanity. Men sleeping in the halls, on tables. . . . What the hell kind of program was that . . . ?"

"But why, Darrell?"

"Election day, why else? He was going to sweep the streets of all drug addicts. Crime in the streets buys a helluva lot of votes. So they swept the streets and dumped them all here. I don't have the staff, the space, the anything. . . . I complained. . . . Nothing but official gobbledygook. . . . I saw the game that was being played . . . just hold tight till after the election. . . . Still another two and a half weeks. . . . Well, I wasn't going to have an incident in here. So I gathered some of the staff together, and I decided that we should issue passes to those oldest residents. . . . In the course of things they would have been eligible anyway. I just speeded up the process and extended the time away."

"Good idea. That way you'd reduce the population of the house. . . ."

"Great idea. . . . But a couple of the guys messed up. . . . There was a mugging of an old man. . . . he was killed." (My heart suddenly jumped into my mouth.) "Turned out he was assaulted by a couple of kids . . . not junkies at all. . . . But the newspapers grabbed it and ran. . . . They jumped all over His Honor—he put them in the front door and let them sneak out the back; that was the gist of it. . . . Well, I want to tell you, Cortina, that phone got red hot. . . . I know I'm through . . . done. . . . Nothing official yet. . . . But 'Who was I to release men at this critical time in the midst of the mayor's holy campaign against that most sordid of all human failings, dope-taking?'" Darrell shriveled in his chair. He mumbled: "But the mayor has been

around a long time. . . . And since it is the art of the possible that
motivates him, he made capital of it. . . . He didn't know of the
overcrowding here—it was inhumane, breakdown in commu-
nications. . . . etc., etc., etc.—he would personally involve
himself—he would order a relocation. You saw them . . .
they're all going to prison. . . . See? Politics. The art of the possible. . . ." He lighted one of those thin, black cigars. "Well, at least
we don't have this God-damned cold in California." He looked up
—his eyes were bleary, the lids ringed with red. "Now, I don't
know about your people, Frank Michael. . . . They could be here
or among the shifted. . . . Who was your . . . ? Ursula. . . .
Right. . . . And isn't she a pain in the. . . . Screaming and wailing about the rights of the residents, mouthing off to the reporters,
and all the while she was happy to get rid of some of them. . . .
The games we play. . . ." He was on the phone. He got her.

Darrell said to me as I started for her office: "I'm taking my degrees and experience and going into ecology, Frank Michael. The
public likes to look at dead fish. . . . It makes them come. Nothing so inspiring as dead fish and shit floating on top of a lake. . . .
You'd better try it, too. . . . Remember, fish and shit . . . ecology,
Frank Michael. . . ."

The excitement had heightened her color, made her eyes shine,
gave a touch of mystery to her otherwise undistinguished features.
She was wearing a mauve mini-skirt, and her legs were blue with
cold. Her hand on her hip, she greeted me with a militant camara-
derie, as if she were a latter-day Jacobin. "How do you like those
bastards? Those political bastards? Coming in here to make their
political moves. . . . Ever see anything like that . . . ? Well, they
won't get away with it. . . . We're taking it to the papers. . . ."
She simmered down for a moment. "Did you see any of it? Outrageous . . . simply outrageous. . . . Dirty bastards. . . ."

"What about Gerard?"

"Gone."

I knew it, but I still felt the wallop. "Just loaded with all the
rest?"

"Oh, yes. . . . What can you say . . . ?" She suddenly sat down and lighted a cigarette, the bracelets on her arm jangling together.

I felt my lip. "He was coming along, you know. . . ."

"Well, yes, of course. . . ."

"His is a world of very small satisfactions. . . . Very simple things meant a great deal to him. . . . I suppose there was no way . . . ?"

"Mr. Cortina, I understand that you've had many years of experience, but you don't reveal great professionalism to me. . . . I'm going to be frank with you. Gerard got a pass to go home. . . . And he didn't come back. . . . All of that group went out and messed up. . . . They shot horse. . . ."

I was incredulous: "Gerard? Abscond . . . ? Use stuff?"

She pointed at me. "That's not a professional attitude. . . . Why not? He's a junkie. . . ."

"Mrs. Chalmers. . . . Did you have a urinalysis taken?"

"It was negative. . . . But he's very, very clever. He could have switched it. . . ."

I stared at her. She looked so young. "And you had him picked up . . . ?"

"No, he was too shrewd for that. . . . He came back on his own . . . two hours late. . . . A good story he had, too. . . ."

I could have knocked her down with one hand. Instead I gripped the back of the chair. I said: "He was late."

"He was clever . . . clever. . . . He had to go. . . . They all had to go. . . . More power to our mayor. . . ."

"No, Mrs. Chalmers. . . . More power to you. . . . Senseless. Senseless. . . . That boy has no sense of time, as I have or you have. . . . He probably thought he had done well by not using drugs, by coming back. . . . He was putting himself on the line. . . ."

Her hands were shaking. . . . She bit her lip until it grew white with pressure. . . .

Sundhollow prison was not the worst place. I had been there before on assignment. I knew the warden. I had no difficulty in gaining entrance. Darrell had made the arrangements. But it was a prison, laced with that unique prison mystique of inflexible struc-

ture and imminent punishment, all reinforced by the visual sym-
bols of steel, stone, high thick walls, and uniformed, belted, club-
carrying staff. Sundhollow did have two social workers on the
staff; they were part of the concession to the twentieth century.

The guard who had been assigned to me was very kind. He offered to help carry my equipment along the endless corridors and
doors we had to go through. He must have been nearing retirement age. At last we came to a small room. He said: "046328 will
be here in a minute. You know him, huh . . . ? No need for me
to sit in here with you. . . . Small enough for you two. . . . I'll
be outside the door."

I set up the equipment, put my package of cigarettes on the
table, . . . waited, feeling that gray prison light and life filter into
me. The door opened; my escort said: "046328, Mr. Cortina."

He stood there, his head shaved, clad in dungarees, blue cham-
bray shirt, heavy work shoes, his hands at his side. No glasses on
his face.

I smiled. "I'm glad to see you, Gerard. . . . I am. . . ."

He was motionless. He looked at me. No recognition in those
cold, hate-filled eyes.

"Can we talk together? Remember, the last time you said that
you'd see me in a month? Well, here it is. . . ." I heard myself
talking. My words struck my ears as if spoken by someone else,
someone profoundly ill at ease, perhaps someone rather shallow
and artificial.

"Sit down, won't you. . . . Tell me about yourself. . . ."

He didn't move. He hardly breathed. He was as still as those
gleaming tiles on the wall behind him.

"You got a bum rap, didn't you? I spoke to Mr. Stoner and to
Mrs. Chalmers. . . . You got a bum rap, kiddo. . . ." I pulled out
a cigarette. I didn't have the nerve to offer him one. It seemed a
mockery. "Won't you sit down?" He remained still.

"Do you have a social worker assigned to you? If you don't, I'm
going to try and get one for you . . . I know the warden. . . ." I
sounded as if I were boasting to this boy. "Gerard, I'm so sorry.
. . . I swear I didn't know. . . ."

"I ain't gonna talk to you no more. You can keep me here. But

I ain't got to talk. No way to make me talk." If it had been clicked
out on a typewriter it would have sounded more life-like. It was
deadly and final. Oh, I tried most of the handles I had developed
over the years, but to no avail; I think I knew before I saw him
that it was hopeless. It was a lost cause. I held out my hand to
him. "I can't make you talk, of course, Gerard. But I feel that I
have lost something. I won't keep you. . . . Will you shake
hands?" And how false, how inane that sounded in my ears. He
didn't budge . . . just that one eye that he couldn't control. It was
out of keeping with the rest of his controlled stillness. I went to
the door. The guard came in. . . . It was the last time I saw Gerard . . . the last time.

Last year I was in that city. . . . I had been called in on a brief
consulting assignment. The city had largely withdrawn from drug
rehabilitation; it was too expensive to maintain staff and facilities;
moreover, methadone was more immediately promising as a tool
and far less costly. The mayor had been very eloquent; it had been
he who had formed the committee to which I had been assigned as
a one-day consultant. The papers reported the next day that the
treatment approach to drug dependence was far too uncertain, far
too expensive for any municipality to undertake without state
money to underwrite it. . . . And I should add that the state in
this instance repeated in its turn the same thing. The state said,
however, that federal money should underwrite it. I was through.
I went back to my hotel. I knew that Darrell Stoner had indeed
changed his field. He was in California. He was working in stream
pollution. I couldn't imagine in what capacity.
    There was a message at my hotel. Just a telephone message. It
told me to refer to a newspaper article of the previous month. It
was signed Ursula. . . . Ursula. . . . Ursula. . . . It came back—
Ursula Chalmers—I remembered.
    The next morning I went down to the newspaper office. I got
the issue. I stood at a counter in the office. It was a bold leading
article: DRUGS STRIKE TERROR AT HEART OF CITY. "A young,
chunky, armed robber shot and killed a bank guard this morning
in an attempted holdup at the Crest Meadow bank. He then

shot the teller. An off-duty policeman, Simon Dolliver, hearing the shots, entered the bank and shot down the killer. Later examination revealed that Gerard Onslow, 18 years of age, was a heroin addict, his arms crisscrossed with tracks. How long must the lives and property of this . . . etc., etc., etc. . . ."

THE
MENSCH

1

"In a stinking war that's immoral, killing innocent women and children and young men, killing a nation, destroying its land, blighting it for the next three generations. . . . And our great leaders with their Victorian minds mealymouth words like honor, democracy, self-determination. No wonder we're in rebellion. Everybody preaching like some Calvinist divine and then fornicating behind the cellar door like the last Roman. Hypocrisy is the word, and this is its time. . . . There's only one imperative: destroy the individual. . . ."

The words came out like saber cuts, nothing delicate in the delivery. She hacked them at me as she moved nervously, restlessly, without pattern, in the space between the window and the door. It was like being in the middle of a fierce tempest without warning.

"Only sixteen men killed this week, the lowest total in five years. Wonderful! Only sixteen of them! The cities crumbling, race pitted against race, starvation, the most appalling deprivations, and we fly another mighty mission of B-52s against a rice paddy and we damn well blow it to eternity." Suddenly she shouted: "So don't you try and give me any of your canned values. Keep them." She sat down, unable to keep her hands still, her legs twitching, her breath coming in short, labored gasps. "Keep your beautiful American world that you made for us, that you struggled to provide us with. Liars, hypocrites, murderers. . . . Lurking behind each one of you is that killer, killer. You're killers. . . . American dream? American nightmare! Just below the surface of every American is a killer. Yes, a killer."

I had seen it before. She was coming down from methedrine, "speed." Sometimes it took days or weeks before the extreme agitation subsided. This was Connie. She was short, with a pale complexion, her dark hair worn in what used to be called a Clara Bow bob. Her face seemed pinched. "Oh, it's too much, it really is, that we should be indicted. . . . We're the only decent thing left. . . . The young people are your conscience . . . your conscience. Otherwise you'd be totally depraved. Yes, we're your conscience, with our syringes and pills and pipes. We're the extreme expression of your outrage. We're forcing you to look at yourselves. . . . Heroin—the junkie affectation is so apt—King Heroin— King Heroin forces us out of Vietnam. . . . Wonderful, isn't it . . . ? Billions of dollars, hundreds of thousands of crippled children and lives, hundred of thousands of deaths, land destroyed . . . blasted, and all the king's horses and all the king's men couldn't make Thieu and Ky loved by the people. . . . But we will overcome, with honor and B-52s, and make the people democratic. . . . So don't try and give me values, Mr. Whatever-your-name-is. . . . And it sounds foreign to me, too."

"Cortina," I said mildly.

"We're the breakout point. We're the part of all you old bastards who have blighted and blunted your nature, we're the cry of outrage. You don't listen, you go along like sheep, fat and contented. . . . Well, we'll bring you up, with our syringes and needles and pills and hair. . . . King Heroin wins the war, and you bastards will pay and pay and pay through the next two generation of children who'll be infested and infected and mutilated by your wonderful dedication to honor and democracy in Vietnam.

. . . So don't you give me any appeal to your small social-worker's bag of values, Mr. Whatever-the-hell-your-name-is. . . ."

"Cortina. . . . Not a social worker. . . ."

"I'm here because I came in. . . . I don't need new values, I need a new basis for humanity. Did you hear that? A new basis for humanity. . . . Because you and the rest are cockroaches with the morality of a pack of rats. . . ." Suddenly she got up and resumed her pacing, jerky, coiled tight like a spring, twisting, turning, twitching, no place of rest. "Don't exhort me with your Billy Graham puerility, Mr. Whatever-your-name-is. . . ."

"Cortina."

"We're saving you . . . all of you old fuddy-duddies, with your honor and body counts . . . saving you with a needle, salvaging your humanity through chemistry!" And then with no accountable sign she suddenly collapsed in the chair, deflated, staring out the window as if fascinated by some unspeakable drama. There was nothing out there but the accidental square of littered space that had been created by the rear walls of four buildings that didn't quite butt together. Perhaps one could have been fanciful and described the dirty patch as a courtyard.

I offered her a cigarette. She accepted it and I struck a match. She said, formally: "Yes, thank you." Her speech—I had heard it on different campuses: Wellesley, Smith, Mount Holyoke, Bryn Mawr, Bennington, yes, a very distinctive drawl. How incongruous it was to hear it in this most municipal of drug rehabilitation facilities. I looked at her shaking hand.

"Speed?"

She nodded her head in agreement. Once started, she couldn't seem to stop its shaking. Her words jarred loose: "Y-es . . . meth-meth-."

"Have they given you medication?"

"Y-e-s I'm-m-m bet-ter to-to-day. . . . Bet-ter."

"How long have you been here?"

"Seven days . . . I think."

"You signed yourself in?"

"I . . . did. . . . My-self. . . ."

"Big decision . . . voluntarily surrendering your freedom. . . ."

She had gotten her shaking under control. "The only candles in the window are the ones you light for yourself." It came out in jerks, shaken from her, but still with that unmistakable speech quality.

"You must have been pretty desperate, to come in on your own."

"I couldn't sleep any more. . . . Couldn't eat. . . . Look at the wall. . . . Be up for four days . . . sleep for an hour. Come down and have the horrors. . . . Take a shot . . . quiet me down. . . ."

"You'd use heroin to come down . . . ?"

"Yes. . . . Or pills if I had them. . . ." She puffed away on the cigarette. "You're in a flash of light, a light created by your own burning. It sweeps up brighter and brighter, and it's suddenly quenched and you sit numbly trying to understand. . . . Up until yesterday I was like a fly on the wall. . . ." She lifted her left hand; it was swollen. "This was like a catcher's mitt. . . . I couldn't pop a vein in my arm anymore so I was shooting in my hand. . . . I needed horse to come down. . . ."

"That happens with addicts, doesn't it? They can't find the veins anymore. . . . You were addicted."

"Yes. . . ."

"How long have you been using?"

"Five years. . . ."

I noticed the scar tissue just above her ankle. "What's that from?"

"A cutdown from my last hospital stay. Septicemia, from a needle. . . . The doctors couldn't find a vein for the transfusions . . . so they cut me there."

A low-flying jet roared overhead, awakening tinny echoes in the room. I looked at her—small, meager, her eyes still focused on the window.

She said: "My arm was so badly infected they discussed amputation. My hands were bloated. . . . And I was sick as a dog going through withdrawal. . . ." The words jerked out of her.

"You've had your troubles. . . ."

"Last year hepatitis. . . . I could set myself up as a pain bank and provide interest."

"Ironic, isn't it? You know, I hear so many times from addicts that they are particularly susceptible to pain, and yet the lives they live are shot through with the most appalling pain. . . ."

"We are susceptible to pain, all kinds, physical and mental. . . . To avoid it, we'll go to any lengths: robbery, assault, shoplifting, theft from your family. . . . The fear of pain motivates all your acts." She turned and looked at me. "The way hypocrisy and self-ishness motivates your life, the way you avoid pain."

"It's just in what you opt for, is that it? In your case, speed and heroin . . . and in mine, what you say, huh?"

"Definitely. . . . We're just more honest."

"Did fear of pain motivate you to robbery and prostitution and things like that?"

She dismissed it and snuffed out the cigarette. Nervously, she got to her feet and went to the window.

"Did you fear death the last time you were in the hospital?"

"That's a good establishment question, Mr. . . . ."

"Cortina."

"I was fearful that I'd lose my arm. I couldn't endure the thought of that . . . a cripple, a grotesque."

"That disturbed you? To be a cripple . . . ?"

"Please spare me your archness. . . . I can feel you mounting a marvelously subtle allusion to my already being a cripple, a lame. . . . Don't be subtle. . . . So it doesn't make sense to you. So I'll have them run out the flag—you've discovered a contradiction. . . . When you live a contradiction, Mr. *Cortina,* the shadings don't particularly faze you. . . ."

"But to lose your arm, that did . . . ?"

"For once and all, it did . . . it did," she said sharply, nervously, and came away from the window.

"I wonder why. . . ."

"Yes, you go on wondering. . . . It'll stimulate you. . . ."

I have to be careful here. I don't want to create the impression that Connie was singling me out as an individual, to heap coals on

my head; she was lashing out broadside, randomly. She felt profoundly distressed, the aftereffect of stopping speed.

"Perhaps it was the idea of your completeness . . . you know
. . . your completeness that you treasured."

It penetrated. For she stopped pacing and sat down. "Completeness?"

"Yes. When you lose an arm, your disability shows . . . your incompleteness is revealed. . . . Now heroin and speed, that kind of
abuse . . . well, that's hidden. That incompleteness is concealed.
. . ."

"Good God, a psychiatric social worker?"

"To have your disfigurement apparent, that jarred you."

"Yes, yes, yes, yes. . . . I would rather have died. . . . I would
have gotten out of there and O.D.'d myself."

"But why, Connie?"

She looked at me, studying my face, her brow furrowed; and
then it was as if she figured it wasn't worth her while to humor
me. She said, rising: "I'm an eccentric."

"But that's the problem. . . . You're not an eccentric. You don't
have the strength and conviction to be an eccentric. You're an incomplete eccentric. A real eccentric doesn't need dope, he has his
uniqueness."

"May I have another cigarette?"

"Sure."

"Where did you get that theory?"

"From a drug-abuser friend of mine."

"I'd like to think about it. . . . It's better than the old saws . . .
emotional immaturity, passivity, lack of motivation . . . self-destruction. . . ."

"I think those things are part of the riddle, too," I said, putting
my cigarette pack on the table.

"Right, and so does every other nickel-and-dime psychologist.
. . . And our society is alive with all the answers, those pat
phrases and explanations that label everything and still land us in
the absolute gutter of ignorance. . . . Never in the history of man
has there been such an articulate mass of ignorant people. . . ."

"Obviously you're a thinker, Connie. You're outraged. I wonder if that sense of outrage comes from what's happening to us as a nation or because of disgust with yourself for using drugs . . . or to justify your use of drugs on account of the war . . . the traditional junkie strategy of making himself into an unwilling victim."

"Mr. Cortina, how fortunate that I was chosen for this series of interviews and not one of the other battered kids upstairs. . . ." It was as close to an evil smile as her extreme physical discomfort would permit. "You're not going to either badger or persuade me into accepting any of your social-work pablum. For once in your life you'll earn your money—and maybe lose some of your sleek Victorianism!"

I watched the brave posturing. She was doing her best to sit still and complete her image as a champion of enlightenment, but she couldn't control her exacerbated nerves. She was on her feet again, prickling with wretchedness.

"I'm glad that you'll be doing this, too. I don't often interview anyone who is so expressive. What was your major in college? Drama, literature, writing?" I waited a moment. She continued her thrashing about. "Obviously, you're not like the majority of the other women here. Frankly, I'm surprised to meet you here. I'd expect to encounter a Connie in one of those private, costly, discreet treatment refuges." I lighted a cigarette. "You know, one of those places where the patient is king? Where the Cadillac is waiting in the wings to whisk you off when you've had enough therapy and indulgence."

"Yes, Mr. Cortina, you must be the very William F. Buckley with those poor slob junkies," she snapped.

"How much were you using a day, Connie?"

"Plenty."

"How did you get your stuff? Prostitution?"

It was with profound disgust that she said: "Wouldn't it be reassuring if you could think that all drug addicts are the dregs? All mentally retarded, all pariahs, all safely removed from your circle of acquaintances? No, Mr. What's-your-name . . . Cortina. Those days are gone forever. The Black ghetto, the poor White slum, they're not the dope cradle any more. . . . The stuff is out, haven't you heard . . . ? The stuff is out, falling like snow in your happy middle class. . . ." She was at the window. She appeared very young, her shoulders hunched, her head against the pane. When she turned around, there was a white mark on her brow from the pressure. "The rottenness has spread, and that's why all of you are so disconcerted. It shouldn't have gotten to those nice, clean, advantaged Americans. . . . Booze, occasional pills, clandestine reefers, the double and triple standards, those are acceptable, but heroin. . . . O, Lord, what have we come to? What's wrong with American youth, the pride of our nation, the cream of the crop, shooting shit in our veins? Disturbing, isn't it?"

"How come you're here, Connie? Why not one of those elite establishments?"

She reached for my cigarettes. "I've been there, too."

"I see. And you've come here to find help?" I paused as she struck a match. "Or to find acceptance . . . is that it? You feel more at home. You were too disgusted with the wealthy addict, they weren't real according to your view?"

"Whatever you say. You wouldn't accept my ideas anyway. . . . Your own are too established."

"Did you come here because you would stand out? Your superiority would get you attention? Is that it?"

Some swift, scathing retort hung on her lips, and then unexpectedly she turned away. "I needed help."

"You used drugs to insulate yourself against the grossness of our society. . . . We're so repugnant, is that it?"

Was it a smile? "The same old question. That standard query. Everyone asks that question because they feel that once it's put, then the addict will begin to think furiously and will be on the road to abstention. Typical middle-class simplicity. . . . How many times have you asked that in your career, Mr. Cortina?"

"Many, many. . . ." I followed her movements about the room. "How many answers have you given to that question? You indicate that you've been in other programs before. . . ."

"It depended on who was asking, what there was in it for me, what the context was."

"Okay. I'm asking. The context is a rehabilitation facility. And what's in it for you is something only known to yourself. So why did you use drugs?"

She returned to the chair and sat down. "I don't know."

"That's reasonable to me. I hear it all the time. I wonder, however, if you can accept that. Whether you can just drop it like that."

"You people are wonderful. You never question why you drink to excess, drive at insane speeds, jump in and out of bed promiscuously, stuff yourself with pills, gorge yourself like gluttons. . . . You never address that same question to yourselves, only to us. . . . Why?"

"But we're not in here seeking help. . . . Perhaps we should be. . . . But you're here . . . looking for help, you said. . . . Why isn't that question relevant?"

"You're refreshing, Mr. Cortina. . . . Skillful as a Jesuit, aren't you . . . ? I can just imagine you with some of the other girls. . . . How your ego must swell with satisfaction."

"Are you saying that you're the product of a culture that requires drugs in order to survive?"

She hesitated, thinking. "I think in a way that's so."

I looked at her. She seemed so small, her face so white; she struck me as being physically undersized. She moved nervously. "Then why are you here? Why shouldn't you just continue to use drugs? Or is it that you're afraid that next time you will suffer amputation . . . ?"

She considered it and said gravely: "I can't control my drug taking. I abuse them. . . ."

"That's perceptive. . . . If you could somehow learn to control your habit, keep it to a safe level . . . then drugs would be all right?"

She shook her head and got up. "But I can't. . . . I've tried. . . . I just can't control my demand. . . . I used to think I could, but I can't."

"Like a disease for you?"

"Like alcoholism. . . . One shot and I'm off. . . ."

"And yet with all the years that you've used, I'm sure that

you've been drug-free on occasion . . . in the hospital, for example; when you were in other drug programs. . . ."

"Every addict has kicked regularly. . . ."

"But you always went back, in the past?"

"Right."

She seemed to have relaxed for a moment, her voice had lost some of its intensity. "So what is it in your case, an incurable physical affliction? Or do you have to dig around inside yourself to find out what it is about Connie that makes her use drugs in order to live?"

She tossed her head, ready to puncture my assertion . . . and then, for some reason, she thought better of it. "I don't know. . . . It's not incurable. . . . People give up heroin every day and a lot of them remain free of it . . . so it's not incurable. . . ."

"Then it must be something in Connie, is that it?"

"Please, don't press it. . . . I can't think of any reason, you know, with quotation marks, any great problem. . . ."

I smiled at her. "So what are we left with? Do we need chicken bones, a crystal ball, and a ouija board? Are we in the realm of the mystical to account for your drug abuse?" She was back at the window. "Speed and heroin, it's a deadly combination . . . as close to suicide as you can get. . . ."

"I've been through therapy and out the back door. Let's not start with that string of beads: 'Why are you self-destructive? What are you trying to do to yourself?' That's a blind alley."

"So it's hopeless . . . ?" I waited. Her face was grim. I said: "You signed yourself in here on a whim. You're like most drug abusers. You enjoy the high but after awhile you're not experiencing it, so you lay up, hoping that by abstaining you'll renew your freshness and when you start back you'll once again feel that old rapture?"

She grabbed the cigarette package. Her hands were unsteady, and she had difficulty pulling out a cigarette. I lighted it for her.

"Isn't that what happens, Connie?"

"For a lot of the kids. . . . Yes. . . ."

"Not in your case?"

She sighed. "I don't know. . . . Something is wrong, screwed up. . . ."

"Why did you come in here?"

"I need help, man. For God sakes, stop acting like a district attorney."

I passed her an ash tray. "I'm really a very good listener. . . . Have you thought of your other options? Methadone, cyclozocine, going abroad where you could become a registered addict . . . ?"

"I don't want that. . . . They're not answers. . . ." And she seemed to be pouting, like a disgruntled child.

"What are you left with? You discredit everything—therapy, drug antagonists, etc. . . . Is it that you think you'll just grow out of drug dependence, is that it? A kind of magical maturation process?"

"It's like a trashy detective story. . . . I'm the victim, the sleuth and the culprit all rolled up in one."

"That sounds awfully slick—jive talk. You've certainly heard other addicts dramatize themselves like that. . . . I will say, you are just a little different from some. . . . You have this very pronounced social consciousness . . . you know, about the war and our tainted values. . . . Perhaps that's a way for you to come to grips with your heroin and speed. . . . You could use that intensity to set us right, to effect change. . . ."

"Oh, Lord, you're going back to your William Buckley routine. . . ."

She was pacing again. "I'm very curious about why you came in here," I continued. "Why this place? It's understaffed, highly structured, it's therapeutic in orientation. . . . The addict that can't go anywhere else is put in here . . . the last stop. . . . And you signed yourself in? That is mysterious. How were you getting your money for drugs?"

"I had an allowance from my parents. . . ."

"They knew that they were supporting a drug addict?"

"They're divorced."

"You lived with one of them?"

"I had my own place. . . ."

"Did you graduate from college?"

"Yes. . . ."

"Do you have much in common with the other women in this program?"

"We all used drugs."

"Aside from that. How many of them have been through college? Had an allowance?"

"I don't know," she said sharply, nettled by the questions. "I haven't been here long enough to start a research project. . . ."

I laughed. "It's a good idea, that. When I come back next month, perhaps you'll have started. That is, if you're still here."

She picked up the challenge recklessly: "I'll be here. . . ."

"I look forward to it, Connie. I just wonder why you picked this place."

Like a shot she was out the door, and I was left alone.

Mrs. Isabella Hartung, who had outtalked, outlived, outworn four husbands, was short and blocky; her dyed red hair showed gray at the roots. Bella didn't merely sit at a desk, she overwhelmed it, as she overwhelmed everything else in life—her staff, the rehabilitants, the municipal bureaucracy that supervised her.

"Do you know what the girls call her?" she asked, in a cloud of smoke. "Grace Kelly."

"She certainly doesn't look like Grace Kelly. . . ."

"Look . . . what's that got to do with it? It's her manner, that pale, pearl-white appearance. And that drawl she's got. It ain't Southern. It sounds like Beacon Hill. . . . Sounds like a girl who's got beaucoup dollars."

"Does she have beaucoup dollars?"

"You didn't get that from her? I'm surprised. She's got to be the most labial cat yet. Talk, talk, talk. . . . She's been here five days. I hate to think what a long-distance talker she's gonna be when she comes off medication."

"She's like a cat in a cage. . . ."

"Like all speed users. . . . But wait; she'll settle down."

"Does she have any friends upstairs . . . ?"

"Friends . . . ? That type, Frank Michael, she don't want

friends . . . maybe a disciple or two. . . . You touch her on any
point and you get clothes-closet militancy. The world is rotten.
The girls told her she should get bombs. . . ." Bella tried to ape
Connie's distinctive speech. It was ludicrous and cruel at the same
time.

"Bella, you're marvelous."

"Subtle I ain't, but it's all me. It's all one piece, it buttons up
the back, and there ain't no bones," she said, standing up to her
full five feet, one hand on her hip and her cigarette hanging from
her lips. Bella had her academic degrees, some ancient and dusty,
but her greatest talent was her patient understanding. For a long
time she *was* drug rehabilitation in her section of the country. She
had been working with drug-dependent people long before it became a subject of national preoccupation. "This Grace Kelly is the
kind who makes you think that the roles are reversed. That she's
here to help me and everybody else. There ain't nothing wrong
with her, it's just us, and the world. We get a dose of Eriksen,
Freud, and stop the world, it ain't a nice place."

"Why should she come here, Bella?"

"Why?" And her cigarette ash plopped to the desk. "Why? Because she ain't a mensch, that's why. She ain't a mensch!"

2

"It must have a tremendous effect on the kids when they walk in
and see the tape recorder propped against the wall, the cables on
the floor, the microphones hanging so artlessly from the chairs.
Wow! Plays right up to a junkie's ornate heart!"

The drawl, the confident ring of the words, the implied
superiority—I understood what Bella meant when she had
talked about the roles being reversed: Connie was in that room to
help me. In the month since our last meeting that restlessness that
withdrawal from speed produces had lessened.

"Aren't all of these gewgaws part of your mystique, Mr. Cortina? You know: 'Smile, kiddies, you're in pictures'? How important, how symbolic the paraphernalia: their words about to be recorded, their words immortal, captured for all posterity. How flattering! What drug addict could resist such a setting."

The scarcely concealed contempt made me understand that she saw through me and my sordid scheme, that it was important that I feel uncomfortable and self-conscious, that I defer to her. It was the incongruity of it. If I'd closed my eyes and just listened to her, I might have imagined some giant, a masterful critic, a dauntless social scientist—that voice echoing in my ears. . . . Yes, if she had just been a voice, she might have gotten away with it. . . . But to see her, small, unfeminine-appearing, I could not rid myself of the feeling that she was stunted.

Her words cascaded out: "Addicts love pageantry. Inevitably they're suckered into it, and the more fabled it is, the more they wallow in it."

"Fabled pageantry. . . ."

"Armor, rich trappings, panoply . . . the baroque. That's the setting for the addict. . . ."

I said: "The way they express themselves. The words they use, the way they can create a world of substance through words. . . ."

"Of course, that's all part of it. . . . Ceremony . . . ceremony, like a primitive tribe. . . ."

"Curious, isn't it?"

She shrugged her shoulders, as if she had tired of the badinage, and said: "That's the way they are."

"It glosses over the tawdriness of their lives, glosses over their passivity, their isolation?"

She lighted a cigarette and with a nervous flick of her wrist extinguished the match. "You're using the wrong words. Drug addiction is now the Number One preoccupation of our glorious republic. Everybody is on the bandwagon. What an irony! That alienated, passive, immature, unmotivated, somehow slimy figure of the drug fiend has turned the country upside down, is giving it nightmares and thrills at the same time and making our best citizens take more pills and alcohol so that they can cope with the

American epidemic. It's really very ironic. . . . This is the way Americans expiate their grossnesses—drug abuse is like pimples, a sign of rich and unregulated living. . . . Drug abuse may be the best thing that ever happened. Perhaps now we'll have to do something about our attitudes . . . our unrealities. . . ."

"I understand. . . . So your becoming a drug addict was essentially a patriotic act? You were going to bring the country to its senses?"

"Really, Mr. Cortina, your sarcasm lacks the proper lightness of touch. . . ."

"Or was it just your parents you were trying to get back at . . . ? You said that they were divorced. . . ."

She scratched out the cigarette. "Ah, enter the therapist." (And, she implied, a nickel-and-dime therapist at that.) "Yes, my parents were divorced. But I had plenty of family left. . . ."

"Oh, you enjoyed home?"

"Yes."

"You had lots of friends?"

"Yes." She was going to develop the whole bubble of interaction and then let sheer indifference and boredom prick it.

"You were a very active child?"

"Yes. . . . A tomboy, a daredevil. I kept things stirred up." She made no attempt to disguise her leading me on.

"What about school?"

"What about it?" she asked sweetly.

"Did you get along well?"

"Splendidly. Excellent student. I graduated at sixteen from high school."

"You were precocious?"

"Yes, yes, yes, yes, yes," she said abruptly, sullenly, her mood swiftly turning into resentment.

I looked out at the small square of dirty yard, a perpetual twilight hovering over it. "And you were always confident and expressive?"

"Always."

"And you had advantages—no economic or social deprivation?"

"Yes." She was bored.

"And you went to college and grew up to become the successful heroin and speed abuser." I said, straight-faced.

"Good God, where were you trained?" she exploded irritably.

"It's so puzzling. The poorest, most battered drug addict can spin out a web of shimmering words, an aura of complete confidence, and yet can hardly pull his zipper up. . . . Excuse me, I mixed my genders here. . . ."

"You must be a winner with those poor slobs upstairs. They probably hang on your every word, marvel at your skill."

I said equably: "Why not? They're poor slobs. They don't know why they use dope. They're just 'lames.' But when I'm confronted by some one so obviously superior in every way, then I'm out of my depth. Yes, you've proved to me how incompetent I am, Connie. Now you can go upstairs and tell the girls that I'm really an inept fraud. You have been triumphant. You can write me off as another failure. Therapy, psychiatry, methadone, American society, the government, all crossed off because they couldn't stand up against Connie's searing superiority. Just think, in a few weeks you can get your influential family to petition you out of this program and you can declare it as another failure. . . . And you can return to your heroin and speed. It's just puzzling . . . puzzling. . . ." I let the words trail away and looked out the window, where the flakes of soot floated down.

She broke the silence: "What's puzzling?"

"How anyone so superior could be so, you'll pardon my crudeness, stupid."

"Stupid?"

I said harshly: "How else would you characterize your hepatitis, your blood poisoning, your near loss of an arm?"

"Hardly as stupidity," she said waspishly.

"Not to sterilize a needle—to infect yourself—hardly seems intelligent." Again I was struck by her appearance of being undersized, dwarfed. Slowly, deliberately, I removed my microphone from around my neck, reached over, and turned off the recorder. I smiled at her and said mildly: "You win. I'm stymied. Why waste your time? My middle-class conscience bothers me when I waste time. So, thank you for your time and indulgence. Let me just remove your microphone and you can go back upstairs . . . triumphant. Thank you. Good luck," I said, unhooking the microphone ribbon from her neck.

She was drawn inward, her face wan, her hands moving nervously. I looked at my watch in the silence. At last she said hollowly, almost in a whisper: "I don't feel triumphant. I don't know why I'm the way I am. I get this way . . . a desperate need to discredit everything."

"And everyone . . . ?" I asked.

She nodded her head, agreeing: "To put down somebody, to shred them away. . . ."

"Was this the way things were handled in your family?"

"Words cloaked so much there. . . . My grandmother, my mother. . . ."

"Interesting, you say your grandmother before your mother. . . . Does that mean anything?"

"She's a very forceful woman . . . and so is my mother."

"She's your mother's mother?"

"No, my . . . my father's. I hardly know my mother's people. They're in Cuba. . . ." She sounded very smug. "Anti-American to even talk about Cuba, you know."

"You said last time that you'd never been in trouble with the police, you never had to do the criminal things that so many addicts have to in order to support their habits—prossing, for the girls. . . . You had an allowance. . . . Did your family know about your drug dependence . . . ?"

"My mother. . . . My grandmother didn't know and doesn't know yet."

"How can you be so sure of that?"

She smiled wanly. "If she knew, she'd be here like a shot."

"And you don't want her to know, but you don't care that your mother knows? Your mother knows that you're here?"

"Yes."

"Must be something for her to know that you're in a city-run program. How does she feel about it?"

"I don't know. I haven't seen her. We're not supposed to communicate with the family the first six weeks. . . ."

"Enforced separation, is that it?"

"I suppose so."

"Did you get along with your mother, Connie?"

It nettled her. "Spare me the approach . . . the pussy-footing, trying to construct a childhood trauma. . . ."

"You said that your mother was a forceful woman."

"She's an outspoken, strong woman who did her damnedest to dominate me. She's very volatile, not surprising in a Latin. She's short-tempered, raises her voice, always in a passion about something. She charges at things. That's the way she handled her marriage. . . . She's a woman with tremendous energy. She's intelligent, competent."

"Is this why your mother and father broke up?"

She had a fixed, abstracted expression in her eyes. "Incompatibility. He's a very quiet, gentle man. Shy, even. She managed him and she tried to manage me. . . ."

"What happened when they were divorced? Your father supplied maintenance?"

"She went out and went to work. She'd been an economist before she got married. . . ."

"She worked when you were growing up, too?"

"No. In those days, she was a typical suburban housewife. You know: teas, lunches, cancer campaign. . . . My father'd catch the train and go into town. . . ."

"What did he do?"

"A banker. His father had been one, too. A family thing altogether."

"Obviously you felt more comfortable with your father."

"Yes, that's so. I could talk to him. He was never too busy to sit down and listen. I used to tell him everything." She rubbed her hands together.

"You couldn't do that with your mother?"

"I didn't want to."

"She was too threatening a figure?"

Connie demurred: "You see, this is what I mean about this kind of confrontation. That kind of question—was I threatened by her—it leads to all kinds of inaccuracies. Of course I spoke to my mother, but never with the freedom that I spoke to my father. I wasn't afraid of my mother, I just felt that there were certain things I didn't want to discuss with her. Isn't that natural? All of us are like that."

"But you had a feeling about it. Were you afraid that she'd swallow you up?"

She toyed with the microphone cable. "Bleach me out, perhaps. . . . She's a very strong personality."

"And you had doubts that you were?"

"Who knows at that age . . . ? What do you remember about your feelings at age nine? I know that my father always appeared tentative at home, as if he didn't belong there, as if he were a visitor. When we sat talking together, I sensed that he was putting on an act. I think he was always protecting himself against her. His life style so, so vastly different from hers. I think I was conscious of that. For one thing, I know that I wanted him to stand up to her. Stand up to her."

"You mean for his own survival?"

"Sure. . . . He was so self-effacing. . . ."

"Couldn't have been a very relaxed atmosphere for a kid."

"Hardly. . . . Hardly." she lighted a cigarette. "My mother would get all pent up and then let fly at him. It could be anything that would trigger her outburst. And in a certain sense, I could understand her feeling. He just wouldn't stand up against her. The more she attacked, the more he would draw back, and finally she'd just blow. . . . Pow!" She smoked thoughtfully, her nervousness barely apparent. "And yet she loved him intensely . . . I know that. Because she would grieve. I heard her crying some nights. But she seemed unable to understand that she was destroying their union by her constant pressure on him. . . ."

"It was always like that?"

"Nothing is ever always . . . the same, Mr. Cortina," she said sharply. "It had its ebb and flow. . . . I think the most devastating thing for me was the trick my father had of hooding over his eyes, his defense, his way of withdrawing. You know, we'd be there together talking and she'd come in, and I could feel him detaching himself, effacing himself, dematerializing. He was always polite, accommodating, but he never was really there, as a presence, when she was around."

"In those days they lived together as man and wife?"

"Conjugally, you mean?" She hesitated. "Yes, I guess they must have, though it's hard to think of my father as a passionate man. . . . Let me put that in another way. However passionate he was by nature, he would have been daunted by her in the marriage act as he was in every other relationship they had together. . . . You know, conditioning works across everything. . . ."

There was some shade that had crossed her face. I asked: "This bothers you? You'd rather we didn't talk about it?"

"Well, I know where it leads. I've been through it before with psychiatrists. Once open the sex bag and we all become little Sigmunds, and we can spin all kinds of erotic traceries and sexual repressions and motivations. . . . Yes, I find it disagreeable, if you must know."

"The discussion of sex in general or just as it affects your parents?"

She stammered slightly: "I just think there's entirely too much exploitation of it as a great and sweeping grab bag for hangups."

"I'll bet there's little reticence about sex upstairs among the other female residents. . . ."

Suddenly Connie got to her feet, walked to the window, drummed against the pane with her nails, moved her head about as if exercising cramped muscles. "I'm off the medication . . . and that nervousness comes over me so I want to climb the walls." She went back to the chair. I gave her a cigarette. She sat and looked at me as if she were trying to get me into focus. "Sex is a preoccupation of theirs. . . ."

"And all kinds of homosexual entanglements, scenes, pursuits. . . ."

"Ad nauseum."

"And you've been propositioned, accosted, sweet-talked. Part of the institutional syndrome, isn't it?"

"Once they're cleaned up, all their appetites return. But so many of them are damaged . . . abused beyond belief by men. I guess every single one of them has been a prostitute at one point. Some of them are pretty badly warped by it. . . . One girl, they call her Gussie, a kind of raw-boned blond of uncertain age, can't talk. . . . She just looks at you . . . and mumbles. . . . I don't

think she's old. She'll suddenly appear next to you and stare. . . .
God knows, sex is a pawing beast."

"You're surely not surprised. You must have expected as much
when you signed yourself in here?"

Her face was as pale as the whiteness of her blouse. "I don't
know what I expected. . . ."

"Disturbs you, doesn't it?"

"It does. . . ." She twitched in the chair. "You can't reason with
them. You just can't make them understand."

"Why should you try?"

She stared at me. "Because we're creatures of reason. That's
why. . . ."

"So that they'll let you alone, not molest you?"

"They let me alone." she said flatly.

"Not only sexually. . . . You're frozen out?"

"They keep their distance."

"And that's what you want?" I asked, watching her pleating her
skirt into folds. "You must have group therapy sessions with them.
What happens in there? They ignore you there, too?"

"They're too busy operating, grandstanding, making a play for
attention. Typical addicts, playing the game, attempting to deceive
one another, and all the while aware that they're twisting, trying
to shift their responsibility. . . . Typical addict maneuvering."

"They're not sincere in seeking help?"

She exploded: "Why do you use phrases like that? What the
hell do they mean in this kind of setup? Most of those girls are
here because they were offered this place or prison. . . . Addicts
are always posing. They have to. They're too uncomfortable in
their own skins. . . . They're always operating, conniving. . . .
They can't help it; it's part of their conditioning."

"And you're like that, too? Posing, conniving?"

She shook her head: "I haven't had their degradations."

"That's right. I'd forgotten. You weren't a street addict. You had
an allowance from your family. . . . But you know a lot about addicts and how they behave."

She glared at me. "I had to be with them to get my stuff, didn't
I? You can't pick your company there. . . . You've got to buy your

stuff in certain places. . . . How can you avoid the street addict?"

"Is it possible that you do have poses, that you are uncomfortable in your own skin?"

"Are we going to get back into the nit-picking bag again?"

"I asked a reasonable question. You say we're creatures of reason. Isn't it possible for us to have poses and not know about them? It's done all the time. How accurate is your perception of yourself?"

"What an absurd question."

"You just said that these girls are always posing. Does this big, raw-boned blond know that she is posing . . . ? What was her name?"

"Gussie." She wrinkled her forehead. "Gussie isn't posing. . . ." Then slowly, "I don't think so. . . . Who would pose by becoming mute?"

"Who would pose by being garrulous . . . ?" I asked. "Besides, isn't the trick to know ourselves when we're posing and what makes us pose . . . ?"

She took what I said very seriously; for the first time she seemed to be caught up in the exchange.

"From what you say, Connie, I would gather that you consider yourself to be open and frank by contrast with these other girls. . . . Is that right?"

"I think I am frank . . . honest. I don't use a group therapy session for an emotional bath or a place to snivel for cheap sympathy. It's a pretty disgusting spectacle to see a forty-four-year-old addict whimpering away like a ten-year-old . . . especially when it's all an act. Just show her a bag and she'd be back off shooting in a second."

"So therefore you don't take any part in the group interaction. . . . You remain aloof?"

"I don't remain aloof. . . . They haven't been interested in me."

"And you wouldn't offer information on your own? Volunteer?"

"I told you that I'm not a street addict. I don't go around crying out my guts."

"But your silence must interest the group leader. . . . Isn't the group leader curious about you?"

She shifted in her chair. "The group leader is a kid, probably just barely out of school. . . . Freud sticks out all over her . . . her social-worker mystique hasn't dried yet. The group gets her so upset about herself that she doesn't come down off the wall. Addicts detect a weakness a mile away. And once they find it, they'll work on it and work on it until they've opened a hole a mile wide. They've got that kid going so hard about her own hangups that she hasn't any time to work on them. . . ."

"Maybe she's really a very skillful therapist. Perhaps she's just leading them on. . . ."

"Oh, Mr. Cortina, you really are too much. Listen, I've been through therapy more times . . . and if that girl is that accomplished. . . . She's just being harassed. She's out of her depth."

"Well, whatever it is, it's diverted her attention from you, hasn't it?"

"I think I'm her security . . . since I never get on her back."

"And that gives you immunity, allows you to remain silent and withdrawn," I said, expecting her anger. Instead she frowned. I drew a cigarette out from the pack slowly, feeling it, "I wonder if it's conceivable that for all of your articulateness, your expressiveness, that you really are an uncommunicative person . . . and you don't know it." I lighted the cigarette. She was weighing what I said. "Did you have many friends outside?"

"Yes, I had friends."

"Close friends?"

"Not really intimate friends . . . kids I ran around with . . . a crowd."

"Boys and girls?"

This made her look up. Something about that phrase disturbed her. "Well, they weren't cats and dogs!"

"How did you manage to get through college while you had a drug habit?"

"I did it."

"Remarkable. . . . I should think that your concentration, your constant need to supply your habit. . . ."

She lashed out: "There's so much gobbledygook about drug addiction, so much ignorance. . . . Everybody's an expert. . . . I went through four years of college, and I used heroin practically every day. . . . And there were others like me. Good God, a little bit of knowledge is certainly a dangerous thing in your case, Cortina. . . ." She turned abruptly in her chair so that her back was to me. "I've known doctors, ministers, teachers, policemen on the stuff . . . and housewives. . . . I've seen them all hanging around in those places you go to to get your stuff, so don't give me your razzle-dazzle ignorance and generalizations," she sputtered, her hands trembling.

"And no professor or college official ever tumbled to the fact that you were using drugs? Remarkable. It says a lot for your powers of dissimulation, doesn't it? Puts you right up at the head of the junkie class. . . . Perhaps, though, your ability to pose, your ability to remain hidden, is natural. You said your father had this gift of hiding."

"My father wasn't talkative."

"Ah, I see. . . . But you are. So he could conceal himself through silence . . . and you conceal yourself through talking. . . ."

"God, how obvious you are . . . and how elementary. I've been through this kind of thing with experts. . . . You're just plain clumsy. . . ."

"It's obvious that you're practiced. No question about it. But you understand that I'm accustomed to working with less advantaged people . . . people who pose, who game, who whimper. . . ." I looked out into the courtyard and asked: "Why do you want to punish your mother so badly?"

"Punish my mother?" She was aghast at my apparent stupidity.

"Yes. Isn't that why you're here? Can you imagine how repulsed she'll be when she visits you here? When she gets a look at your company: whores, lesbians, thieves, pickpockets . . . the whole underbelly of society. God, how that will grab her!"

She said primly: "Perhaps she'll never come. . . . I'm of age. I have to invite her. . . ."

"Oh, there's no doubt of it. . . . You'll invite her. That's why you came in here, isn't it?"

She sighed: "If you say so. . . ." She lighted a cigarette.

"You said yours was like a trashy detective story. . . . You said that last time, didn't you . . . ? This may be a clue. . . . I tell you that you came in here to debase your mother. You chose the most degraded setting you could imagine so that your mother would have to come in and see her daughter and be degraded. . . . You want to abuse your mother. . . ."

It was almost dreamlike, the quality of the response: "Is that why I came here?"

She had her head turned from me. "Your mother knew that you were a drug user, you said. Had she sought help for you before? I think you said that you had been in a psychiatric institution. . . ."

"My mother knows me. She discovered that I was using heroin. At that time I was very upset about it. I was riding myself because I was an addict. I went home. I kicked there. She remained with me for eight days while I went through withdrawal. The doctor kept coming and going. We talked together as we hadn't talked in years. She was trying, I was trying. The best that was between us came out in those eight days, but it soured. I don't know why. After that, I agreed to go into the psychiatric institute. . . . But it was all false and I knew it. . . ." She looked up at me. "If you're trying to get me to say that there is something screwed up in my relationship with my mother . . . of course there is. . . . Isn't it obvious? I've really never forgiven her for driving my father out. Breaking up our home. But my mother couldn't endure that. She's so purposeful. She had to coax me into private therapy. It was her way of handling her feelings . . . her guilt. . . ."

"She wasn't considering you, trying to help you?"

Disgustedly, she said: "Of course! But that was not the whole story. I was her indictment. I was a dope fiend! Don't you understand? You're not going to untangle all of these threads, Mr. Cortina. You're not going to card them and make them into a nice sequence of motivation and response, and then come up with a startling result as to why Connie uses drugs. It doesn't work that way. . . . We're not question-and-answer summations! We're not. If we were, I wouldn't be here. For I've asked myself the questions . . . and I've come up with some answers. . . . But I still used dope. . . . And I'd go right back out there and use all over again. . . ."

"Perhaps it's all in the way we view our experience. Maybe a slightly different perspective. . . ."

"If it will keep you happy, you view from any angle you want. . . . Just go ahead and view. . . ." She had become very nervous again.

"Well, we've almost run off the tape. We'll stop now."

She said crossly: "I'll bet you're relieved. . . . I'll bet you are."

"Yes, I am, frankly. I hardly thought you'd show up for this second interview." I turned off the machine and removed my microphone.

"You don't know me, Mr. Cortina. I'm not in any way overwhelmed by you. I know your type. . . ."

I leaned forward. "Would you be pleased to have me say that you're hopeless, that I'd just as soon not have to go through another session with you? A kind of confession of total defeat?" I asked. "Is that what you want?"

"I don't know what I want. . . ." And it was said petulantly, like a spoiled child. She took off her microphone and put it on the chair. She walked out.

"Are you leading any therapy groups these days, Bella?"

She was smoking in that unrelenting way she had of doing everything. She never flicked off an ash, it always fell from the cigarette. "I'm leading one special group. Who gets time for anything? I'm the director, Frank Michael. That means I sweep the floors, clean the johns, hold hands, make beds, fight with city hall, try to get more staff, try to piece out the money. . . ."

"I think you ought to take Connie into your group."

"She shouldn't be here. Our debutante has money, she could pick and choose, she could find herself some nice, posh place. Why does she have to come here and slum . . . ? She shouldn't be here."

"But she signed herself in, Bella. . . . Don't you think that significant?"

"She's trying to find out how the other nine-tenths lives. . . . She's getting a smell of life. . . ."

"But she hasn't tried to cop out of the program, has she? So it's got to be more than just an impulse. Take her into your group, Bella."

"Her kind is the most difficult kind. You know that. There ain't nothing there to work with. She's tasted it all, she's jaded. What have we got for her here? With the rest of them there's always something you can work on, something. This is a plastic; she ain't no mensch, this Grace Kelly."

I stared at the ash bending from the cigarette. "Bella, she's more defenseless than any girl you've got here. Defenseless and cut off. . . ."

"So, with her dollars why should she care? Huh? We're going to give her a new life? Grace Kelly herself with her snooty ways, so far above all of us. I'll give you her file and you can drool over it. . . ."

"I don't want her file. She'll tell me. . . . Take her into your therapy group."

The ash plopped on the desk. "She's a speed user. She's part of a special pattern. Beaucoup dollars, beaucoup advantages, beaucoup screw-ups. A plastic she is, Frank Michael." She took in a massive breath, smoke coming from between her lips. "I'll take a hundred ghetto girls to one like this . . . any day . . . any day . . . to trying to work with one like this. . . ."

3

Outside, that steady, sluicing sound of heavy rain. The courtyard was blackened by it—and though it was early October, the weather was so unseasonably cold that the window panes were steamy.

She looked pale; she had bluish pouches beneath her eyes. She had been shifting restlessly throughout the playback, as if she were chilled. At last the tape slipped through the drive puck.

"I'm cold." She shivered. I got my topcoat from behind the door and passed it to her. She took it as if it were her property. It was obvious that she felt miserable as only methedrine users can.

"No more medication, Connie?"

"I refused it. . . . I told you that last time. I just get so cold. . . ." She hunched herself into my coat. "My skin prickles with it."

"How's it going?"

"Dreary."

"This place?"

"Everything."

"Does your father know that you're here?"

"No."

"Why shouldn't he know?" I watched her moving inside the topcoat, that bobbed head, the small ears. "Does he know about your drug taking?"

"No."

"Why is it that neither your father nor your grandmother know? They're to be spared?"

"I don't know."

"But your mother knows because of the time when you went through your withdrawal at home. Perhaps even she wouldn't know unless. . . ."

"I was very sick then; I had to go home. I wouldn't do it now." The drawl was there but it was subdued.

She seemed so disconsolate. "You don't feel well, why don't we forget it for this time?"

For the first time she looked me in the face. "I'm just cold and revolted."

"Revolted by what?"

"Everything. . . . This place . . . these people . . . their primitive, slimy lives."

"Is there any way you can get out of this program? I mean, can you be transferred to another . . . ?"

"Anything can be managed. . . ."

"Then why stay?" And I tried to sound inoffensive, because she was suffering.

"It's so gross," she muttered into the coat.

"Not as gross as a penitentiary, Connie."

"Even the simplest things are brutal. To be observed as you uri-
nate."

I nodded my head, affirming that. "Why not? You know how
specimens are switched, how girls use this as a device for all sorts
of things—to get rid of unwanted loves or hates, to be busted, to
conceal cheating, messing up. . . ."

"But, oh, God. . . . And the constant conniving and cunning,
the coarseness, intolerance . . . the spitefulness, the need to hurt
others." She shuddered. "Oh, my God, how hateful they are!"

"Giving you a real hard time?"

"They live on the most primitive level. . . . Food, clothes, cigarettes, radios, shampoo, cookies, candy bars, perfume—all items
of exchange or intimidation or extortion. Everything is inverted.
. . . It's a jungle . . . it's savage."

She had shrunk inside the coat, her face blanched by revulsion.
She began to mutter, more to herself than to me, "They grab the
food, kick you, stab you . . . lie about you. . . . Stand there, lifting
up their breasts for you to suckle. . . . Animals. Oh, my God.
Their sex play, old women trapping the young ones, drooling with
their lust, and the cries of victory. . . . To watch their eyes undress
you and fondle you, their whispers, their promises, their breath
. . . with their bad teeth. . . ." She looked up, her face drained of
all color, pinched, her eyes huge. It was appalling to see her without defenses, without resources, almost hallucinating in her terror.

Still, she had signed herself into the program. It was this act
that was etched out by the acid of her agony. I watched her, waiting there quietly, waiting for her to surface.

She muttered: "People are not like that. . . . Not human. Animals. . . . Filth. . . . In their dunghills. . . ."

I said quietly: "If the girls could see you now . . . if they could
see you now, Connie, they would help you. . . . They would, you
know. . . ."

She stared at me dully, shaking her head, biting her lip, and
then a vast sob rose from her and shook her inside the coat. . . .

I watched the rain stream down the window, a steady plopping
striking the floor from a crack in the window sash. She was crying

now . . . only an occasional sob wrenching out. Undoubtedly it had been building up for months—perhaps years. God alone knew what those tears were cleansing. All I could do was wait.

At last she stammered: "I'm going to call my grandmother; she'll take me away from here. . . . My grandmother will take me away from here. . . ."

"Is that what you want . . . now . . . ? You're through the worst of it."

Suddenly she caught sight of the reels moving, I had forgotten that I had turned on the machine. She said, snapping it off: "How could you? How could you . . . ? What a horrible thing to do. . . . What kind of a man are you? What kind of man . . . ? You're heartless. Who are you to sit there in judgment? Listening with all of your detachment. . . ."

I smiled. . . . I smiled in relief, genuine relief. She was angry at me. I smiled, and to cover my own feeling of inadequacy, I lighted a cigarette. She shook herself out of my topcoat and left the room.

Sometimes it was difficult to remember that Bella was far beyond retirement age. I had known her for twenty years, and she had not been young then. But now she must have been in her seventies. Even in repose, Bella was energetic. She never took her breath properly, she always had too many words to get out, and as a result she always gasped out the last of them.

"So she crashed. . . . Crashed, smashed. . . . So?"

"It was long overdue."

She shrugged and puffed on her cigarette. "She ain't my style . . . I told you before. . . ."

"Bella, that drawl is for real. . . . She can't help it. She actually talks that way. Even this morning, when she was really broken, she drawled. . . ."

"So she's consistent. What's that?" And she gave me one of her famous glances, one of those glances that cut right through you, as if to reach your heart. It was that glance that had brought many a practiced addict down to utter ruin. "Maybe, Frank Michael, in your old age you're getting softheaded. . . . Maybe she gamed you."

"Perhaps. . . . But if she did, it revealed a very different girl. . . . I think this one is really helpless, Bella. Like a crab without a shell. . . ."

"Poetical, he is, too. . . . The girls have been slamming her hard . . . shootin' her down. . . . They can't take that beaucoup dollars and background. It's the nearest thing they got to break up. . . . She'll either make it or she'll break. . . . And it ain't no use to sit here and be sorry for her. That don't help her to get to be a mensch. . . . What was her complaint?"

"She's never been locked before. . . . She panicked."

Bella puffed the ash away. "Sex?"

"That and everything else. . . . The whole thing. . . ."

"See, like her, that kind. . . . The mother, absolutely the mother . . . the mother cripples 'em. . . . No mensch . . . Look for the mother. . . ."

"Did you take her into your group?"

"She's been there twice. . . . Getting her feet wet. . . . She started like she wasn't ever going to stop. . . . Talk, talk, talk. . . . Beaucoup words. . . . The girls in the group sit back. . . . You know that they're waiting for this chicken. . . . And they slammed her, Frank Michael . . . like, they slammed her." She gasped for air. "What else could they do . . . ? They put it on. . . . Sure, there's homosexuality—name me an institution where it ain't? We do what we can to keep it under control. . . . What we need, we ain't got—one staff for every resident. . . . This is a treatment facility. . . . You ain't gonna find no better in the country, bar none, I don't care where you look," and her breath ran out. "But Miss Rich Drawers ain't in approval of the human race. . . . Institutions shouldn't be. . . . All right, so let her make everything all over, like it should be different. . . ."

"Bella, do me a favor. . . . Drop in accidentally and see her now. . . . Don't let her duck it."

"So I got nothing else to do but futz around with rich people's daughters. . . . God help us if she's the Great Society . . . better we go back to the slums. . . . Not ghettos I ain't said, but slums. . . . Spinoza came from a ghetto."

"Thank you, Bella." I reached over for her hand.

"Now he does that. . . . Twenty years ago it never occurred to him. . . . Now you do it. . . . So long, Frank Michael."

4

Funny, but I had never seen anything animate in that courtyard: sparrow, mouse, cat. Only paper cups, tin cans, bottles, a broken umbrella, some bags, bricks, things unrecognizable, and the coarse grass. I wondered whose responsibility it was, that little plot of spoliation? And would it feel the urge of Indian Summer? New grass growing in the atypical November warmth?

I heard the footsteps and sat down abruptly. She came in. I made the overture: "Good morning, Connie. How are you?"

"You're not going to make me listen to that last episode are you?" she said with asperity, a ring of petulance back in the drawl.

"Whatever you say."

Some of that hint of chubbiness was gone. Her face was almost gaunt. She sat down, crossed one leg over the other, clasped her hands together and said: "I've had the flu. I think I must have been coming down with it the last time. I'm not trying to water down my exhibition. But I'm not quite ready for a strait jacket yet either. But get one thing straight—I don't like this place. I don't like the people here. But I can't sign myself out."

"Perhaps you have to go through these crises. Part of getting a hold of yourself."

"Thanks for the sop. . . ." She lighted a cigarette to show me that her hand was steady.

"Did you get in touch with your grandmother?"

"No, I didn't. I could call my mother. I didn't need her. Mrs. Hartung subtly snapped at me that if I needed to talk to a grandmother she would qualify. . . ."

"Well, you know, she is a grandmother. She didn't tell you to call her Bella?"

"Oh, yes, she gave me her number three spiel, I think: the staff sergeant with the heart of gold. What a caricature."

I smiled. "Mrs. Hartung is a remarkable woman. . . . I think you make a serious error to pass her off as a caricature. She's responsible for helping more girls find themselves over the years. . . ."

"Find themselves in bedlam?" she snapped.

Suddenly I laughed, not at the rejoinder, and Connie realized that. "What's so funny?"

"I was just thinking of what Bella's opinion of you might be. . . . Caricature was what you said of her. . . . I can just imagine hers. . . ."

"Somehow I'll survive."

"That's reassuring after the last time," I said callously.

She peered at me, stung by my remark. "I suppose if I come here I have to take what I get?"

"What would you like? Seriously, what would you like? To have me extend sympathy? To offer to smuggle a letter out to your grandmother? To get the newspapers to run this place down because of what it's done to you? Tell me, what would you like?"

"To be spared your crudeness. . . ."

"You said that you were a leader. . . . I wonder how come you led yourself into this program. . . . Had you some idea that you were going to find a kind of coarse roughage that had been missing from your life? You know—the very kind of experiences that appalled you so greatly last month. . . . Maybe you were seeking this. . . . Is that possible?"

She stubbed out the cigarette. "Place any construction you want on it."

I clasped my hands behind my head. "There is a great similarity between you and most of the girls, actually. I can see it. . . . I'm not trying to twit you now. I genuinely think that you're blind to it. I said that you were an incomplete eccentric and you are. You don't have enough self-belief, or energy or direction or cantankerousness to be a real eccentric. . . . You're like the rest of the drug band. Easier to sit back and appear aloof, superior, somehow above all the rest of us dopes. But you're not sitting back, you're lying back, prone, because you don't have it. Every other junkie I talk to has the same innate capacity for crumbling, only they're more honest than you. But you're the same as they. You gripe at their crudeness, at their cruelty, their singling you out. . . . You're guilty of exactly the same. Underneath, for all your advantages, for all of your superiority, you're immature, unmotivated, selfish, passive, and tainted by your own view of yourself." I smiled. "I can't think of anything else at the moment . . . other than that I'll speak to Mrs. Hartung, if you like. I'll give her a professional opinion. I'll suggest that you need a psychiatric milieu. . . . She'll buy that. She has to think of the rest of the residents . . . their well-being. You could be a pernicious influence."

She said tiredly: "I didn't come in here to trade insults with you, Mr. Cortina."

"Nor I with you. It's playing to your long suit again. I'm outmatched. You want me somehow to overcome your repugnance for everything that's happened to you, and yet you want me to do it in such a way that you'll look good in the course of it, you'll be justified, you'll be vindicated. . . . Or that somehow I'll come and sit next you and murmur: 'Yes, you've been victimized. Poor Connie.' I'm sorry, but that's what I feel. I can talk to you like this because you're a most intelligent and articulate young woman, able to entertain the most sophisticated ideas . . . but with a kind of hopeless disregard for doing anything. . . ." Her eyes never left my face. She made no attempt to get up. I wondered if any of my taunts would provoke a response. We sat there, only the sounds of the building echoing remotely. At last, very deliberately, I took my handkerchief out, spread it open and waved it aloft. "A truce, a truce, please. . . ." It must have seemed so ludicrous to her, perhaps almost a confession of weakness on my part, that she smiled.

"You've mentioned your grandmother frequently. . . . What kind of woman is she?"

The question hung. Connie was deciding, I guessed, whether she would indulge me, toss me a scrap. "An intelligent, energetic,

strong woman. . . . A woman who guided the family business
after her husband died . . . who expanded it. . . . A woman who
believed in family. . . . In a way, my grandmother is the family.
. . . Her house is center for family. . . ."

"And your father was her only child?"

She gave me a swift, suspicious glance. "How did you know?"

"You implied as much. . . ." And I knew that she was wondering whether I had been searching her files.

"Yes, he was an only child."

"She sounds very much like your mother . . . the attributes.
. . . Is that so?"

Connie seemed disarmed. "In a way. . . . Yes, in a way. You
could say that."

"So you had trouble getting along with her. . . . She wanted to
dominate you?"

She was considering. "I didn't think of it in that way. . . . We
were very close. I used to spend a lot of time with her. On the
weekend I'd go to her house and stay with her. Cousins would be
there . . . nieces . . . family friends. It was a big house, always
lots going on. . . . Play croquet or badminton or go swimming
. . . or she'd take me down to the office. . . ."

"This was before your mother and father were divorced?"

"Before and after. . . . Perhaps it was more so after, or maybe I
remember it that way."

"Your father worked for your grandmother, is that it?"

"She was the chief stockholder. . . . She had been on the board
of directors. . . . And when my grandfather died she took over. It
seemed very natural. . . . My father worked for her, yes. . . . After
the divorce, I don't know, I guess she decided that he would be
happier at a branch office. . . . He went to Denver. . . ."

"Your grandmother was fond of you?"

"I was the apple of her eye. You can understand, being the only
grandchild for a while. . . . We were very close. Even when I was
a little girl, my grandmother talked over very serious things with
me. I think she was grooming me for the future. Sometimes I almost got the impression that she thought of me as a son. . . . Curious . . . that just occurred to me."

"Did your mother resent your grandmother's attention to you?"

"I don't think so. . . . Perhaps she did. . . . I must make you understand. My mother spent a great deal of time at the big house, too. We lived only a few streets away. It was a closely knit family. . . ."

"Your mother and father would have been at your grandmother's . . . ?"

"Yes . . . together. . . . And then when Arlette came along . . . four of us would be there. . . ."

"Arlette was your sister?"

"Uh-huh. . . ."

"You enjoyed being in your grandmother's company?"

"She's a wonderful woman. Very natural. . . . There was never anything covert. . . . If she had something to say, she'd come out with it. . . . Never deliberately harsh or crude . . . but candid and firm. . . ."

I offered her a cigarette. She accepted it. "Your father and mother. . . . I've forgotten. . . . What happened between them?"

She looked at the glowing ash. "My mother didn't understand him. She couldn't realize that he was a man, that it was important to him to appear as the man. . . . You know, I don't think my mother ever realized that my father had been trying all of his life to work up enough gumption to break away . . . I mean, to break away from my grandmother. . . . You know, you can be tied down with strands of silk just as tightly as you can be with wire. . . . I used to think this. . . . My father should never have been what he was. He loved sports. Great tennis player, golfer, sailed. He would have been supremely happy as a physical ed. teacher in some boys' school. Really, he was that kind of man. . . . I can remember one time, he'd been drinking, he made this crack about the seats on the toilets always being down. . . . He shouted: 'If I could once go to the jake and find the seat up.' I remember laughing at it. I think it's one of the few times I ever heard him voice rebellion against his female world. . . ."

I must have sounded very pedantic and dense: "Your mother didn't understand that he was in rebellion?"

"I don't think so. . . . I've thought about it a great deal. . . .

He'd come home at night. His jacket would be draped over a chair, one shoe on the floor, another one on an end table, his tie on a light sconce. Everything higgledy-piggledy. His way of breaking the thralldom. . . . I'm sure he hated the conservative suits . . . the formality of his life. The clothes thrown off . . . a very poignant symbol. . . . It bothered her, my mother, and yet in a curious way I think she understood that he was struggling against his mother but it didn't help her to find the right way to capitalize on it. . . . Because she resented my grandmother, too. She felt that she was dominating the family. . . . Sometimes it's like being inside of a bubble that you've blown. You're trapped inside. . . . All you need is to pierce it to be freed . . . and yet you don't. . . ."

"Puzzling that your father should seek out in a mate a strong, energetic individual?"

"Yes, it is. . . ." She said wryly. "Flying into the face of destiny."

"Or knowing instinctively what is needed."

"Perhaps it's the same thing."

"Was your mother all that strong?"

"She must be that strong, otherwise she couldn't have broken him away. . . . And the irony of it, my grandmother would say to me when I was this little girl: 'Do you think your father is looking as well as he might?' or 'Don't you think he's awfully restless?' You know, telling me, as if I were an adult and responsible for him and his well-being. . . ."

"Must have been a strain when your mother and grandmother got together . . . kind of a tug of war. . . ."

"It wouldn't have been so bad if it had been out in the open, but it was always smoldering below. And I don't know to this day whether they were aware of their fierce enmity. . . . It was combat . . . real combat . . . without the wholesomeness of blows and physical pain. . . . For instance, sometimes my grandmother would say, almost as if it were spontaneous: 'Claire, should Billy be so nervous at his age?' Now, on the surface it sounds like a standard maternal-type utterance. But you knew that it was anything but that. You had to know that my mother was seven years older than my father, for instance, something my grandmother would never understand. You had to know that my father had had several of his early crushes demolished by my grandmother. You had to know that my mother was exotic in the eyes of my grandmother. . . ."

"Exotic?"

"That was her way of looking at it. My mother comes from Cuba. . . . I don't think in her worst imaginings about her son, my grandmother ever conceived of that."

"Your father gets more provocative all the time. . . ."

"All that redolent Maryland tradition suddenly grafted onto a Cuban vine. . . ." Connie smiled. "She had sent him to Cuba for a vacation—actually it was her way of throwing a monkey wrench into one of his entanglements. . . . He met my mother and that was it. . . . Now, look at the threads—he was away from his mother, smarting, ripe for some maternal solace. . . . It's too much . . . too obvious. . . . And yet consider how involved it became."

"I suppose that it's too simple to say that your father was a dependent individual. . . ."

"You can say it. He obviously was, but that's hardly saying anything. . . . It's in the mixture, you know. . . . For instance, he'd take me to see a Sunday ball game. I think I was a son to him because I was a tomboy for a while. . . . He'd let himself go. He never used anything but the most proper language at home, but at the game, wow, he'd get scorching . . . taking his fist and pounding it into his hand: "Hit it, you bastard, hit it.""

"Your mother became aware of her being someone triumphant on the rebound, as it were. . . ."

"Oh, yes. My grandmother told her. . . . Again, in a very open way, so you'd never imagine there was insinuation or innuendo. . . . My mother was never comfortable there at the house. . . . She tried in the early years, I know, to get us away . . . in the years before my sister was born. . . . We were going to go to Denver. We'd packed and everything. The house was up for sale. . . . But something happened. . . . The position was filled at the last minute by someone else. . . ."

"But I thought it was a family business. . . ."

"It was. . . . And my mother asked him how it could happen since they had control of hiring and firing. . . . She of course could not talk quietly. . . . Even when she was at her most reasonable, she would let fly with an intensity that turned my father around. He'd wince . . . I could sense it. . . . She just misread it. . . . Sometimes I think if she had been quiet and helpless, he might have gotten his back up. . . ."

"But then, how could she . . . ? She felt under attack."

"Yeah. . . . She was under attack . . . and not at all equipped for that kind of battle. . . ."

"Was she a good mother?"

"She was a very good mother. . . . But you see, she was always competing. . . . She could never relax. Our house had to be just so. . . . End tables uncluttered, dusted, the rugs straight, bric-a-brac carefully distributed, the pictures just so. . . . It must have been that she felt that this was the way Anglo-Saxons expected a home to be. She was always after the maid. We had a regular parade of maids . . . because of my mother. And lurking at the back of her mind was that fear that her mother-in-law would drop in and find something out of place. . . . She was forever casting herself up in a sum . . . trying to pass muster in Grandmother's eyes."

"Exotic. . . . Perceptive observation. . . . What was your mother's background?"

"Her father was a prominent jurist in Cuba. She had four brothers and four sisters. . . . College graduate. . . . She'd gotten her advanced degree in economics in the States. As far as tradition goes, I think her family was genuinely more aristocratic than my father's. After all, his grandfather had been a rifle smuggler on the Mexican border." Connie laughed. "My grandmother thought that to be a fact of enormous social value. She'd drop it into any important discussion—to cast light on the family strength and drive."

"Must have been a helluva life for your mother?"

"It was . . . and yet I couldn't see it. . . . Somehow I felt that it was all her fault. . . . She should have stood up to my grandmother."

"As your father should have stood up to your mother?"

"Yes. . . ."

"And you? You sound like a hostage."

She stared at her cigarette pack. "Hostage? Oh, yes, I see. . . . I guess so. . . . But the tugs were velvet, do you understand . . . nothing really overt. . . . I had lots of feelings of having always to decide. . . . I'm going to my grandmother's; I should stay home with my mother. I'm getting this present from my grandmother; I'd better conceal it from my mother. Nothing was ever really spontaneous, free, an act just for itself. . . . School for example. I told you I was a good student. I had to be; it was expected of me. My mother expected that. . . . It had to be . . . after all, I was an exposed flank of hers. Suppose I had been slow or disruptive . . . just think how that would have told against her in my grandmother's eyes. . . ."

"It's amazing that you didn't louse up."

"But I did, didn't I, Mr. Cortina? It just took a little longer. . . . Sometimes I think how much better it would have been if I had gone to pieces then. . . . But it hardly would have been in the tradition. . . . Everything was always done without fanfare . . . except for my mother and her rages. . . ."

"And your sister?"

"She was very small when the whole thing went to smash. My mother had changed, too. . . . I think she was relieved that the contest was over. Not that she wasn't affected. My mother was crazy about my father. I think he came into her life when she had just about resigned herself to being single. It must have flattered her to have a man seven years younger than her meet her and marry her all in the space of five weeks. . . . God knows what was going through his mind. . . . Perhaps mind wasn't involved. . . ."

"Just chemistry. . . ."

She snorted: "Yes, just chemistry. . . . I can remember one year when we were taken down to Cuba. . . . The climate, the colors, the opulence of life, as if everything were in a state of continuous ripening. . . . I think for the first time I saw my mother in her proper environment. She bloomed. My mother is Junoesque . . . all woman. . . . See her in that setting, and you knew what chemistry meant. . . ."

"You said that you had friends in those days?"

"I had companions. . . . I was good at athletics . . . I played shortstop on a boys' team. . . . I was always managing people though. . . . That disturbed me . . . made me feel self-conscious. I was never one for dolls and little sets of dishes or miniature ovens. Barbie doll was not my thing."

"What precipitated the final breakup between your parents?"

"My grandmother, I'm certain. She never disguised the fact that she felt my father was not getting what he needed from his marriage. I know, because I saw it on occasion, that she'd talk to my father as if he were an adolescent. She'd comfort him, give him solace. . . . That thread she wove between them got stronger and stronger. . . . Lots of nights he'd come home only after he'd stopped in at my grandmother's first. . . . Of course he'd say it was business and I suppose it was, at least on the surface. . . . About that time I did something. . . . It was a very cruel, irrational thing . . . but now it doesn't seem quite that way. . . . My mother had taken Arlette and me into town. She left us in the car while she went in to do some shopping. . . . Arlette was about two. . . . I burned her cheek with the cigarette lighter, and then I began to scream. . . . You can imagine the rest. I tell you, Mr. Cortina . . . I was afraid as I've never been since of what I would do to my sister. . . . I was always thinking anyway . . . but now I was panicked . . . You know, tormented by thoughts of stabbing her, or some other horrible thing. . . . I was really in agony. . . . And always trying to make up and always clumsy about it. . . . It all came together, my mother and father just holding on, barely holding on. . . . I had overheard her accusing him of seeing another woman. . . . I had heard her trying to choke down this knowledge when she spoke to my grandmother. . . . Uptight. It's a good phrase. . . . Everything was uptight. . . . Not much tremor needed to blow everything sky high. We went to my grandmother's right after the mutilating of my sister. . . . My mother was there . . . my grandmother and father and the woman whom my father finally ran off with, a few other relatives. . . . For some reason, I kept trying to get my mother to touch me. . . . I'd try snuggling over near her. I must've put out my hand. It knocked the coffee cup from her grasp. . . . It was just sheer reflex on her part, the head of steam going. She slapped me with the back of her hand and knocked me down, and I bit my tongue and lip . . . unheard of in that place where everything was beneath the surface. . . . And I screamed and screamed. . . . I wasn't hurt, but the screams just poured out of my mouth. . . . That was it. . . . My mother sat there, struck dumb, and watched my grandmother pick me up and rush me off. . . . When I looked back, there was my father with distance between him and her . . . well away, as though he and she were strangers. . . ." She stopped and looked at me. "Mr. Cortina, I'm suddenly very tired. . . . May we stop now . . . please?"

I just poked my head into her office on my way out. "Bella, I'll bring you one of those Sumatra cigars the next time. . . ."

"Enthusiasm, Frank Michael . . . ?"

"Keep after her. . . . The ice has cracked, Bella."

"And so are you," she said with a wicked grin. "Cracking, that is."

5

"Wow. . . . Oh, wow!" she exclaimed.

The tape of the previous month had nearly run its course. From watching her, seeing her attempt to keep her body still, to keep her hands from thrashing about, to prevent herself from getting up and pacing the room, or leaving, I understood a little what exorcism meant.

I placed a fresh tape on the spindle and busied myself threading it through. It gave her a chance to pull herself together. When I regained my chair, she was puffing on a cigarette. "Wow!" Her hands shook.

"Speed . . . ?"

"That tape . . . that tape. . . . Whew! But the speed is part of it, too. It affects me like a bout of malaria. . . . That wild restlessness—sometimes it would hit me in a lecture and I just couldn't linger. I'd have to go. It's an insane compulsion. . . . So it's partly speed flashback, but that's not the handle. . . . It's my recollections. That's the first time that I've ever shared that much of myself with anyone. . . . When I left you last month, my head was spinning, literally. I thought it was a recurrence of the flu . . . and of course the speed . . . but it wasn't. The rest of that day and on through the evening I was lightheaded. A feeling of oppression had numbed the balance center of my brain. I lay there, flat on my back, perspiring and panting."

"Oppressed by the sense of having lost some of your oppression?" I suggested.

"Exactly. . . . That's exactly it. I'd lived so long with this burden of the past. . . . I made myself come down here this morning . . . forced myself . . . because I knew that I would have to listen to that account. . . . I needed to hear it outside of myself . . . objectively . . . to criticize it, to criticize my telling of it, to correct omissions or distortions. . . . I wasn't interested in an apologia . . . just a true accounting. . . ." She reached for the ash tray. "A true accounting from my angle."

"If it were played for your parents, or your grandmother . . . would they reject it?"

"Reject it . . . ? Oh, no. They'd squirm but they'd recognize it in substance. . . . It's always been there, but it's never been organized and packaged before. It's like a study of tidal action: you see the force of the tide, you know erosion and waves and sheer power, and the pull of the tide, but you don't understand the dynamics of tidal influence. . . . No, they would squirm. . . ."

"Would you consider playing this for them?"

"Oh, God, no." Her voice was numbed. "No."

"Why not?"

"What purpose would it serve? They didn't crumble under it. They didn't escape to drugs. . . . I shouldn't need their solace."

"You rule that out?"

"Solace? It was through solacing myself that I'm where I am. . . ."

"Your parents crumbled . . . so did your grandmother. They escaped. It's the how of it. . . . They solaced themselves. I don't know how, but they did. . . . We have to, it's part of that recurring cycle within us . . . part of the process by which we add dimensions to ourselves . . . or. . . ."

Thoughtfully, frowning, she said: "Or survive. Those kids upstairs . . . nearly every one of them . . . cases of survival."

"Doesn't it have to do with the choices you make, Connie? And how free is one to choose? It's not at all simple, with instinct which can be corrupted, reason which can be conditioned, and imagination which can be seduced. . . . Not at all simple. . . ."

"And survival powerful, powerful. . . . Why did you suggest playing the tape for my people?"

"I was thinking of your need . . . not theirs."

"My need for them to understand me, what's happened to me?"

"You don't need this out in the open? So that you've destroyed this refuge that you've cultivated and operated from?"

She was puzzling it out: "So that I can't fall back on it again. Is that it? Destruction of a culture?"

"A coming of age, is that possible?"

"Hummm. . . ."

"What would happen if you played that tape for Mrs. Hartung and the group?"

There was a mulish expression on her face. She was ready to do battle. "I can't conceive of it."

"Pride? Shame? Destruction of a cover?"

She snapped: "You sound like a group therapy primer. . . ."

"Come off it, Connie. . . . For Pete's sake. . . . I'm not going to play the tape for them. It's your tape . . . your choice."

She attempted to smile—a forgotten social device? "I beg your pardon, Mr. Cortina. . . . It's not exactly an agreeable prospect."

"What do the other girls talk about?"

"Everything and nothing, and at the same time. . . . And after,

on the floor, they gossip and cut it all up and use it for their
purposes. . . ."

"Is that surprising?"

"It's painful. . . ."

"Isn't that a necessary part of it? Didn't your grandmother do
pretty much the same thing . . . and your father . . . and your
mother?"

"But these girls . . . they couldn't possibly. . . . And Mrs. Hartung. . . . She's a devil . . . cunning and smooth. . . ."

"But you're cunning and smooth, too, Connie . . . only you
practice your adroitness against yourself . . . and the girls do, too.
. . . They use your revelation to conceal their own, to hide . . . to
play the game . . . transference . . . to 'shift.' You've heard them
say a hundred times that they don't want to ring all the changes
on themselves. You've heard them say that. . . . Is it any different
from what you say?" My cigarette package had been mangled. I
pulled out one of the butts and tried to straighten it. "Your father
was running around with another woman?"

She was still thinking of what I said, I guessed by the expression
that passed over her face, as she said abstractedly: "Oh, yes. . . .
We knew her. . . . She was there in that big living room that
day. . . ."

"Was that brazen . . . ?"

"It was my grandmother, I'm certain. . . . She was good at stag-
ing things. Do you know who she was? She was the woman, the
one my grandmother had rejected before. A little shopworn . . .
she'd run through two husbands since the time she had been
thrown over by my father's getting married to my mother. . . ."

"Your grandmother sounds like a kingmaker."

"Yes, she was . . . in a sense. . . . She was the center of that
family. Everything. There was nothing that happened in that
whole network of cousins and brothers and in-laws that she didn't
affect. That was the clearing house. It was her preoccupation."

"Her security?"

"Yes, that's what it was. . . . Her security, her purpose. . . .
When my mother and father broke up, were divorced . . . where

do you suppose my mother would telephone at night? To my grandmother."

"After all that had happened?"

"Sure. . . . It was at my grandmother's house that my mother had met her second husband."

"You never mentioned a stepfather."

Her voice was husky: "I'd blotted him out . . . almost completely. But he exists." She smiled ruefully. "Alive and well. . . . My father mated with her choice, then my mother to be taken care of with another man." She shivered all of a sudden. "It really happened that way . . . looking back on it now. . . ."

"You mean she planned it?"

"Planned . . . improvised. Looking back on it, it comes to the same thing. She was a woman of energy, she was purposeful, and she saw ends. . . ."

"But she must have had feelings, too. She must have felt regret and a sense of guilt. . . . Good Lord, it was a family she had tampered with. . . ."

"She had feelings . . . strong feelings, but there is such a thing as conviction. She was a person with enormous conviction about herself and her role . . . accustomed to success, able to demonstrate that her management of anything resulted in success."

"You make her sound like a monster."

"But she wasn't. . . . I just haven't told it right if that's your feeling. She cried . . . she would rebuke herself . . . she would repent, but at the same time she would do. . . . She was an activist." She lighted a cigarette. "She had chosen the college for me. She had talked about where I would fit in the company business. She wasn't blind to the fact that my father could never succeed to a place of importance, run the business. . . . I was picked for that. . . . I was a whiz in math. . . . I really didn't need financial help to get through college. . . . I had four scholarships offered me because of my talent for mathematics. . . ."

"How could she arrange your mother's life . . . ?"

"Again, when you look back it seems like arrangement . . . it seems planned, but I don't think she sat down and coolly thought out an approach. Rather, it occurred to her that my mother was too much by herself. She invited her over regularly . . . talked about the children . . . how things were going. She invited people to the house at the same time. Everything really was just the same, that was the atmosphere generated, even though my mother and father had been torn apart. . . . To the world it appeared to be just a slight realignment, nothing more. So into this going concern a new figure makes an appearance. I was always at her house. . . . My mother was out working. She didn't have to. It was her pride. In any case, what's more natural than for a teen-ager to tell her mother about the good-looking man at Grandma's . . . ? He had been transferred from one of the branch offices. I was the one who was the courier. I told my mother about him. He was so handsome and polite. He was interested in so many of the things my father had been taken up by. He made a fuss over me. Why not? I was the grandchild of the owner. . . . There was a birthday celebration for Arlette held at my grandmother's, he was there, we were all there . . . even my father and his new wife. . . ." She crushed out her cigarette. "And on the surface all smooth, all harmonious— though I knew my mother was picking apart my father's wife, pitting herself against her. . . . And my mother, Mr. Cortina . . . that chemical part of her could radiate sexuality. It was her revenge. . . . And I didn't know what it was, but I could sense something. And it was powerful, so powerful that that pale, slender blond woman seemed a stick. . . . It was my mother's triumph . . . and my grandmother's frustration. . . . I'll swear she was conscious of it. . . . And anything like that, a situation in which she found herself daunted, only stimulated her, made her more ingenious. . . . That ancestor selling his rifles to both sides. . . . So Mr. Sayles was introduced. . . . Mr. Sayles had graduated from Cornell. Mr. Sayles had been in San Francisco for four years. Mr. Sayles was a whiz in oil investment. Mr. Sayles was a championship golfer. Mr. Sayles . . . Mr. Sayles. . . . It had to succeed, Mr. Cortina. It had to. You see, my grandmother took what most daunted her in my mother, her sexuality, and turned it to her success. . . ."

"Couldn't your mother see?"

"I suppose so, but she thought that maybe she could pull it off, or maybe she thought it might be a way to recapture my father.

. . . But it didn't work. . . . My grandmother was too foxy. . . .
My father and his wife became very scarce. We hardly saw him
any more. If I wanted to see him, Grandma would take me down
to his office. . . . And that was a charade, because he was so embarrassed that he would say things and make promises to me that
he couldn't keep, it was not part of him. . . . He was someone else
. . . a stranger to me. . . ."

"So your mother remarried?"

"That was something. . . . Married in my grandmother's house
in the spring . . . you know, music, lobster, champagne. . . ."

"Just like that? Sprung on you by your mother?"

"Oh, no. . . . We had the traditional mother-daughter scene.
. . . You know: 'You and Arlette are grown up now. (I was almost sixteen.) . . . And I'm lonely. . . . Even though you and
Arlette mean everything to me. . . . A woman gets lonely.' And
Mr. Cortina, she had my head against her, I could hear her heart
pounding away, I could feel her breast under my head, and I got so
choked up, I pulled away from her and wanted to vomit. . . . She
was like a cat in heat. . . . I was furious—my temper tantrums
were old hat by now. I think my mother was afraid of me. It probably took all of her courage to tell me about Miles and herself. I
must have seemed a savage to her. I upbraided her about driving
my father away because of her treatment of him. . . . Wow!" Connie was breathing heavily. "I wouldn't go to the wedding. I hid
away at the last minute. . . . When she left with my sister, I came
back and packed. . . . and I cleared out."

"Where did you go?"

"My grandmother had a summerhouse on the property. I stayed
there all afternoon and until late at night. I heard all of the wedding noises, the laughing and music, the cars going off, a drunken
guest urinating out in the garden. . . . And when it was all over
and quiet, I went up to my grandmother's room. . . . She soothed
me. . . . I slept in her bed that night. She explained to my mother
that in time, in time . . . I would accept."

"You loved your mother?"

"Yes, I loved my mother . . . and I missed her. . . . A few
miles separated us. . . . I stayed with my grandmother for six

months and then I went back. . . . I was wooed back, wooed by myself. . . . I was going to break up that marriage. It was just about then that I first started to drink. . . ."

"You never talked this over with anyone?"

"Then? At that time? No. Oh, no, I nursed my grievances in private. I remember I got drunk on wine one time and sounded off to another girl. . . . She didn't understand."

"What kind of a man was your stepfather, Connie?"

She smiled: "I hated him!"

"With reason?"

"For the best reason—he brought things into focus."

"What was he like?"

"Kind, dull, unimaginative, sort of awkward around a couple of young girls, awkward to find himself in a female ménage—exactly the way my father was. But I didn't trust him."

"Did he ever make a pass at you?"

"Miles?" It flabbergasted her. "Oh, no, Mr. Cortina. Anything but that. In some ways he was more of a father to me than my own father had been. He took his responsibility very seriously. He made my mother happy. I'd hear her singing. . . ."

"That provoked you?"

"You've heard addicts describe their behavior as being outrageous—they get to a place where they're just insufferable. That's the way I became. I'd come home at three or four in the morning, usually looped. I'd eavesdrop. I'd crouch outside their door listening. Once I heard Miles talking about me. He was persuading her to seek psychiatric help for me. But she couldn't come right out and tell me. My own mother!" she said savagely. "No, it was Miles in his dull, plodding, firm way that explained to me that I needed help to 'overcome' a difficult adjustment." She shook her head. "He really was concerned . . . really concerned about me . . . talking to me about what I was doing to myself, the pain I was giving my mother . . . and the pain I was giving him. . . . I made life hell for him and her. I ranted about their trying to put me away. . . . I was going to tell my grandmother, I was going to run away. . . . Finally it was the family doctor who persuaded me. . . . Because I had gotten frightened by myself, Mr. Cortina. You know, hoist with my own petard. Some of the old torment about hurting Arlette . . . being unsure of what I might do. . . ."

"Your grandmother didn't know?"

"I don't remember how that came about. . . . She found out about it later on when I was in the sanitarium. . . . But I imagine that Miles handled it. He was a determined man. . . ."

"So you went in?"

"Yes, I was there for some weeks. . . ."

"It wasn't like this setup?"

"Oh, no. . . . It couldn't have been more of a contrast. . . . The weekly bill must have been astronomical. You've been in that kind of place, Mr. Cortina. The superb meals, the private air of well-being. The room that has chintz and comfortable chairs, the stationery that crackles with distinction. . . . And the patients. . . . No, just a soft womb." She glanced at the courtyard. "I was so adroit. It didn't take me very long to size up my position of strength. Tears were my best device. I was able to completely destroy any help that I might have gotten by just my own cleverness . . . just through observation, just through surface play. That poor doctor. I'd throw something out and he'd hold it for a minute, then I'd embroider it, and suddenly cry. . . . Or I'd have a temper tantrum. He knew, he knew I was spinning a web, using him. I remember just baiting my hook with a little piece of the father-mother-stepfather situation. . . . I was trying even there to break up their marriage. . . . I'd play to it . . . work myself up into such a frenzy that they'd give me a pill. . . . Even that I learned to exploit. . . . In spite of the letdown, I'd spin out at half-speed the 'trauma'. . . ."

"Didn't that create a backlash . . . ?"

"Sure it did . . . all inside of me. . . . But then it seemed to suit my purpose. . . . The doctor was a good man . . . I've never forgotten him. But he couldn't do anything. . . . I gloated over my own dexterity. . . . Somehow he was to be defeated, as I lived to defeat Miles . . . and, I suppose, my father. . . ."

"Your father knew about it?"

"Oh, yes, he visited me. Poor guy was so totally uncomfortable that he stuttered. He stuttered. That was something he used to do when my mother got on him years before . . . something he would do in front of my grandmother. . . . But I used him. . . . I told him that he had broken up our home. How could he do that . . . ? But it had a backlash, Mr. Cortina. . . . It did. . . . When they released me and I went back home, I think I really was disturbed. . . . Disturbed in the sense that I could hardly stand myself, I hardly knew any longer who I really was and what I really felt. . . ."

"You went home?"

"Oh, yes. . . . The pressure from my grandmother to relieve my mother of me . . . the weak attempts on the part of my father . . . all of these succeeded in getting up my mother's defensiveness. Like the old days, she was on the spot. . . . Her own pride made her insist upon my going back to her house. . . ."

"That must have been a prospect for Miles."

"The things I've done to that man. And he was so square. . . . You know," she outlined a square in the air with her finger and drew a slash through it. "He actually loved my mother . . . and cared for me. . . ." She shook her head. "I was out of the house more than I was in it. Running around with every discontented kid. Smoking pot . . . finally trying heroin . . . and mind you, using these things as tools, devices. I remember bringing home a joint to show my mother. Telling her what she had done to me."

"Did you tell her about the heroin?"

"Well, I told you she found out about it the time I came home to kick. . . . But tell her about it then? No, even I wasn't that ruthless, but I insisted to myself that I was using drugs because of what she had done to me. . . ."

"It couldn't have been a very happy home."

"I made a shambles of it. . . . I had my mother so that she would talk to Miles self-consciously, deceitfully just to protect me. . . . I was breaking them apart. . . . But Miles was a strong man —though square. . . . I think he finally opened my mother's eyes by pointing out to her that I was damaging Arlette. It was a stroke of genius. That impressed her. . . . That, and I think it was he who appealed to my grandmother for help. It was a challenge she couldn't refuse. So I went with her. . . ."

"You stopped using drugs?"

"No, I continued . . . but not heroin. . . . I fooled with it that last year in high school. . . . But that backlash I told you about . . . I was living with it. I was frightened of myself. I built all kinds of rationalizations. . . . I banged up the new car my grandmother had gotten me. . . . Drinking, running around . . . estranged from everything. . . . She got my father to see me. He was totally inadequate. He talked to me in what he thought was a serious father-to-daughter way. . . . I was high on pot at the time. . . . We talked, you know, 'rapped,' for hours. . . . I think he felt somehow that he had at last fulfilled his duty and expiated for all his sins. And when he led me to my room and kissed me . . . and closed the door, I went out the window, down to the lawn, and ran for the summerhouse. . . . I was smoking a reefer as his car lights disappeared down the driveway. . . ."

"But you got to college?"

"Yes, I got to college. . . . I think that I was the first resounding failure of my grandmother's life. And that gave me satisfaction . . . at the time. . . . She hadn't been able to work a miracle, she'd been frustrated. That expression of relief on her face when I climbed aboard the plane must haunt her to this day—the knowledge that she had been defeated. . . . How it must have rankled her."

"And you?"

She sighed and shook her head. "Me . . . ? I was devastated! It hadn't happened at all the way I thought it would. . . . I was devastated. If ever there was a child making a lonely journey, it was I. I should have been under the care of the stewardess in that plane. . . . I knew, Mr. Cortina, there at twenty thousand feet, that I was just about twelve years of age. . . ."

The tape slipped through the head and flapped against the head. I turned it off. Then I sat down and offered her a cigarette. Her finger touched my hand. It was icy. We sat quietly smoking. She got up and walked to the window and stared out at the courtyard. "I understand what you mean about blowing my cover. . . ."

"You did come here. You could have gone elsewhere. Where it

would have been easier. . . . It must have been for a reason, Connie. . . . Instinct, perhaps?"

"If you'll let me have that tape of last month, I'll ask Mrs. Hartung about playing it. . . ." I handed her the reel. She said huskily: "Though you know, it's going to kill me to sit there with all of them and listen to it. . . . It will kill me, Mr. Cortina." She turned abruptly and left the room.

I decided against seeing Bella that trip.

6

"She has that drawl for real. It's natural with her. It ain't no pretence. You were absolutely right, Frank Michael. For once I was wrong." She gave me an evil smile. I laughed. This was the vintage Bella: thickset, powerful, a majestic study of clashing colors, from the dyed, almost red hair to the wild yellow blouse and purple skirt, the speech that has been described as South Plainfield, New Jersey, the cigarette hanging from her lips, the poor breath control that never permitted her enough air to finish a sentence. "This Grace Kelly is very damned courageous. Drawl or no drawl, cut it any way you want. It took what you're supposed to have and what she ain't got as a female to do what she did." Bella glowered at me. It was apparent that Connie had impressed her. "You know, she stopped those stupid broads with their stale games, made them sit up and take notice, made them shut up and listen—and more, more, she made them feel. . . . Now some of them beauties, they ain't really felt for nobody else in a generation. . . . Oh, you know the old cries about being concerned and you're moving me, baby. . . ." Bella gasped for air. "Merde . . . merde. . . . All they feel for is themselves—and why not, nobody else ever cared except to use them. But Grace Kelly she made them feel. . . . So at last after all these years you justify the expense, Frank Michael. I shouldn't say you—that little piece of celluloid on which is a voice. Now all my counselors they want a taping machine and microphones. . . . So everybody all of a sudden will be Lowell Thomas. . . . It was beauti-fool. It was, Frank Michael. It occurred to that slinky mind of yours that this is the making of a plastic . . . huh? That the way to no feeling is through abused feelings . . . or am I beaucoup nosy—you're saving that for a book. . . . So I gotta hand it to you . . . even with your drawl. . . ."

I had to laugh at her. She was . . . well, I had to laugh. "Last thing she said was that it would kill her to do it. . . ."

"Some hyperbole she's allowed. She ain't old enough to know that only death kills you. But you coulda knocked me over when she goes through all the chain of command to come see me. . . . It ain't like I expected of her. To demand she wants to see me— not in the least. . . . She gets her supervisor on the ward to call the general supervisor to call the supervising. . . ." The rest of the sentence was choked off for lack of breath. "So that's how she touches all the bases and gets to see me. Now I know, Frank Michael, that I ain't her type. . . . I conceal my Jane Austen education very cleverly. . . . For our Grace Kelly I am coarse and crass and insensitive. . . . This was a hurdle for her. . . . You told her to come see me . . . first . . . right?"

"Yes, of course, Bella."

She mimicked me: "You knew, you pirate, that if she could get over her disgust with me that she had it made. . . ."

"I didn't know what she'd do, frankly. . . . But the momentum was there. . . ."

"When do we hear the next tape . . . that's the one you made last time. . . ."

"That's up to her, Bella. . . ."

Bella was fantastically sensitive; her little eyes bored into me. "You don't like that. . . . You don't feel that's kosher for some reason . . . ? You think that maybe it should now carry on in the group without hearing no more of the tapes . . . ?"

"Exactly. . . . Next time the girls will look upon the tape as entertainment. . . ."

"You ain't really so stupid, Frank Michael. . . ." And she stroked my hand. "Now don't talk so fast and listen to what's happened." Her cigarette ash hissed into the open container of coffee on her desk. "I spoke to Grace Kelly after that momentous therapy session . . . nicely as usual. I suggested to her that she could see that no walls caved in, no ceilings fell down. . . . She told you . . . she told all them stupid broads, she told me. What was next to be done? Then in that charming drawl . . . she's a very bright girl, she knows precisely where I am gettin' to—a family therapy round table." Bella rested her head on the side and looked at me. "They shoulda been in here. . . . If they'd all come in here twenty years ago that Grace Kelly would nevera wound up the way she did with all of them undiagnosed feelings that led her to fool around with stuff that she should. . . ." And she had no breath left.

"Did you invite the grandmother, too?"

"Oh-hoho. . . . She is a robber baron, that one. . . . Just as nice as you please she would have your heart and make out like she's given you chicken fat for nothing. . . . She is a frontier woman. Thank God they ain't made that way no more. With her, Woman's Lib needs nobody else and you men better get for the hills and find a Che Guevara to protect you against her. . . . Frank Michael, what she radiates . . . such radiations. . . . Ming! Power. Robber baron. . . . As she's little, mind you, little . . . short little thing . . . maybe an inch less than five feet she is. . . ."

That would have made her the same size as Bella.

"And the men. . . . Well, that father he's been dry-cleaned too many times. He ain't got them; the grandmother she cut them off. . . . The wife of the father—what he ain't got she don't need. No blood. . . . Now the stepfather. . . . He's hmmm . . . like Yale '42 . . . a few years in the Navy . . . nice . . . nice . . . but black is black and white is white. . . . You know: 'I'm telling you this for your own good. Give up these filthy drugs, they ain't no good to you. They'll kill you, they'll ruin you. . . .' That kind of man." And Bella began to choke from her own vocal exertions. She took a quick swig of the ash-laced coffee. "Youach. . . ."

"What about Connie's mother . . . ?"

Bella sat down dramatically, wiped her mouth, and seemingly composed herself. "That is Ceres . . . Ceres. . . . She's got to be fifty or near it. . . . But that is Ceres, Frank Michael. . . . A zoftische mama, if ever you saw one. . . . She is sex, lucky darling, and she ain't got nothing to do with it. . . . But there it is and that is the problem, because any one of them men coming within three miles of the little robber baron and the zoftische mama they are gobbled up. . . ."

"And so is Connie?"

"Precisely."

"And you said in the beginning that she wasn't a mensch. . . ."

"So what did that require from my remarkable academic training?"

"Who led the session?"

"Who else should lead it but me? You don't let no kid handle matches around dynamite, when every false step could lead to catastrophe. . . . I was very adept and very subtle. . . . In five minutes I had them all hating me because of my coarseness and my insensitivity. So they had to forget their personal hatreds and just join in hating me. Now Connie, she could feel that since I was doing all her hating for her, she could keep her powder dry until she had to commence shooting. . . . What a session; it was there and then that you should have had your machine with its piece of celluloid. . . . That old robber baron—boy, can she fight. . . . God help socialism with that captain of industry. But she was tough, let me tell you, tough. . . ."

"What came out?"

Bella lighted a cigarette and, with a kind of aching sadness in her voice, replied: "Wreckage . . . what else could come out?"

"Connie stood up under it?"

"With me by her side, well, even you could stand up."

"One session only?"

"Oh, no, we've had three battles so far. . . . Another tomorrow night. . . ."

"Has everyone come for all three sessions?"

"Except for the father and that piece of celery who's his wife. They came to the first. . . . I think Grandma saw to it that Caspar or whatever his name is was sent to Romania or somewhere on business. I can't blame her—who wants to leave his back door open with his heart on the table? But he's supposed to be here this time. . . . This I insisted on. . . ." She looked at me shrewdly. "See, everything is worked through the old robber baron. She can't step down; she don't turn and run. For her it's a duel. . . . She ain't gonna be put down by no upstart like me. Even though she is an old lady in her seventies, she is tough. So all I got to do is shoot my arrow in her and the rest comes along. . . . But this time they will have them other charming families of them other charming broads to sit down with. . . . The colors in that room will be like the colors in my hair. . . . We will have a mixin' of the races and such a mixin' of family problems. . . ." Her breath was exhausted again.

"What about Connie, Bella?"

"She's good . . . good. . . . After the first time, she got stronger. . . . Grace Kelly will do all right. Like you said, though it was no great perception, mind you, her instincts brought her here. . . . Here she met me." She grinned and patted my hand. "Now . . . Grace Kelly . . . she can't make it with the men. . . . I'm talking to Dr. Lowndes about her. . . . But it has got to be handled with the utmost in finesse—do you understand? The ultimate in finesse on accounta she's been burned by psychiatric fiddle-faddle. . . . It ain't necessary for her to be losin' what she's gained. . . . You see, she still ain't a mensch, Frank Michael. . . . She feels that . . . but she don't know it yet. . . . When she knows it . . . and why it is so . . . so why will she need heroin? Now go see Connie and make with your machine!"

All she lacked was the mantilla to be the girl in the Goya painting—its name I couldn't recall. Her skin was clear, pearly, and her face thin. The playback of the previous tape had just finished.

"Are you trying to lose weight?"

"Wow. . . . These last few weeks, since I saw you last, . . . I've been through a wringer. . . . I think I've cried away my tissue. . . . Like . . . like. . . ." She threw up her hands. "I can't absorb it. . . . You were very accurate. When oppression is lifted, you feel oppressed. Now I'm really frightened, because all the things I've consciously and unconsciously struggled against or rebelled against are out in the open. . . ." She looked at me helplessly. "I feel awful . . . awful. . . ."

"Awful enough to cut and run?"

It was a half-smile. "That's your subtle way of asking me if I have a yen for drugs! That's part of the awfulness, because I don't know what I would do if I were outside this minute."

"And isn't that impressive? To be uncertain? To be uncertain after years of drug dependence?"

She examined my face and then looked out toward the court-yard. "You are. Did you know that? You are. I thought of you during that first nightmare of family therapy. . . . You are, Mr. Cortina."

"So is that dirty courtyard, but I take it as a compliment any-way."

"I mean, such frightful things, things that you imagine but never believe can happen, come out. There they were, sitting about expectantly, all their experience and instincts telling them that they were certainly prepared to cope with this.

"But they weren't: unpleasant, disagreeable, embarrassing to be exposed to this kind of confrontation—and in such surround-ings. . . . Girls of all colors shuffling along the corridor in that woeful way they have of not caring how they look, lost all pride. . . . Things that shouldn't be for my family, where it is known that if you make an effort, brush your teeth, and have determina-tion, everything else will be added unto you. . . . And then, too, they had been through things with me before. . . . But really this . . . that it had to come to this—a kind of public washing of family linen. . . . It was awful. . . . And Mrs. Hartung . . . ciga-rette ash slopping over her, crouching, yelling, browbeating them, that voice of hers that she abuses. . . . They weren't prepared for that. But I thought of you. . . . When I got down to it, I had no anger for them. I was angry at Mrs. Hartung. . . . She was so crude. . . . I fell back on aloofness. . . . I was crawling inside myself. . . . My grandmother sitting there so calmly, so securely . . . my mother trying not to look at me, my father, his face blotched with his distress, his wife somehow wondering how she had gotten involved, and Miles interested in a very stolid way, as if he were being invited to authenticate a new oil discovery. . . . It was incredible. . . . And then to hear Mrs. Hartung: 'We ain't here to listen to no chamber music, kiddies.' " Connie laughed. "That's what she said. And with that she pointed to me, her cigarette smoke in her eye, 'Grace Kelly, what you got against them . . . ?'

"Unorthodox, unreal, they couldn't take it in. . . . My mother had been in conferences with me before . . . the psychiatrist gently leading, suggesting . . . all somehow within the bounds of decorum. . . . But Mrs. Hartung . . . like one of the Dead End Kids."

"She's a brilliant woman, Connie. . . ."

"Yes, she is. . . . Everything that was felt and unspoken in that room, including my own bottled-up conflicts, all crystallized in our resentment of her. I finally started to talk in order to somehow protect my family against her. . . . But it was ghastly. I couldn't look at my mother or father. . . . I was ashamed and felt like a spoiled kid. . . . I couldn't understand where that passion of resentment was . . . all the injustice, the stupidity and selfishness. . . . To understand that people, however many advantages they've had, still do things through instinct, without awareness of motive and planning. . . . It was a thoroughly uncomfortable experience . . . far more uncomfortable than listening to the tape being played back in front of all the girls. . . . My mother just fell apart . . . fell apart, all of her defenses gone—and this collapse in front of her most detested adversary, my grandmother. . . . Incredible. That made me furious . . . it made me furious . . . when I saw that. Then I whirled on my father . . . calling him weak and dependent . . . accusing him of copping out in every way he could. . . . My grandmother, poised, her eyes cold. . . . I accused her of manipulating people's lives, destroying them. . . . And Miles, coming into a family and taking over as if his Mr. Clean attitude could wash away all the past—a kind of Boy Scout Pledge philosophy.

. . . I caught myself breathing as hard as if I had been running a
mile. It just came pouring out. It was hardly a confrontation as
much as it was sheer expurgation. . . ."

"How long did it go on?"

She drew in her breath. "Forever it seemed, after it was over.
. . . Forever. . . . But I suppose for a couple of hours. . . . It was
astonishing how completely I could recall the smallest details of
things that happened way back . . . way, way back. . . . Playing
with me, using me, turning me . . . Grandmother . . . as if I were
some minor tool. Trying to make me into a son. . . . The things
that came out. . . ."

"What happened?"

"You know, they're people who are accustomed to talking, to
exchanging ideas . . . really very verbal. . . . But they crumpled.
. . . And I was appalled for them. I was. My sheer emotionalism
overwhelmed them. . . . And I knew that I was putting my
mother through hell. . . . I could see my father's face breaking out
in those red blotches. . . . It was awful, Mr. Cortina."

"Bella didn't say anything?"

"After she got the pot boiling, all she did was to chain smoke.
. . . She stopped it . . . finally. She just got up and said something
about it was well to remember that for all their faults—my
family's—it was well to remember that they were not in here
for using heroin and speed. That was a dash of icy water in my
face. And then she reminded them that they would have to come
back in a week. She told them that the next time would be less
harassing. . . ." Connie began to smile. "She wouldn't let me pass
any time with them when it was over. She put her arm around my
shoulder, a kind of hint of restraint, as she told them with that
smile of hers that when they got to know her they would learn to
hate her. . . . Wacky . . . wacky. . . . Like Alice in Wonderland.
. . . But she was very good to me. . . . When it was all over . . .
she said: 'You're gonna feel that you loaded it on, Grace Kelly'
—I don't get that at all—'so feel it. . . . It'll balance out. . . .
So go upstairs and go to bed.' "

"And the next time . . . which was . . . ?"

"Last week. It was quieter. . . . My father didn't come, or his wife. . . . I suspect that my grandmother saw to that. . . . But I understand, I guess. . . . I honestly came to respect my mother. She admitted that she always felt under pressure. She shouldn't have, she should have been able to cope with that. She turned to my grandmother and told her that she was sorry to wound her but felt her always to have been opposed to her, actively trying to forge a wedge between her and my father . . . always felt that she was looking down on her, always felt that she had struggled to wrest her children away from her . . . always was sitting in judgment on her. . . . And my grandmother sat there, finally saying that one did what one felt had to be done even sometimes when one was wrong . . . but she had had to do something. It was her way, her outlook, her whole conditioning. . . . Early in her life she had learned that to talk and not to do was equivalent to dependence. . . . She talked about my grandfather. . . . He had not been active. . . . It had fallen on her shoulders to do. She had become that way. Someone had to be active. . . . She was impressive, Mr. Cortina. She wasn't asking for quarter. She took it. She spoke in her own defense. She took what blame there was. . . . She said to me: 'I had no intention of hurting you. I love you.' Wow! I split wide open. . . . And then Miles, he could be counted on with his even-tempered squareness. . . . He explained that he looked upon me as if I were his own flesh and blood—that, for him, was getting almost carnal—and his home was mine. . . . But I had to forego some of my ways. There was order in everything. . . . Once one accepted basic discipline. . . . Life is a game, rough-and-tumble, you had to learn to be a professional. It may sound as if he was like one of the Rover Boys, but he was so sincere. . . . How could you hate him for saying what he thought and the way he expressed what he thought . . . ?"

"What did any of this mean to you?"

"It filled me with respect for every one of them, Mr. Cortina. . . . I'd never seen them before. As the girls say upstairs: maybe I should have given them a whirl years ago. . . . Yes, it was revealing. . . . And so now, here I am, in the middle, just like Mrs. Hartung predicted. . . . I'm back alone. . . . And it's all down on my head . . . and it's awful . . . awful . . . because I don't know. . . .

I keep asking myself what was left out of me . . . or what was perverted in me, that I got so mixed up? I look at these kids upstairs. . . . They never had a chance from the word go. They never had anything. And look at me. . . . You once asked me what we had in common, do you remember? Failure. . . . Failure. . . . Only in my case . . . I should be ashamed to say it."

7

"These aristocrats look so good, they just hang in there so you get tired first, you think you got them on the ropes, and all of a sudden you fall down from exhaustion and they won. . . . They didn't land a punch, but still they won because they wore you down. Now it's exactly this process that is taking place with Connie. They're all hanging in there except her father, he couldn't take it —the robber baron sent him off. . . . So now you can see how Connie gets thrown for a loop—so how come with all these suffering, accepting, repenting, dignified people can she make out a case for herself having used dope? You know? Like, what a mountain of guilt she's left with. And you know why, Frank Michael? All on accounta them aristocrats. They stick together, united front, they suffer so elegantly. They hate each other like hard pieces of liver but bunch together under attack. Connie has betrayed them!"

"Betrayed them? How, for Pete's sake?"

"For Pete's sake, by coming in here, by exposing the family. . . ."

And I added: "By using drugs. . . ."

"The drugs they could handle," said Bella with a sweeping gesture. "They coulda handled them by sending her to a dozen different, ritzy places. . . . It ain't the drugs, Frank Michael. It's making public the family hanky-panky. That's Connie's unforgivable transgression. That's her stain, her betrayal of the code. That's it. So this kid is left with nothing. She feels totally adrift, cut off."

"But she's been alienated anyway, Bella. She cut herself off. . . ."

"It was her way of surviving. . . . A wholesome response it was. Survival." Bella blew ash from her cigarette. "You know, this kinda thing ain't a fight, it's an engagement. You don't use passion and force, your heart and feelings; it's fought with tradition and according to their code. Ordinary weapons like curses and blows and recriminations, they don't cut no ice here. So what is this girl left with? They look like such marvelous people: Jesus Christ, Mrs. Gandhi, Queen Victoria, and Leo Tolstoy couldn't be more forgiving. They don't point no fingers, they don't say that she's a bum. . . . So what's she left with? Hopeless, crushing guilt. . . . She's got to be a freak. . . . That can be her only conclusion because with what she's getting as feedback from them, it's the only explanation," said Bella, gasping.

"You're saying that by the family's blandness Connie is prevented from reaching any kind of satisfactory understanding of her own behavior."

"And what else have I been saying? It took you long enough to phrase my own thoughts which I had thought I had been saying all along." Again she winded herself. "It's a deadly thing for that girl, Frank Michael. There's no breathing place for her."

"She mentioned in our last interview that she had misread her family. That they had impressed her, they had emerged well from the family therapy. She felt that something must have been left out of her personality. . . ."

"See, already it's what I've said. That's what comes from this damned breeding. Like those puppies that're so highly pedigreed that you can't give them no bones because they ain't got the teeth to gnaw it with." I lighted Bella's cigarette. "These other kids here . . . with them it's possible to start rehabilitation or maybe habilitation, because no matter how balled up they are, underneath they will respond to common feelings, when you can cut them out of their webs. You know, like they been abused by men or women, or their father attacked them, or they got underdeveloped parts, or they feel they're ugly, or they can't read, or any of the thousand and one things that they can't cope with—now, once you get them to see this themselves, give them some support, bring in their families for recognition and more support, let them tie their shoe laces for themselves three-four times so they get an idea of success, and mazel tov. . . . Pretty soon, it's 'Look, ma, I'm human.' But with Connie . . . it ain't like that. . . . All her feelings has been used up, totally. You know, like it's worse than jaded . . . surfeited on feelings, and the simple, crushing truth is, she ain't never had a chance to experience really developed feelings. . . . They were always wrenched from her by these damned aristocrats. . . ." Cigarette ash plopped on her bright green blouse. "She's a plastic, this kid. What the hell else is a plastic but somebody whose feelings is all played out? The slum girls, you got all kinds of options . . . all kinds of handles. A girl like Connie, how many do we get in here, in a place like this? Like you, of course, working sometimes in them fancy dens, like maybe you're accustomed to them types. . . ."

I had to admit that this was not my experience.

Bella resumed: "Look, Frank Michael, even me, when I'm with these people, even me, I get somehow a nagging idea that maybe we should have a screen around us to protect them from the vulgar gaze. . . . How does that grab you, huh? Even me, I am uncomfortable. . . . So what must it be like for that girl who don't know what the score is? I ask you," she said breathlessly. She gave me that piercing glance; she was weighing my understanding, trying to make me discover for myself, as it were, what it was she knew about this situation—the act of this transference of knowledge would somehow prepare me to deal with it (a typical Bella tactic, designed to make her people feel competent and secure).

She puffed away. "Like her heart has been made small, like it's been squeezed small. It ain't been exercised. It's the smallest part of that kid. . . . It could be a full-sized heart, Frank Michael. Dr. Lowndes says there ain't nothin' the matter with her. Nothin'. She just talks, everything has been put upstairs in her head. Everything is intellectualized. . . . But she has a full-sized heart; it needs to be seized by something. . . . That's what happens with that kind of family set-up—those aristocrats with their shadow play took away that child's full-sized heart. That's why I say she ain't no mensch. No boy ever took her to the movies and tried to shove his hand inside her blouse to feel her breast. He wouldn't dare. His hand would freeze off."

"Hummm. . . . How to make her see it?"

"Naturally. We ain't got to see it. We see it. It's that child who's got to see it. . . ."

"That child of twenty-two. . . ."

"Sarcasm, it don't become you, Frank Michael. . . . She'll be a child until she becomes a mensch, for all her sophistication, for all her intellectualizing, for all her education. You came to me and said she was defenseless. A hundred percent right you were. You saw it first. . . . Maybe she thinks she's ready to go now. . . . The family thing is out in the open, she thinks, it's all said. . . . Said . . . said! But she'll go right back to escaping . . . right back. The job ain't done. You got to give her a full-sized heart." Bella patted my hand.

Snow, a strange, sooty, streaked snow, covered the littered courtyard. I followed the flakes in their descent. The machine reproduced: "It filled me with respect for every one of them. . . . I'd never seen them before. . . . I keep asking myself. . . . Perverted in me. . . . Failure . . . failure. . . . I should be ashamed." Like the snowflakes, her words fell between us. The tape concluded, and that special quiet of institutions descended: slamming doors, shuffling feet, telephone bells, laughter, humming machinery, voices, all quivered in a metallic cadence. I replaced the tape. It would have been a mistake to interpret her motionlessness for repose. The grey dress with its high neck, the blackness of her hair, the glints of earrings couched in her ear lobes set off the pallor of her face. She was small, still, silent—bloodless. An under-sized heart? Bella's concept.

"You look gravely elegant this morning, Connie. You remind me of an elegy. . . ."

She looked at me and nodded her head: "Interesting fancy . . . my being in mourning. . . ."

"Don't you find the girls upstairs wearing clothes to typify their moods? Somehow they're always very conscious of the appearance they're making—or of an image they're projecting."

"That's the way addicts are. . . ."

"So what should I conjecture about your appearance this morning?"

"My mother sent the dress . . . and the stones came from my grandmother."

"How simple or symbolic can we get about that . . . ? You know: rapprochement? Acceptance, capitulation, defiance?"

"That's what's troubling me. . . . I don't know. . . . Upstairs I could always tell after a girl had had a visit. She'd come back with new clothes or food or a radio or some kind of present. She'd flaunt it, a boast to show that she belonged to somebody, had a connection with a family, she wasn't just an unattached vagrant. . . ."

"How accurate is that observation?"

"As far as I'm concerned?" She shook a cigarette from her pack.

"Or is that the riddle? What you can't decide?"

"I watch them up there. . . . For all of their knocking around, their air of being equal to anything—to getting in the first word and the last to show that they're proof against any kind of slight, real or imagined—they're incredibly responsive. On visiting day something unreal happens. . . . They become just creatures. . . . Quarrels, fights, temper tantrums, They talk up the number of bags they used to shoot up, all the pleasures of an old 'high' . . . anticipating and fearful of the visit. . . . And those who don't have a visit or have no one to visit them . . . even the older women . . . their feelings are close to the surface then. . . . I've come to hate Sundays, Mr. Cortina. . . . For all the given tokens of expressed guilt—cigarettes, cookies, candy, treats—it's a sad evening. All those regrets and forced resolutions, the gaiety of false promise. I watch this little girl, she so big with her pregnancy that you forget for a while that she's only fifteen. . . . She tells me about her 'man,' . . . he's coming to see her. They're going to talk about the 'baby,' his future, their marriage, the apartment, the car. And he never comes. . . . You learn he's a pimp. He wouldn't be allowed in even if he ever intended to visit her. But it's always the same with her. . . . He's coming. . . . She labors along with that mountain in her stomach. . . . He's coming. . . . He's coming. . . . And that night. . . . She has all the excuses framed. Like your tape there, they just play out of her. And you know that inside she's totally scraped and raw. . . . And all of us know it. . . . You suck in this continuum of hope-despair, hope-despair, and it's always set to some grotesque surface behavior." She scratched out the cigarette. "So elegy is the right mood."

"This kind of direct response . . . like skimming life right off the top . . . could it be that you were looking for this and that's why you came in here?"

"I came in here . . . just as I said last time, because I felt that I was a failure. And perhaps my own failure wouldn't be so glaring. . . ."

"Bottom of the heap?"

She nodded, and sighed deeply. . . . She looked toward the courtyard and bit her lip, tears in her eyes. "But there's no bottom to that heap for me, Mr. Cortina. You can go down even deeper. . . . It's bottomless. . . . Not for the others . . . but for me. . . . I'm still going down."

"But you compare yourself to them? You can't figure out why you should have messed up?"

"Right. . . . Right. . . . I've been through the family therapy now. . . . I'm clean, I'm well. . . . Everything that I had to get out . . . I've gotten out with them. . . . I've said it. . . . I tell myself and the group, I'm ready to go. I've got myself together. 'Why did you use stuff?' they'll ask. 'Because I felt inadequate . . . because I couldn't get a part of my mother or my father, I couldn't reach any kind of place of peace with them, I couldn't be myself. . . . I was too busy reacting.' "

"You couldn't handle the pressures. . . ."

"Sure. . . ." She glared at me. "But so what? So what? How does that do anything . . . ? I've spent two months now in family therapy. . . . The family has come through like a winner. . . . And me, I'm kaput. . . . I'm completely kaput. . . ."

"More so than the little girl on your floor with the swollen belly, talking about her 'man' who'll never come?"

"They've come. . . . I shouted and yelled. I accused them. I didn't let them overlook anything. I ran it for them. I stripped them. Every grudge I ever had against them I hurled at them. They took it and they accepted it. They accepted it. It's all over and done with. They're contrite, they want me back. . . . Oh, Mr. Cortina, it's no good. No good. . . . It doesn't do it. . . ."

"And now you feel thrown back on yourself for an explanation . . . ?"

"You know, I've harbored this, . . . always thinking to myself: 'If only my mother or if only my father or grandmother or my sister. . . .' This has been that secret bank account that has allowed me to squander myself in self-pity and self-justification. . . ." Her eyes were enormous in that pale face. "At least Merle's man hasn't come. . . . She can hold on to her deception."

"You've had your deception exploded, . . . that's what crushes you?"

"What else have I?"

"Seven months of freedom from drugs. Your health restored. Meeting your family without disguising that you've been a drug addict. Not trying to buy your way out of here." I reached for my cigarettes. "Seems to me you've got a great deal. . . . Pretty much in the way you look at it . . . don't you think? Or is it perhaps that you haven't been honest with yourself? Is that what's chewing you up?"

"Honest with myself?"

"You're an extremely intelligent girl, accustomed to reasoning out things. Not like the rest of these kids, whose emotions and instincts dominate their lives. Your way is to intellectualize. . . . I can suggest certain things to you without fear of your collapsing."

"What did you mean about my being honest with myself?"

"Perhaps you won't accept the fact that you are a dependent person, egocentric, self-seeking. . . ."

She blinked her eyes. Was I being gratuitously callous, was I trying to abandon her? She was considering it. She said, a note of waspishness in her voice: "In an oblique way you've returned to the old saw about a drug addict being immature, passive, and unmotivated . . . isn't that it?"

"Does that fit . . . ? Now, just a minute, shall I rewind the tape to let you hear what you said . . . see how it strikes you?"

"I remember what I said."

"Doesn't it sound like you're being victimized?" She squirmed in her chair. "Isn't that why you burned your sister's cheek?"

She thought about it. "To draw attention? Your attention?"

"What happened after that?"

"After burning my sister? My mother was appalled. She thought there was something the matter with me. . . . She felt she had to do something. . . ."

"Something had to be done?"

"But I admit now that everything that's happened has been my fault . . . not my family's fault but mine. . . . I'm not trying to evade my responsibility."

"But you are content with a feeling of guilt . . . of despair . . . of disregarding what has happened to you in these months. Be frank, Connie. If you were outside right now and you felt the way you do, would you be able to cope with it?"

She lighted another cigarette. "You're asking if I would go for a shot of dope. . . . Humph." She breathed deeply. "I don't know. . . . I might."

"So hepatitis, blood poisoning, the months in here, the family therapy. . . ."

"You're only confirming my own feeling, Mr. Cortina."

"And what is that feeling? Spit it out. . . . Don't think about it, don't try and intellectualize. . . . What feeling?"

"I hurt. . . . I hurt," she cried.

"Because you don't know what to do?"

"Because I'm all alone with me. . . . I'm all alone with me. . . ."

"You have money, you have a family, you have your health, you have everything that most of these other girls have been denied. . . . And I know that you're going to wamble all of this to say that this is your plight."

She puffed on the cigarette nervously. "Then I'm victimizing myself?"

I beat her to it: "What do you know about yourself, Connie, that demands that?"

Her brow furrowed, she murmured, more to herself than to me, "I don't measure up."

"In your own eyes?"

"Must be, mustn't it?"

"What're you measuring yourself against?"

"Yes. . . ." She was worrying the notion. There was substance to it.

"The girls here?"

She smiled wanly: "Hardly."

"Not in your league?"

"It just boxes me in to be compared with them. You said it before. They want what I've got. Take the whole bag of their denial—it's what I've got."

"Okay, then who? Your sister? Your father? Your grandmother . . . ? Your mother?"

She was shaking her head. "I can't see it."

"Because none of this is valid or because you're not able to?"

"Oh, I don't know," she said petulantly. "I don't know. . . ."

"You're not as powerful as your grandmother? Not as conventional as your sister? Not as irresponsible as your father? Not as handsome as your mother?"

She breathed heavily.

"What have you measured yourself against so that you can declare yourself a failure?"

Her eyes searched the wall. "Must be something I feel about myself."

"Or not feel. . . . It could be the absence. . . ."

"Or the absence . . . something missing. . . ."

"Let's back away, Connie. Let's talk about school. Your friends . . . your boyfriends. . . ."

"Boyfriends . . . ?"

"Yeah . . . right, your boyfriends." I said. "You've never mentioned them."

She shrugged it off. "I've had boyfriends."

"You say that like you'd say that you had colds. . . . Unhappy experiences with them?"

She said exasperatedly: "I've had boyfriends. What else do I say . . . ?"

"Do you have one now, a particular boy?"

"No."

"Did you have one before?"

"I had heroin. . . ."

"Have you had sexual relations with a boy?"

A flash of color blazed on her cheeks; she was angered. "Back to Freud, are we?"

I smiled at her, opening my hands. "I don't know, Connie. . . . We're trying to find some clues. You were the one who said to me that you were like a detective story . . . the sleuth and the victim. . . . You've exhausted some of the other leads. . . ."

"I've never had relations with a boy. . . ."

"Is that significant? I mean, to you . . . ?"

"For all the flamboyance about sex and everything connected with it, there are girls who still feel there's something tawdry about being promiscuous. . . ."

"They don't upstairs, though."

"But they do. . . . Three-quarters of those girls upstairs have been trollops most of their lives. They had to be to get their stuff. They're so hung up about sex that they don't know anything about themselves and sex any more. . . . With heroin you don't need sex. There's one girl up there, Gussie, she's been a whore for twelve of her twenty-eight years. She's so repressed by it she can't talk. . . . She can't talk. . . . You get a few words out of her. . . . And then they're flat and dead, as if even her words are crushed. . . ."

"So in that way, you're not like those girls . . . right?"

"I've never been a prostitute. . . ."

"In everything else though, you've had more than they. . . . You could buy heroin. You didn't have to commit criminal acts to get it. So if you had no money, you most likely would have been prossing, too, huh?"

She straightened up. "Never. . . . never."

I imagined that her grandmother could not have appeared more superior at that moment. "So this is an area of great difference, isn't it? You said before that you could hardly measure yourself against them—you'd had so much more. . . . Not experience with men?"

"You know that when you're on heroin, sex doesn't mean anything . . . you know that. . . . So why beat a dead horse, Mr. Cortina?"

"And maybe one goes to heroin for that reason. . . . Is that possible?"

"You're playing games . . . trying to shilly-shally."

"I'm sorry. . . . Connie, tell me about your best boyfriend. . . . Who was he?"

"It's a blind alley, Mr. Cortina. I'd tell you, if it had any meaning. It's a blind alley. . . . I've been honest with you. . . . I've been franker with you than with any other person. It's a blind alley. . . ."

"Like your father who hooded his eyes and ran away?" I leaned forward. "He was always protected by someone running interference for him: you, your grandmother, your mother, and now this new wife . . . someone always covering for him. . . . He was unmanned by a woman's world, huh?"

"My father never had a chance. . . . He was never cut out for doing what he was made to do," she said grimly.

"But he never used drugs. . . ."

"He didn't have to. . . . There was always somebody there he could depend on, someone always ready to steady him. . . ."

"So then your mother would appear to be overpowering him, huh . . . ? Or your grandmother . . . ? Or even you, huh?"

"I suppose so. . . ."

"You always wanted him to fight back and he wouldn't, I recall your saying that. . . . He couldn't even stand up to the family therapy. . . . I remember your telling me about the toilet seats always being down and his crack about that . . . unmanned by a woman's world. . . ." The snow was falling heavily in the courtyard. I watched it, sensing her tension. "Is it possible, Connie, that you don't respect men very much?"

"It's something I haven't paid much attention to."

"But you had boyfriends . . . but no relations with them."

She said by rote: "Boyfriends but no relations."

"You discouraged this kind of promiscuity. . . . The situations were controlled by you?"

"Yes."

"Never any moment of such wild passion that your control weakened . . . when your own emotions ran away with you . . . ?"

Her face set, she shook her head stubbornly.

"But you were always very intellectual . . . in control. Maybe you didn't inherit your mother's passionate nature?"

She was struck by this. "What do you know about my mother's 'passionate' nature . . . ?" The Grace Kelly drawl!

"Just what you've said—her anger, her energy, her approach. . . . Did I use the wrong word? She's not passionate. I beg your pardon."

Connie was sulking, her face puckered, her lip held between her teeth.

"So here we are. Stalemated. I've been off on a wild goose chase. I've agitated you to no purpose. . . . All we know is that you've measured yourself up against something—and you've found yourself wanting. . . . Some cryptic failure. . . . Hidden. . . . What you measured yourself against. . . . I'm sorry that I've given you pain. I haven't been skillful. . . ." I put out my hand to touch her arm. She pulled back violently, wrenching the microphone cord from her neck accidentally as she rose. Her face was chalk white. "I beg your pardon," I said, bending to pick up the microphone. I was going to wish you a Merry Christmas. . . ."

She turned and left.

8

Those first few minutes of renewed acquaintance quiver with mystery. Just the bare bones of the device—the separation of two

people for a month—can cover worlds of experience. For me
there is always speculation—will the subject return to pick up
the thread? Neither penalty, reproach nor disfavor hangs over his
head to force him to resume, so will he come back? Then, too, how
successful will I be in selecting that cord which will tie together
the gap of separation and encourage continuation of the exchange.
It is a most tenuous membrane, particularly with drug abusers,
who must be in some ways the most mercurial of subjects—most
particularly those confined to large institutions, for there the facade
of regimentation hides most deceptively the feverishness of that
kind of existence. . . . So when Connie entered the room, I was
impressed by her valor—she could have ducked the confrontation. Again she was dressed somberly, but there was something tentative about her. I had not perceived this in her earlier. And something else—she shook hands with me; this had never happened
before. I held up the tape that we had made together the previous
time, giving her the option of skipping the playback.

"I want to hear it, Mr. Cortina."

She sat quietly, her features betraying only her profound interest
in what was being reproduced—that tentative quality had vanished. Outside I could hear a steady drip in the courtyard—high
up and out of sight, snow was melting from the cornices and falling down on the litter. I was startled by her saying over the playback: "Would you play that section over again?" I backed up the
machine.

"Never any moments of such wild passion that your control
weakened . . . when your emotions ran away with you. . . . Maybe you didn't inherit your mother's passionate nature. . . . What do
you know about my mother's passionate nature . . . ? So here we
are. . . . Stalemated. . . . Agitated you to no purpose. . . . Some
cryptic failure . . . hidden. . . . What you measured yourself
against. . . ." The tape hissed for a moment and passed through
the head and flapped on the take-up reel. I put on a new tape.

"Mr. Cortina . . . it's been a harrowing month for me." It was
still that drawl. "It's my voice, my experience, my interpretation of
that experience. I've spent a whole month trying to overturn that.
I analyzed it from as many angles as I could, gave myself as many

cop-outs as I could. You know them . . . I was running the game, ringing the changes on you, I was lying, I was trying to project an image, trying to arouse sympathy, I was trying to shift the weight. . . . I went through all of the accepted junkie techniques. It was a revelation. . . . I had every one of them down pat—so they can't be junkie techniques alone, just adaptations of common human devices everybody uses to defend. . . . I tried this with the group therapy session with the girls. I convinced them, I convinced them! I convinced them that you, Cortina, with the making of these tapes, in effect suggested these situations that I exploited. I had them agreeing with me, aroused them to anger. That's how persuasive my own powers of manipulation are. . . . Once my mother, in sheer desperation, said to me that I could fool Jesus Christ. I'd never heard her talk that way before or since, but she was completely distracted by me. . . . I have this ability . . . to alter reality, to alter my perceptions. . . . So I gamed the girls up- stairs and I felt satisfaction, and then I insisted upon seeing Mrs. Hartung. . . . And I thought I was so clever. I launched into my attack on you and the whole tape bag. That you put off self-exami- nation by offering suggested avenues of escape, opportunities to de- velop cover, marvelous chances to spin webs. And then I really came down on the sex bag that you had opened up. She was so sympathetic—for her—so quiet, so eager to support me. I had it made. When I left her, I felt that I had demolished you, wiped you out. . . . I couldn't reconcile my triumph with my feeling of desolation. I was desolated. I could hardly get myself to move, Mr. Cortina . . . that's how utterly I felt shattered. . . . And this was triumph? You know, it was all of a piece, the whole thing. I wouldn't have to see you any more, I had discredited you. You would suffer. That was very important, to make you suffer. . . . But how to understand that feeling of utter desolation. . . . I'm not a cusser, but I delighted in calling you a dirty fuck to Gussie. . . . She doesn't talk, I mentioned that in the last tape. . . . And Gussie, who has to be the least demonstrative individual in the world, just rolled her eyes. Even Gussie I had influenced. . . . But oh, my God, I was shattered. . . . And then I was on my way to the chow room and Mrs. Hartung passed me. . . . She said, terribly casually for her—you know how she clubs you with her subtlety—she said: 'It was your voice though, huh, Connie, on that celluloid . . . ? It was your voice though, huh, it wasn't Cortina who made that up? I'll give him hell when I see him, Connie. He ain't helpin' none by this kind of tampering. . . . It was your voice, though, he didn't make that up?' "

"It was so oblique, so unexpected. It burst the balloon. . . . It was my voice. . . . Everything else I could demolish but that. . . . And then what else was there that was I? The whole pattern of defense, that was mine. . . . And what an eye opener that was. It was exactly my method of operation. It had always been that way . . . pitting my mother against my father and both of them against my grandmother, and Miles against my mother, against Arlette, against Miles. That whole textbook of my strategies. . . . Wow! What I told you would add up." She looked at me intensely: "It would add up. . . . I don't think I deliberately tried to mislead you. But the way I put the figures together, that was it. . . . And then, of course, why should I falsify the record, or alter it? Who were you, and what did Cortina mean to me? Like Hamlet, you know, 'What's Hecuba to him or him to Hecuba?' So why? Why? I altered things . . . I altered them. Not knowing, myself, why I did and when I did. As heroin alters things, but I must have been altering things long before I used any drugs. . . . Mr. Cortina, perhaps we alter things as a reflex, like a soul defense . . . so that we don't know. . . . How could I have taken so long to see that I have been twisting . . . ? Twisting. Alteration up until one month ago was my way of living and perceiving my world. Do you remember my telling you in one of our very early tapes about my mother grieving for my father? That was fact . . . absolute fact. . . . But let me extend that fact for you . . . show you how from another angle an entirely new fact emerges. . . . She wasn't crying, Mr. Cortina, though I took it for tears. . . . She was crying out in ecstacy. She was in orgasm. . . . She had reached her sexual climax . . . and she was crying out. . . . I had crept along the hall. . . . I was frightened. . . . The night light was on. I could see into their bedroom through the keyhole. . . . She was on top of him, thrashing around, crying and groaning and grunt-

ing. . . ." She swallowed. "Slightly different perspective, isn't it
. . . ? But I had forgotten that. . . . I had, until you talked of
her passion. . . . It was not the only time I spied on them. . . . I'd
come down in the morning, her face would be flushed. . . . My
mother is like a tropical flower. My father couldn't stand up under
it. Not the way he came up. He was crippled, Mr. Cortina . . .
crippled. . . . So he ran. . . . Sure, it must have been that origi-
nally he ran to my mother, his own manhood would be redeemed
by his sexual adequacy, that must have been his instinct, healthy.
. . . But my mother . . . a tropical flower. . . . You know, I could
come into a room and for no apparent reason begin to act like a
monster . . . yelling, and rolling on the floor, drawing all kinds of
attention to myself . . . and why? My mother would be there, just
radiating her sexuality. Every man in that room would be attracted, and not know it. . . . I remember when we were in Cuba
that time, I saw the ripe papayas hanging from the stems. . . .
That orange richness, the fragrance, the oozing of the sweet juice.
. . . Mr. Cortina, my mother didn't know any more than the pa-
paya knew. . . . I have to go back through everything . . . everything . . . erasing a little bit here, straightening a line there. . . .
I have to refocus what's in my past. You were right. It's there, I
have to go back and review it. . . . Every relationship I've ever
had has been squashed by my nervous haste. . . . As if I couldn't
bear to have you examine me too closely . . . or you would discover me lacking. . . . Lacking. I never had a real boyfriend as
such. I dazzled them. My words poured out. I was so superior. I
don't know what I wanted with a boy, something was unreal. . . .
My heart would pound and I would imagine him about to touch
me. . . . My instincts made me turn and run, or laugh him off.
. . . They couldn't touch me, though I would watch my friends
petting or playing as kids will, and then I would suddenly become
the daredevil, let's raise hell. . . . Though in my room I would
read Balzac and Boccaccio and just drool with desire . . . drool
with lust. . . . Some part of me was my mother. . . . I massaged
my breasts for years, always hoping that they would grow round
and ripe like my mother's. . . . But if a boy came close to me,
though I most desperately wanted it, I would cripple his passion by

my taunts. . . . So they worked one against the other, these urges, Mr. Cortina, though I didn't know. . . . I didn't know. . . . After a while, you know, one takes the shadow for the substance. . . . The boys didn't want me. . . . They sensed the barrier. . . . And I, looking in my mirror, could see this flat-breasted, straight body. . . . But I could talk you into my being Cleopatra, I could reason you into my being Madame Curie. . . . I could talk and talk and talk. When I was high on heroin, I would mumble out my hatred for family. . . . I would mumble my conviction that they had forced me into using drugs because of their messed-up lives. . . . If only the family had remained together, if my mother hadn't been so dominating, if my grandmother hadn't been so interfering, if Miles hadn't entered the picture, if Arlette hadn't been born. . . ." She leaned forward and said softly: "All true to a point . . . to a point. . . . Even heroin couldn't relax the blockout of my own mixed-up sexuality. . . . I had been ravaged by my own sense of frigidity. . . . I. . . ."

I lighted a cigarette and passed it to her. She took it and began to smoke, barely aware that she had done it. "You said I couldn't compare myself upstairs to the girls when it came to men? Of course not. . . . I must have sensed that. I couldn't understand their constant sex references, their coarse sex terms. I made myself sick, not understanding why I was so repulsed. . . . Oh, I'd intellectualize about the return of the sex urge once the heroin had been flushed from my system. I even carried it off with something like sophistication. The girls would say: 'Get her' or something like that. . . . But it never occurred to me that my urge also should have returned. . . ." She smiled to herself. "I could never have been a prostitute . . . if it had meant giving up heroin. I couldn't have been a prostitute. I would have destroyed myself first, Mr. Cortina." She took a deep breath. "So you see, I have done some thinking since our last get-together."

"Have you shared this with anyone else?"

"No. . . . I wanted you to know first. . . . But I'm going to bring it up in the group therapy session."

"And in family therapy?"

She shook her head. "Not there. . . . I don't need to hurt them any more. I don't need that kind of vindication. How can you blame them for what they don't realize . . . ? No, they've been hurt enough. . . . Guilt doesn't succor, Mr. Cortina. . . ."

"But you feel that you should share this with the girls in your group . . . ?"

"Just to reveal myself. . . . Not for anything that they will say to me, or for any help that they can give me. . . . I must tell them, just to give a piece of myself, Mr. Cortina. *To give a piece of myself.*"

Her hands were trembling. I said: "Why not take the tape? Do you have to . . . ?"

She didn't give me the opportunity to offer her a crutch. "I used the tape once. . . . I can see now that it was a stratagem. I must do this in person. I'll tell Gussie first. . . . She can't talk. . . . Next to you, she's the best listener there is."

It didn't require a long preamble. Bella, I'm convinced, knew just as soon as I got inside of her office. She said to me, her little eyes flashing: "You and that piece of celluloid, Frank Michael. . . . So you've earned your money, my dear."